AF327990

An Anthology of
MAINE LITERATURE

An Anthology of
MAINE LITERATURE

Edited by

Robert Lecker *and* Kathleen R. Brown

University of Maine at Orono Press

1982

First edition

Manufactured in the United States of America

ISBN: 0-89101-050-5

9 8 7 6 5 4 3 2 1

CONTENTS

ACKNOWLEDGEMENTS

For their advice and expertise we wish to thank the following people: Hilda Fife, Burton Hatlen, Constance Hunting, Nancy MacKnight, Shirley K. Richard, Richard Sprague, and the librarians in Special Collections at the Fogler Library, University of Maine at Orono.

From *Rosier's Relation of Waymouth's Voyage to the Coast of Maine, 1605,* by James Rosier. With an introduction and notes by Henry S. Burrage. Portland, Me.: The Gorges Society, 1887.

The passages from *The American Notebooks* of Nathaniel Hawthorne reproduced herein are from the edition by Claude M. Simpson published as Volume VIII of the Centenary Edition of the Works of Nathaniel Hawthorne, edited by William Charvat, Roy Harvey Pearce, and Claude M. Simpson, and are copyright © 1932, 1960, and 1972 by the Ohio State University Press. All rights reserved.

From "Life in the Open Air," by Theodore Winthrop. *The Atlantic Monthly,* 10 (August, September, November, and December, 1862).

"Pericles to the People." From *Elijah Kellogg: The Man and His Work,* by Elijah Kellogg, edited by Wilmot Brookings Mitchell. Boston: Lee and Shepard, 1903.

Excerpt from "Ktaadn," in *The Maine Woods, The Writings of Henry D. Thoreau* by Joseph J. Moldenhauer (ed.) CEAA edition (copyright © 1972 by Princeton University Press), pp. 62-71. Reprinted by permission of Princeton University Press.

"The Queer Folk of the Maine Coast," by Holman Day. Copyright © 1909 by Harper's Magazine. All rights reserved. Reprinted from the September 1909 issue by special permission.

"A Clump of Posies." From *The Penobscot Man,* by Fannie Hardy Eckstorm, © 1972. Reprinted by permission of New Hampshire Publishing Co., Somersworth, N.H. 03878.

From *Northern Farm* by Henry Beston. Copyright 1948 by Henry

Beston. Reprinted by permission of Holt, Rinehart and Winston, Publishers.

"The Winter of the Great Snows" (pp. 53-59) in *Essays of E.B. White.* Copyright © 1971 by E.B. White. Reprinted by permission of Harper & Row, Publishers, Inc. Originally appeared in *The New Yorker.*

Excerpt from Chapter III, "But You Don't Live Here All the Year 'Round?" (pp. 61-67) in *We Took to the Woods* by Louise Dickinson Rich (J.B. Lippincott Company), Copyright 1942, renewed 1970 by Louise Dickinson Rich. Reprinted by permission of Harper & Row, Publishers, Inc.

From *Touch of Wildness* by Lew Dietz. Copyright © 1957, 1960, 1961, 1963, 1964, 1965, 1967, 1968, 1969, 1970 by Lew Dietz. Reprinted by permission of Holt, Rinehart and Winston, Publishers.

"Letters LIV and LV." From *The Life and Writings of Major Jack Downing, of Downingville,* by Seba Smith. Boston: Lilly, Wait, Colman & Holden, 1833.

"Interview with President Lincoln." From *The Complete Works of Artemus Ward,* by Charles Farrar Browne. New York: G.W. Dillingham Co., 1898.

"Farming in Maine." From *Remarks by Bill Nye,* by Edgar W. Nye. Chicago: A.E. Davis & Co., 1887.

"How to Buy Wood." From *Twelve Grindstones,* by John Gould. Copyright © 1970 by John Gould. By permission of Little, Brown and Company.

From *The Pearl of Orr's Island,* by Harriet Beecher Stowe. Boston: Houghton Mifflin Co., 1896.

"A White Heron." From *Tales of New England,* by Sarah Orne Jewett. Boston: Houghton, Mifflin and Co., 1895.

"Rusticators at the Cove." From *Cap'n Simeon's Store,* by George S. Wasson. Boston: Houghton, Mifflin and Co., 1903.

Chapter V of "Red and White" from *Arundel* by Kenneth Roberts. Copyright 1930 by Kenneth Roberts. Reprinted by permission of Doubleday & Company, Inc.

"The Piano." From *Fraternity Village* by Ben Ames Williams, published by Houghton Mifflin Company. Copyright 1949 by Ben Ames Williams. Reprinted by permission of the publisher.

"And the Sun Stood Still." From *The Sun Stood Still and Other Dud Dean Stories,* by Arthur R. Macdougall. Bingham, Me.: Arthur R. Macdougall, 1939. Reprinted by permission of the author.

"The Lonely Day." From *American Earth,* by Erskine Caldwell.

Copyright 1931 by Erskine Caldwell; copyright renewed 1958 by Erskine Caldwell. Reprinted by permission of McIntosh and Otis, Inc.

"Lost and Found." From *Mostly Maine: Short Stories and Other Writings,* by Edward M. Holmes. Orono, Me.: University of Maine at Orono Press, 1977. Reprinted by permission of the publisher.

"A Psalm of Life," "Mezzo-Cammin," "The Evening Star," "My Lost Youth," and "My Cathedral." From *The Complete Works of Henry Wadsworth Longfellow,* Household Edition. Boston: Houghton Mifflin Co., 1902.

"Eros Turannos," copyright 1916 by Edwin Arlington Robinson, renewed 1944 by Ruth Nivison. "The Dark Hills," copyright 1920 by Edwin Arlington Robinson, renewed 1948 by Ruth Nivison. "Mr. Flood's Party," "Lost Anchors," "Many Are Called," copyright 1921 by Edwin Arlington Robinson, renewed 1949 by Ruth Nivison. "The Sheaves," copyright 1925 by Edwin Arlington Robinson, renewed 1953 by Ruth Nivison and Barbara R. Holt. Reprinted with permission of Macmillan Publishing Co., Inc. from *Collected Poems* by Edwin Arlington Robinson.

"Luke Havergal" and "The Clerks" from *The Children of the Night* by Edwin Arlington Robinson. Copyright 1897 by Charles Scribner's Sons. "For a Dead Lady" from *The Town Down the River* by Edwin Arlington Robinson. Copyright 1910 by Charles Scribner's Sons; renewal copyright 1938 by Ruth Nivison. Reprinted by permission of Charles Scribner's Sons.

"Islands in Penobscot Bay," "Kennebec," "Fisherman's Last Supper," "He Too Wore a Butterfly," "Perusing Mallarmé in Maine." From *Selected Poems* by Marsden Hartley, ed. Henry W. Wells. New York: Viking Press, 1945. Reprinted by permission of Norma G. Berger.

"The Paving Quarry," "Harbor," "Thelma Maloney," "Visitor," "A Maine Winter's Night," "There is an Hour at Evening," "After a Storm," by Wilbert Snow. Copyright © 1923 (renewed 1951), 1926 (renewed 1953), 1932 (renewed 1960), 1940, 1957 by Wilbert Snow. Reprinted from *The Collected Poems of Wilbert Snow* by permission of Wesleyan University Press.

"Renascence," "Passer Mortuus Est," "And you as well must die, belovèd dust," "Pity me not because the light of day," from *Collected Poems,* Harper & Row. Copyright 1917, 1921, 1923, 1945, 1948, 1951 by Edna St. Vincent Millay and Norma Millay Ellis. Reprinted by permission of Norma Millay Ellis.

"Winter-Piece," copyright 1932 by Macmillan Publishing Co., Inc., renewed 1960 by Margaret Coffin Halvosa. "The Woodland Orchard," copyright 1935 by Macmillan Publishing Co., Inc., renewed 1963 by Margaret Coffin Halvosa. "A Mess of Clams," copyright 1937 by Macmillan Publishing Co., Inc., renewed 1965 by Margaret Coffin Halvosa. Reprinted with permission of Macmillan Publishing Co., Inc. from *Collected Poems* by Robert P. Tristram Coffin.

"The Ledge in the Forest" and "November Farmyard" reprinted with permission of Macmillan Publishing Co., Inc. from *Country Poems* by Elizabeth Coatsworth. Copyright 1931, 1933, 1934, 1935, 1938, 1942, 1945, 1946 by Elizabeth Coatsworth. Copyrights renewed. "November Farmyard" originally appeared in *The Christian Science Monitor.*

"The Swan" from *Atlas and Beyond* by Elizabeth J. Coatsworth. Copyright 1924 by Harper & Row, Publishers, Inc.; renewed 1952 by Elizabeth Coatsworth. Reprinted by permission of Harper & Row, Publishers, Inc.

"Medusa," "Statue and Birds," "Winter Swan," "Division," "The Cupola," "The Mark," "Old Countryside," and "To Be Sung on the Water" from *The Blue Estuaries* by Louise Bogan. Copyright © 1923, 1929, 1930, 1931, 1933, 1934, 1935, 1936, 1937, 1938, 1941, 1949, 1951, 1952, 1954, 1957, 1958, 1962, 1963, 1964, 1965, 1966, 1967, 1968 by Louise Bogan. Reprinted by permission of Farrar, Straus and Giroux, Inc.

"For a Lamb," "The Groundhog," "Rumination," "At Night," "The Horse Chestnut Tree," "Seals, Terns, Time," "Sea Burial from the Cruiser *Reve,*" "A Wedding on Cape Rosier," "Old Tree by the Penobscot," from *Collected Poems 1930-1976* by Richard Eberhart. Copyright © 1976 by Richard Eberhart. Reprinted by permission of Oxford University Press, Inc., and by Chatto and Windus Ltd.

"Chartres," "Penobscot," "The Occurrences," from *The Collected Poems* of George Oppen. Copyright © 1962, 1972 by George Oppen. Reprinted by permission of New Directions Publishing Corporation.

"From the Window Down," "Union Soldier," "Squaring the Circle," reprinted from *Passage: Selected Poems 1943-1978* by Louis Coxe by permission of the University of Missouri Press. Copyright 1979 by the Curators of the University of Missouri.

"The Seals in Penobscot Bay." From *An Armada of Thirty Whales,* copyright © 1954 by Daniel G. Hoffman. New Haven: Yale University Press, 1954. "The Hermit of Cape Rosier." From *A Little Geste and Other Poems,* copyright © 1960 by Daniel G. Hoffman. New York: Oxford University Press, 1960. "In the Cove," "Moving Among the Creatures," and "The Summerhouse." From *Striking the Stones: Poems,* copyright ©

1968 by Daniel Hoffman. New York: Oxford University Press, 1968. Reprinted by permission of the author.

"3 poems on tomatoes & immortality": "Abundance, and imagine when you press them," "The fields of vegetable-and-literature Drenched," "A future Italian envisions the miracles" by John Tagliabue first appeared in *Kayak,* September 1979.

"For years, many, I've succumbed to them" and "Another vegetable occasion to thank the Chutes" by John Tagliabue first appeared in *Chicago Review* Vol. 32, No. 4, copyright 1981 by *Chicago Review.*

"Lettuce does not let us alone" and "Related to the presents from the Mt. Vernon poets and farmers" by John Tagliabue. Reprinted by permission of the author.

"Barred Islands" from *Letter from a Distant Land* by Philip Booth. Copyright © 1955 by Philip Booth. "Raker" from *Letter from a Distant Land* by Philip Booth. Copyright 1953 by Philip Booth. Originally appeared in *The New Yorker.* "Shag" from *Margins* by Philip Booth. Copyright © 1956 by Philip Booth. "Jake's Wharf" from *Margins* by Philip Booth. Copyright © 1958 by Philip Booth. Originally appeared in *The New Yorker.* "Voyages" from *Margins* by Philip Booth. Copyright © 1964 by Philip Booth. "Stove" from *Available Light* by Philip Booth. Copyright © 1975 by Philip Booth. Originally appeared in *The New Yorker.* Reprinted by permission of Viking Penguin Inc.

"The End of the Lilacs." From *The Place Where I Am Standing,* by Theodore Enslin. New Rochelle, N.Y.: Elizabeth Press, 1964. "Ballad of the Goodly Company: Birds" and "Apple Tree Study." From *To come to have become,* by Theodore Enslin. New Rochelle, N.Y.: Elizabeth Press, 1966. "The Fan Poem." From *The Poems,* by Theodore Enslin. New Rochelle, N.Y.: Elizabeth Press, 1970. "Cobwebs." From *Ländler,* by Theodore Enslin. New Rochelle, N.Y.: Elizabeth Press, 1975. Reprinted by permission of the author.

"Fever." From *After the Stravinsky Concert and Other Poems,* by Constance Hunting. New York: Charles Scribner's Sons, 1969. Reprinted by permission of the author. "New England," "Poem Overheard in a Maine Doctor's Waiting Room" and "The Lost Boy" From *Nightwalk and Other Poems,* by Constance Hunting. Orono, Me.: University of Maine at Orono Press, 1979. Reprinted by permission of the publisher.

INTRODUCTION

The literature of Maine is so rich and varied that it is difficult to condense its history into a single anthology. Ideally, every anthologist hopes to produce a collection which has both depth and breadth. But the fact remains that no anthology can satisfy these diverse needs. This book is no exception: some readers will wonder why their favorite writer has been omitted; others will complain that the work we have selected is not representative enough. We did not limit ourselves to authors born in Maine; the collection covers serious writing produced both by native Mainers and by those from outside the state who have been creatively inspired by Maine life. In many cases we decided to select non-representative poetry and prose in the hope of presenting significant Maine literature which is not widely available.

The book is organized to facilitate appreciation both by genre and from a historical perspective. Five major sections (Travel Accounts, Essays and Sketches, Humor, Fiction, and Poetry) allow the reader to explore specific kinds of Maine writing in their relation to literary traditions that bear no allegiance to place. The chronological arrangement of these sections also illuminates the writers' shifting approach to genre over time.

Because our emphasis is on the history and development of Maine writing, we have consciously avoided treating much of the important and growing body of Maine literature produced after 1970. The contemporary writing scene in Maine really demands a separate anthology which can do justice to the fertile output of the last decade. And just as we must look to new collections devoted to an evolving and dynamic literature, so too must we recognize past works which have grappled with the task of articulating Maine's literary heritage. In many respects this anthology is complemented by, and should be viewed in conjunction with, three books of signal importance: William Storrs Lee's *Maine; A Literary Chronicle* (Funk & Wagnalls, 1968), Richard Aldridge's *Maine Lines* (Lippincott, 1970), and Henry Beston's *White Pine and Blue Water* (Down East Magazine, 1950).

In identifying the impact of frontier consciousness upon the development of Maine literature, Beston points to a motif which lies at the heart of our section on travel accounts. Beston writes that "Those who would understand the particular quality of Maine must first, perhaps, take thought of this element of the frontier." The frontier, of course, refers not only to the geographical wilderness which confronted the first Maine settlers and authors, but also to a state of mind. The frontier was a metaphor that encompassed visions of human potential thriving in pristine woodlands. These surroundings, it was thought, would return man both to nature and to a pastoral state of innocence. From a literary perspective, the frontier metaphor evokes a string of connections which transcend the local and particular: the early Maine writers were not alone in equating the New World with promise, paradise, Utopia, or kingdoms teeming with evidence of the divine.

James Rosier's *A True Relation* is a good example of the combination of frontier voyage and holy excursion. In his account of the riches to be found along the Maine coast Rosier pays homage to "the All-creating God" and His veritable "garden of nature" waiting for true Christian settlers. If Rosier's narrative had concentrated only on "acknowledging the Deity of the Almighty giuer" it might have remained the utilitarian promotional-religious tract it was designed to be. But because Rosier had a sensitive eye for details which were clearly not divine, and because he focused on the habits of Indians who were ignorant of Christian purpose, his record has a peculiar tension that makes it readable today.

This tension between realism and idealism, between secular and sacred experience, also informs Nathaniel Hawthorne's "Notes from Augusta" and Theodore Winthrop's "Life in the Open Air." Hawthorne's narrative, rich in particulars about the people and places he visited in 1837, is filled with regional lore and bustling action. Hawthorne frequently steps back from all the activity to search for pastoral simplicity, but no sooner does he settle into silence than he is reminded of progress and change:

> My position is so far retired from the river and the Mill-Dam, that, though the latter is really rather a busy scene, yet a sort of quiet seems to be diffused over the whole. Two or three times a day, this quiet is broken by the sudden thunder from a quarry, where the workmen are blasting rocks for the Dam; — and a peal of thunder sounds strange in such a green, sunny, and quiet landscape with the blue sky brightening the river.

Hawthorne had the language to cope with this "strange" experience; his account is believable and engaging because he refused to adorn his Maine travelogue with Romantic diction and cliché. Winthrop was less certain about how the landscape should be rendered. In fact, it is Winthrop's pervading uncertainty that makes his account so fascinating. At one moment he is the Realist describing his boat as "a great, ugly, three-tiered box that walks the North River, like a laboratory of greasy odors." But no sooner has he deflated the ideal than he casts the Adirondacks in conventionally picturesque terms: "It is well to go to the Adirondacks. They are shaggy, and shagginess is a valuable trait." Having assigned this value to the landscape, Winthrop rationalizes his perspective: "Picturesque is a curiously convenient, undiscriminating epithet. I use it here." By the time Winthrop climbs "Katahdin," he has produced a medley of imaginative responses to the environment which combines myth, allegory, and empirical observation, and culminates in a Wordsworthian vision "of solemn joy that the man of soul recognizes as one of the surest intimations of immortality, stirring within him, whenever he is in the unearthly regions, the higher world." Winthrop's narrative has a conversational tone that makes it accessible to the modern reader. "Life in the Open Air" also had a popular audience when it first appeared in *The Atlantic Monthly;* it was appreciated not only as a travel piece, but also a tract which dealt with serious questions about man's conception of nature.

These questions are also explored in the second section of the anthology which is devoted to essays and sketches. In many cases the line between essay and travelogue, or between essay and fiction, is a fine one; our division is in some cases arbitrary. We have approached the essay as a form of literature which achieves what George Orwell described as "pleasure in the firmness of good prose or the rhythms of good story." A characteristic feature of the essay is its emphasis on persuading us to see the narrator's point of view; but it is also a very flexible form which, like the sketch, allows the writer to evoke a particular idea, or scene, or character through any technique that seems appropriate to his purpose.

Elijah Kellogg's purpose is clear: his declamations, inspired by Roman history and myth, were designed as parables meant to inspire moral rectitude and strength of character. We may question Kellogg's rhetoric, but the historical importance of his work cannot be denied: his essays were used extensively in nineteenth-century schools and were read by thousands of schoolchildren.

Certainly a moral stance is also implicit in the selection from Henry Thoreau's *The Maine Woods,* but the similiarities stop there. Unlike Kellogg, Thoreau looked directly at the present for inspiration. "Climbing Ktaadn" is a good example of Thoreau's ability to present "sacred and mysterious tracts" of nature with direct, refreshing simplicity. He had a painter's eye for pattern, shading, and perspective. Again and again in his account he returns to the question of man's identity in its relation to nature:

> Think of our life in nature,—daily to be shown matter, to come into contact with it,— rocks, trees, wind on our cheeks! the *solid* earth! the *actual* world! the *common sense! Contact! Contact! Who* are we? *where* are we?

When Thoreau did invoke mythology (the crags of Ktaadn reminded him "of the old epic and dramatic poets, of Atlas, Vulcan, the Cyclops, and Prometheus") the association added irony to his realization that it was "primeval, untamed, and forever untameable *Nature*" he was confronting.

Holman Day captured a different aspect of nature in his essay on "The Queer Folk of the Maine Coast." Day identified the "human curiosities" he saw with the irregularities of a coastline marked by "deep gashes" and "crooked coves." Day's picture, however, is not so much philosophical as photographic in intent: he wanted to record the habits and stories of "squatter people" who, removed from society, had evolved their own private mythology. And he succeeded in presenting his account of the strange rituals, folktales, and dialect peculiar to the region he visited as a journalist for *Harper's Monthly Magazine.* Like Day, Fannie Hardy Eckstorm was also interested in the diverse legends and people which make Maine unique. Therefore it's not surprising to find that her character, O'Connor, was also described by Day in his volume entitled *Pine Tree Ballads.* Eckstorm wrote a number of books on history, language, and legend. One of her most successful books, *The Penobscot Man,* includes "A Clump of Posies," an essay which reveals Eckstorm's ability to color her studies with ornithological and botanical observations.

Henry Beston's landscape is starker than Eckstorm's. The direct prose in *Northern Farm* accentuates the shifting colors and bold contrasts of a Maine winter landscape when "the whole country lies quiescent in the cup of winter's hand." Beston contemplates this "rural scene of farm and open land," and is led to reflect on the idea that "We may not belong to the Golden Age or the years of the Golden Bough, but we can observe and rejoice, and in such natural joy and natural response lies one of the profoundest secrets of human happiness."

E.B. White has long been known as a sophisticated essayist whose work can be studied for its elegance as well as for its wit, perspicacity, and complex texturing. The narrator in "The Winter of the Great Snows" wonders "if a gull will eat a smelt." The question may seem comic; certainly, the opening paragraph doesn't lead us to expect the smelt question to take a serious turn. But soon we realize that White is really dealing with the question of survival; he wants to see "if a man can stay alive in the cold" of Maine winters. As White traces the rituals which do allow man to survive — and enjoy — the winter, the essay turns into a metaphorical tale about telling tales; it suggests that one means of survival involves the creative writing process itself. Written in 1971, the piece also deals with problems that will affect our survival in the future: "Feeling about oil is running high," the narrator says. We sense the relevance of this observation as the essay concludes by raising the possibility of "a refinery on Sears Island . . . bringing barges and 200,000-ton tankers slithering through the fog-draped, ledge-encrusted, tide-ripped waters of one of the most beautiful bodies of water in Maine or anywhere."

"The Winter of the Great Snows" complements the excerpts from *Northern Farm* and Louise Dickinson Rich's *We Took to the Woods.* Inverting the traditional equation between winter, silence, and death, these three writers find inspiration and solace in the year's coldest months. The section is rounded off by Lew Dietz's "Wild Animals I Have Known — And Vice Versa." Dietz's central purpose is to show that as humans "we have for centuries attempted to shore up our egos by attributing to animals characteristics we find unbecoming in ourselves." Through his sensitive observations of the animal world Dietz suggests that we have been wrong, and that "we have come too far too fast," a sentiment that such writers as White, Beston, and Rich would certainly seem to share.

A different perspective unites the authors included in our section on humor. Maine has produced several writers who gained popular appeal by commenting on the comedy inherent in daily life. Seba Smith, who was known to his readers as Major Jack Downing, began his career by satirizing Maine customs and characters. Later, he lampooned the state's political system, and finally broadened his attacks by sending Major Downing to Washington, a move which allowed the mockery of *The Life and Writings of Major Jack Downing* to be enjoyed throughout the country. The two letters we have included show Smith in his best ranting form. Take the letter of February 1, 1833 (the day appointed by South Carolina for enacting a nullifying ordinance): " . . . I've been up top to the Congress house five or six times today and listened and listened, but all the firing I could hear was inside the Congress house itself, where the members were shouting their speeches at each other." The satirical tone persists in the next letter, in which "Cousin Ephraim" explains to his Uncle Jack "the science of Land-Speculation." The Maine legislators, we learn, "were flying about from one room to another, like so many pigeons shot in the head."

Artemus Ward (Charles Farrar Browne) needs little introduction. His articles were known internationally, he was much in demand as a lecturer, and his contributions to *Punch* were eminently successful in their popular appeal. Ward capitalized on the art of buffoonery; indeed, his contrived illiteracy was consciously directed toward undermining the literary and social pretentiousness which he thought marked his age.

Ward was imitated by many other writers of his generation, but none of them attained his success; their humor was too obviously derived from Ward's innovative approach. Bill Nye refused to adopt Ward's style. This refusal made him an original humorist determined to offer his own views on American life. Nye relied on irony, exaggeration, and caricature to make his audience laugh. A good example of these techniques appears in "Farming in Maine," which rambles through several casual observations about Maine's soil and climate, only to conclude with an apparent non-sequitur: "This shows that the moose is a humorist."

If the moose is a humorist, so then is the state with which it is most closely identified. John Gould displays this humorous quality in "How to Buy Wood." To know how to buy wood, Gould implies, one must first understand the legends, tall tales, and customs which make Maine different. That's why most of his account is filled with stories, jokes, and character sketches. In the end, Gould suggests that how you buy wood is really a function of how you *talk* about buying wood:

> Booker—You going to have some wood for me this season?
> Mason—Eyah.
> Booker—Good.
> Mason—Same amount?
> Booker—Eyah.
> Mason—Same price?
> Booker—Eyah.
> Mason—Will do. It's as good as on the cars.
> Booker—See ya!

Gould's piece focuses our attention on the qualities of a particular region. Many of the fiction writers included in this collection have also concentrated on the local aspects of Maine consciousness. Sarah Orne Jewett is frequently referred to as a 'local colorist' whose important book, *The Country of the Pointed Firs,* has been called a masterpiece of regional fiction. Similarly, George Wasson has long been appreciated for his attention to the Maine landscape. However, none of the fiction in this anthology should be approached strictly in terms of its regional impact. Our selections are intended to demonstrate that the development of Maine fiction reflects the trends of world fiction in its movement from allegorical, didactic modes toward formal realism, with its emphasis on believable character, setting, and situation. In this context one can fruitfully compare the overt sentimentality in *The Pearl of Orr's Island* with the close attention to individual character and speech so evident in Edward Holmes's "Lost and Found." Between Harriet Beecher Stowe and Holmes, we find a range of fiction writers whose work can be explored in several ways. "A White Heron" is a complex story which reveals Jewett's ability to draw effectively on symbol and archetype. Wasson's "Rusticators at the Cove" has a moral dimension that is as important to the story's meaning as is its emphasis on landscape. *Arundel* displays Kenneth Roberts' journalistic attention to historical research, his skills at presenting action, and his tendency to heighten that action by using light imagery. Ben Ames Williams' fiction can be understood in terms of its author's concern with rendering "potency of place." "The Piano" also reveals Williams' interest in the mysteries which prompt people to make, and live by, certain moral choices. Erskine Caldwell wrote several stories set in Maine. "The Lonely Day," which develops a series of contrasts between exuberance and repression, experience and youth, has a freshness about it which illuminates not only Katherine's rebellious antics, but also the rural scene which lies at the root of her private frustrations.

If Maine fiction is varied, the sixteen poets represented in the anthology reflect the even more extraordinary range of verse produced in Maine over the last two centuries. There is Longfellow, the sentimental experimentalist who was perhaps the most popular nineteenth-century poet in America, and Edwin Arlington Robinson, a sophisticated writer whose work was of uniform poetic excellence. Robinson used traditional metrical forms, but he infused his character portrayals and dramatic monologues with insight and psychological complexity. Of course, such poems as "Eros Turannos," "For a Dead Lady," and "The Clerks" reveal more than characters' dreams and obsessions; they convey Robinson's profound concern with the effects of time:

> And we who delve in beauty's lore
> Know all that we have known before
> Of what inexorable cause
> Makes Time so vicious in his reaping.

A similar concern with transience and mutability inspired Edna St. Vincent Millay to write, in "Passer Mortuus Est," that "Death devours all lovely things," and to listen, in *Renascence,* to "the ticking of Eternity." Louise Bogan's poetry also has metaphysical strains, and she too deals with man's perception of time:

> The diagram of whirling shade,
> The visible, that links to spin
> Forever webs that time has made
> Though momently time wears them thin
> And all at length are gathered in.

Bogan's intricately balanced lyrics find their texture in the poet's ability to apprehend the immediate world through metaphors based in myth, philosophy, and religion. Philosophy and religion also influence Marsden Hartley's "He Too Wore a Butterfly," Wilbert Snow's "There Is an Hour at Evening," and Richard Eberhart's "The Groundhog":

> I stood there in the whirling summer,
> My hand capped a withered heart,
> And thought of China and of Greece,
> Of Alexander in his tent;
> Of Montaigne in his tower,
> Of Saint Theresa in her wild lament.

It's a long way from "Saint Theresa in her wild lament" to Robert P. Tristram Coffin's "Winter-Piece," with its attention to "sucking pigs . . . kneeling / with lemons in the mouth," or to Elizabeth Coatsworth's "November Farmyard," with its emphasis on "the farmer's steps from shed-door to barn-door." And Constance Hunting's elegant, symbolic verse stands in sharp contrast to Theodore Enslin's visual and verbal meditations. Or compare the sparseness of George Oppen's "Chartres" with Daniel Hoffman's long-limbed "The Hermit of Cape Rosier." We can distinguish between poets who find their ideas in nature and those who apply their art to understanding nature. We can speak of one poet's affinity with a particular school of thought, a philosophic stance, or a stylistic pre-occupation. But one must first read the poems and experience them before attaching the convenient labels. Through this anthology we hope to encourage that kind of reading experience. Most of all, we hope that this book encourages readers to explore Maine's literature further, to find out more about the authors whose talent can only be suggested here. We've touched some of that talent; more of it remains to be enjoyed.

PART I:
TRAVEL ACCOUNTS

JAMES ROSIER
c1575–1635

The territory of Maine was visited by several of the early explorers, including John and Sebastian Cabot (1498–99), Bartholomew Gosnold (1602), Martin Pring (1603), and Pierre du Guast, sieur de Monts (1604). In 1605 Thomas Arundell, Ferdinando Gorges, and John Popham underwrote the cost of a voyage to locate a possible site for a permanent settlement. The *Archangel,* captained by George Weymouth, studied spots along the Maine coast. On the ship was James Rosier, who wrote a promotional account of his observations entitled *A True Relation of the Most Prosperous Voyage Made This Present Yeere 1605 by Captaine George Waymouth* (London, 1605). His report was glowing enough to encourage George Popham and Raleigh Gilbert to attempt to establish a colony at the mouth of the Kennebec River in 1607. The settlement lasted only a year, but Maine continued to attract other explorers and fishermen during the next few decades.

From *Rosier's Relation of Waymouth's Voyage*

Thursday, the 13 of June, by two a clocke in the morning (because our Captaine would take the helpe and aduantage of the tide) in the light-horseman with our Company well prouided and furnished with armour and shot both to defend and offend; we went from our ship vp to that part of the riuer which trended westward into the maine, to search that: and we carried with vs a Crosse, to erect at that point, which (because it was not daylight) we left on the shore vntill our returne backe; when we set it vp in maner as the former. For this (by the way) we diligently obserued, that in no place, either about the Ilands, or vp in the maine, or alongst the riuer, we could discerne any token or signe, that euer any Christian had been before; of which either by cutting wood, digging for water, or setting vp Crosses (a thing neuer omitted by any Christian trauellers) we should haue perceiued some mention left.

But to returne to our riuer, further vp into which we then rowed by estimation twenty miles, the beauty and goodnesse whereof I can not by relation sufficiently demonstrate. That which I can say in generall is this: What profit or pleasure soeuer is described and truly verified in the former part of the riuer, is wholly doubled in this; for the bredth and depth is such, that any ship drawing 17 or 18 foot water, might haue passed as farre as we went with our light-horsman, and by all our mens judgement much further, because we left it in so good depth and bredth; which is so much the more to be esteemed of greater woorth, by how much it trendeth further vp into the maine: for from the place of our ships riding in the Harbour at the entrance into the sound, to the furthest part we were in this riuer, by our estimation was not much lesse than three-score miles.

From ech banke of this riuer are diuers branching streames into the maine, whereby is affoorded an vnspeakable profit by the conueniency of transportation from place to place, which in some countries is both chargeable; and not so fit, by cariages on maine, or horsebacke.

Heere we saw great store of fish, some great, leaping aboue water, which we judged to be Salmons. All along is an excellent mould of ground. The wood in most places, especially on the East side, very thinne, chiefly oke and some small yoong birch, bordering low vpon the riuer; all fit for medow and pasture ground: and in that space we went, we had on both sides the riuer many plaine plots of medow, some of three or foure acres, some of eight or nine: so as we judged in the whole to be betweene thirty and forty acres of good grasse, and where the armes run into the Maine, there likewise went a space on both sides of cleere grasse, how far we know not, in many places we might see paths made to come downe to the watering.

The excellencie of this part of the Riuer, for his good breadth, depth, and fertile bordering ground, did so ravish vs all with variety of pleasantnesse, as we could not tell what to commend, but only admired; some compared it to the Riuer Seuerne, (but in a higher degree) and we all concluded (as I verily thinke we might rightly) that we should neuer see the like Riuer in every degree equall, vntill it pleased God we beheld the same againe. For the farther we went, the more pleasing it was to euery man, alluring vs still with expectation of better, so as our men, although they had with great labour rowed long and eat nothing (for we carried with vs no victuall, but a little cheese and bread) yet they were so refreshed with the pleasant beholding thereof, and so loath to forsake it, as some of them affirmed, they would haue continued willingly with that onely fare and labour 2 daies; but the tide not suffering vs to make any longer stay (because we were to come backe with the tide) and our Captaine better knowing what was fit than we, and better what they in labour were able to endure, being verie loath to make any desperate hazard, where so little necessitie required, thought it best to make returne, because whither we had discouered was sufficient to conceiue that the Riuer ran very far into the land. For we passed six or seuen miles, altogether fresh water (whereof we all dranke) forced vp by the flowing of the Salt: which after a great while eb, where we left it, by breadth of channell and depth of water was likely to run by estimation of our whole company an unknowen way farther: the search whereof our Captaine hath left till his returne, if it shall so please God to dispose of him and vs.

For we hauing now by the direction of the omnipotent disposer of all good intents (far beyond the period of our hopes) fallen with so bold a coast, found so excellent and secure harbour, for as many Ships as any nation professing Christ is able to set forth to Sea, discouered a Riuer, which the All-creating God, with his most liberall hand, hath made aboue report notable with his foresaid blessings, bordered with a land, whose pleasant fertility bewraieth it selfe to be the garden of nature, wherein she only intended to delight hir selfe, hauing hitherto obscured it to any, except to a purblind generation, whose vnderstanding it hath pleased God so to darken, as they can neither discerne, vse, or rightly esteeme the vnualuable riches in middest whereof they live sensually content with the barke and outward rinds, as neither knowing the sweetnes of the inward marrow, nor acknowledging the Deity of the Almighty giuer: hauing I say thus far proceeded, and hauing some of the inhabitant nation (of best vnderstanding we saw among them) who (learning our language) may be able to giue vs further instruction, concerning all the premised particulars, as also of their gouernours, and gouernment, situation of townes, and what else shall be conuenient, which by no meanes otherwise we could by any obseruation of our selues learne in a long time: our Captaine now wholy intended his prouision for speedy returne. For although the time of yeere and our victuall were not so spent, but we could haue made a longer voyage, in searching farther and trading for very good commodities, yet as they might haue beene much profitable, so (our company being small) much more preiudiciall to the whole state of our voyage, which we were most regardfull now not to hazard. For we supposing not a little present priuate profit, but a publique good, and true zeal of promulgating Gods holy Church, by planting Christianity, to be the sole intent of the Honourable setters foorth of this discouery; thought it generally most expedient, by our speedy returne, to giue the longer space of time to make prouision for so weighty an entirprise.

NATHANIEL HAWTHORNE
1804–1864

Born in Salem, Mass., Nathaniel Hawthorne spent part of his boyhood in Raymond, Maine. Hawthorne graduated from Bowdoin College, which provided him the background for his first novel (*Fanshawe,* 1828), and three long-lasting acquaintances. Henry Wadsworth Longfellow became a literary friend; Horatio Bridge secretly financed the publication of his *Twice-Told Tales* in 1837; and Franklin Pierce appointed Hawthorne consul to Liverpool after he wrote a campaign biography for the politician. In spite of mundane jobs, Hawthorne managed to produce such masterpieces as *Mosses from an Old Manse* (1846), *The Scarlet Letter* (1850), *The House of the Seven Gables* (1851), and *The Blithedale Romance* (1852). While Hawthorne has often been depicted as a solitary individual preoccupied by the enigmas of evil and moral responsibility, his account of a visit to Maine in July and August of 1837 reveals a different aspect of his personality. Delighted to be with his friend Bridge, Hawthorne viewed several towns, observed immigrant laborers, admired Bridge's pretty maid, and discussed fishing stories in a tavern.

From *The American Notebooks*[1]

July 5th, 1837.

HERE I am settled, since night before last, with Bridge, and living very singularly. He leads a bachelor-life in his paternal mansion, only a small part of which is occupied by a family who do his washing, make the beds &c. He provides his own breakfast and supper, and occasionally his dinner; though this is oftener, I believe, taken at the hotel or an eating-house, or with some of his relatives. I am his guest, and my presence makes no alteration in his way of life. Our fare, thus far, has consisted of bread, butter, and

[1]Hawthorne, Nathaniel, *The American Notebooks.* Edited by Claude M. Simpson. Vol. VIII of the Centenary Edition of the Works of Nathaniel Hawthorne, edited by William Charvat, Roy Harvey Pearce, and Claude M. Simpson (Columbus, Ohio: Ohio State University Press, 1972), pp. 32-70.

cheese, crackers, herrings, boiled eggs, coffee, milk, and claret-wine, besides a plentiful variety of liquors, should we desire them. He has another inmate in the person of a queer little Frenchman, who has his breakfast, tea, and lodging here, and finds his dinner elsewhere. Monsieur Schaeffer does not appear to be more than twenty-one years old—a diminutive figure, with eyes askew, and otherwise of ungainly physiognomy; he is ill-dressed also, in a coarse blue coat, thin cotton pantaloons, and unbrushed boots; altogether with as little of French coxcombry as can well be imagined; though with something of the monkey-aspect inseparable from a little Frenchman. He is, nevertheless, an intelligent and well-informed man, apparently of extensive reading in his own language;—a philosopher, Bridge tells me, and an infidel. His insignificant personal appearance stands in the way of his success, and prevents him from receiving the respect which is really due to his talents and acquirements; wherefore he is bitterly dissatisfied with the country and its inhabitants, and often expresses his feelings to Bridge (who has gained his confidence to a certain degree) in very strong terms.

Then here are three characters, each with something out of the common way, living together somewhat like monks. Bridge, our host, combines more high and admirable qualities, of that sort which make up a gentleman, than any other that I have met with. Polished, yet natural, frank, open, and straightforward, yet with a delicate feeling for the sensitiveness of his companions; of excellent temper and warm heart; well-acquainted with the world, with a keen faculty of observation, which he has had many opportunities of exercising [. . .] and never varying from a code of honor and principle, which is really nice and rigid in its way. There is a sort of philosophy developing itself in him, which will not improbably cause him to settle down in this, or some other equally singular course of life. He seems almost to have made up his mind never to be married—which I wonder at; for he has strong affections, and is fond both of women and children.

The little Frenchman impresses me very strongly, too—so lonely as he is here, struggling against the world, with bitter feelings in his breast, and yet talking with the vivacity and gaiety of his nation;—making his home from darkness to daylight, and enjoying here what little domestic comfort and confidence there is for him; and then going about all the live-long day, teaching French to blockheads who sneer at him; and returning at about ten o'clock in the evening (for I was wrong in saying that he supped here—he eats no supper) to his solitary room and bed. Before retiring, he goes to Bridge's bedside, and, if he finds him awake, stands talking French, expressing his dislike of the Americans—*"Je hais—Je hais les Yankees!"*—thus giving vent to the stifled bitterness of the whole day. In the morning, I hear him getting up early—at sunrise or before—humming to himself, scuffling about his chamber with his thick boots, and at last taking his departure for a solitary ramble till breakfast. Then he comes in cheerful and vivacious enough, eats pretty heartily, and is off again, singing a French chanson as he goes down the gravel-walk. The poor fellow has nobody to sympathize with him but Bridge; and thus a singular connection is established between two utterly different characters.

Then here is myself, who am likewise a queer character in my way, and have come here to spend a week or two with my friend of half-a life-time;—the longest space, probably, that we are ever destined to spend together; for fate seems to be preparing changes for both of us. My circumstances, at least, cannot long continue as they are and have been; and Bridge, too, stands betwixt high prosperity and utter ruin.

I think I should soon become strongly attached to our way of life—so independent, and untroubled by the forms and restrictions of society. The house is very pleasantly situated—half a mile distant from where the town begins to be thickly-settled, and on a swell of land, with the road running at a distance of fifty yards, and a grassy tract and gravel walk between. Beyond the road rolls the Kennebec, here two or three hundred yards wide; putting my head out of the window, I can see it flowing steadily along, straightway between wooded banks; but arriving nearly opposite the house, there is a large and level sand-island in the middle of the stream; and just below this island, the current is further interrupted by the works of the Mill Dam, which is perhaps half-finished, yet still in so rude a state, that it looks as much like the ruins of a Dam destroyed by the spring freshets, as like the foundation of a Dam yet to be. Irishmen and Canadians are at work on it, and the echoes of their hammering, and of their voices, come across the river and up to the window. Then there is a sound of the wind among the trees round the house; and when that is silent, the calm, full distant voice of the river becomes audible. Looking downward thither, I see the rush of the current, and mark the different eddies, with here and there white specks or streaks of foam; and often a log comes floating down, glistening in the sun as it rolls over among the eddies, having voyaged, for aught I know, hundreds of miles from the wild upper sources of the river, passing down, down, between lines of forest, and sometimes a rough clearing, till here it floats along by cultivated banks, and will soon pass by the village. Sometimes a long raft of boards comes down, requiring the nicest skill in navigating it through the narrow passage left by the Mill-Dam. Chaises and wagons occasionally pass along the road, the riders all giving a passing glance at the Dam, or perhaps alighting to examine it more carefully, and at last departing, with ominous shakes of the head, as to the result of the enterprise. My position is so far retired from the river and the Mill-Dam, that, though the latter is really rather a busy scene, yet a sort of quiet seems to be diffused over the whole. Two or three times a day, this quiet is broken by the sudden thunder from a quarry, where the workmen are blasting rocks for the Dam;—and a peal of thunder sounds strange in such a green, sunny, and quiet landscape with the blue sky brightening the river.

I have not seen much of the people; there have been, however, several incidents which amused me, though scarcely worth telling. A passionate tavern-keeper, quick as a flash of gunpowder, a nervous man, and showing in his demeanor, it seems, a consciousness of his infirmity of temper. I was a witness to a scuffle of his with a drunken guest; the tavern-keeper, after they were separated, raved like a madman, and in a tone of voice having a queerly pathetic or lamentable sound mingled with its rage, as if he were lifting up his voice to weep. Then he jumped into a chaise which was standing by, whipped up the horse and drove off rapidly; as if to give his rage vent in this way.

On the morning of the fourth of July, two printer's apprentices, lads nearly grown, dressed in jackets and very tight pantaloons of check—tight as their skins; so that they looked like harlequins or circus clowns, yet appeared to think themselves in perfect propriety—a very calm and quiet assurance of the admiration of the town. A common fellow, a carpenter, who, on the strength of political partizanship, asked Bridge's assistance in cutting out great letters from play-bills &c, in order to print Martin Van Buren Forever, on a flag;—but Bridge refused. "Let every man skin his own skunks," says he. Bridge seems to be considerably of a favorite with the lower orders, especially the Irishmen and French Canadians, the latter accosting him in the street to ask his assistance as an interpreter, in making their bargains for work.

I meant to have dined at the Hotel with Bridge to-day; but having returned to the house, leaving him to do some business in the village, I found myself unwilling to move, when the dinner hour approached; and therefore dined very comfortably on bread, cheese and eggs. Some little Canadian children were peeping out between two buildings; they would have talked French, had they been old enough to talk at all.

Nothing of much interest takes place. We live very comfortably in our bachelor-establishment, on a cold shoulder of mutton, with ham, and smoked beef, and boiled eggs; and as to drinkables, we had both claret and brown sherry on the dinner-table to day; but we are neither of us such thirsty souls as we once were. Last evening we had a long literary and philosophical conversation with Mr. Schaeffer. He is rather remarkably well-informed for a man of his age, and seems to have very just notions on ethics &c though damnably perverted as to religion. It is queer to hear philosophy of any sort from such a boyish figure—"we philosophers," he is fond of saying, to distinguish himself and his brethren from the Christians. One of his oddities is, that, while stedfastly maintaining an opinion that he is a very small and slow eater, and that we, in common with other Yankees, eat immensely and at a great rate, he actually eats both faster and longer, and devours, as Bridge avers, more victuals, than both of us together. . . .

Saturday, July 15th

Went with Bridge yesterday to visit several Irish shanties, endeavoring to find out who had stolen some rails of a fence. At the first door where we knocked (a shantie with an earthen mound heaped against the wall, two or three feet thick) the inmates were not up, though it was past eight o'clock. At last a middle-aged woman showed herself, half-dressed, and completing her toilet. Threats were made of tearing down her house; for she is a lady of very indifferent morals, and sells rum and [wears frilled] dresses. Few of these people are connected with the Mill-Dam, or at least, many are not so; but have intruded themselves into the vacant huts which were occupied by the Mill-Dam people last year. In two or three places hereabouts there is quite a village of these dwellings, with a clay and board chimney, or oftener an old barrel smoked and charred with the fire. Some of their roofs are covered with sods, and appear almost subterranean. One of the little hamlets stands on both sides of a deep dell, wooded and bush-grown, with a vista as it were into the heart of a wood in one direction and to the broad sunny river on the other; a little rivulet crossed by a plank, at the bottom of the dell. At two doors we saw very pretty and modest-looking young women; one with a child in her arms, and another in her belly. Indeed they all have innumerable little children; and they are invariably in good flesh, though always filthy of face. They come to the door while their mothers are talking with the visitors, standing straight up on their bare legs, with their little plump-bellies protruding; in one hand a small tin sauce-pan, and in the other an iron-spoon, with unwiped mouths, looking as independent as any child or grown person in the land. They stare unabashed, but make no answer when spoken to. "I've no call to your fence, Misser Bridge." It seems queer that a man should have the right, unarmed with any legal instrument, of tearing down the dwelling-houses of a score of families, and turning the inmates forth without a shelter. Yet Bridge undoubtedly has this right; and it is not a little striking to see how quietly these people contemplate the probability of his exercising it—resolving indeed, to burrow in their holes as long as may be, yet caring about as little for an ejectment, as those who could find a tenement anywhere. Yea less. Yet the women, amid all the trials of their situation, appear to have kept up the distinction between virtue and vice; those who can claim the former will not associate with the latter. When the women travel with young children, they carry the baby slung at their backs, and sleeping quietly. The dresses of the new-comers are old fashioned, making them look aged before their time.

Mr. Schaeffer shaving himself, yesterday morning. He was in excellent spirits, and could not keep his tongue or body still, more than long enough to make two or three consecutive strokes at his beard. Then would he turn, flourishing his razor and grimacing joyously, enacting strange antics, breaking out into scraps and verses of drinking songs—"A boire! A boire!" &c—then laughing heartily and crying "Vive la gaiete!"—then resuming his task, looking into the glass with grave face, on which, however, a grin would soon break out anew; and all his antics would be repeated with variations. He turned his foolery to philosophy, by observing that mirth contributed to goodness of heart, and to make us love our fellow-creatures. Conversing with him in the evening, he affirmed, with evident belief in the truth of what he said, that he would have no objection, except that it would be a very foolish thing, to expose his whole heart—his whole inner man—to the view of the world. Not that there would not much evil be discovered there; but as he was conscious of being in a state of mental and moral improvement, working out his progress onward, he would not shrink from such a scrutiny. This talk was introduced by his mentioning the "Minister's Black Veil," which he said had been translated into French, as an exercise, by a Miss Appleton of Bangor.

Seeing by the river-side, late in the afternoon; one of the above described boats going up the stream, with the water rippling at the prow, with the strength of the current and of the boat's motion. By and bye comes a raft down the stream, perhaps twenty yards long, guided by two men, one at each end; the raft itself of boards sawed at Waterville, and laden with square bundles of shingles and round bundles of clapboard. "Friend," says one man, "how is the tide now?"—this being important on their onward progress. They make fast to a tree, in order to let the tide rise a little further. It would be pleasant enough to float down the Kennebec on one of these rafts, letting the river conduct you onward at its own pace, leisurely displaying to you all the wild or civilized beauties along its banks, and perhaps running you aground in some peculiarly picturesque spot, for your longer enjoyment of it. Another object, perhaps, is a solitary man, paddling himself down the river in a small canoe, the light lonely touch of his paddle in the water making the silence appear deeper. Every few minutes, a sturgeon leaps forth, sometimes behind you, so that you merely hear the splash, and turning hastily around see nothing but the disturbed water; sometimes he darts straight on end out of a quiet black spot in the water, on which your eyes happen to be fixed; and when even his tail is clear of the surface, he falls down on his side and disappears. On the river-bank, an Irishwoman washing some clothes, surrounded by her children, whose babbling sounds pleasantly along the edge of the water, and she also answers in a sweet, kindly and cheerful voice, though an immoral woman and without the certainty of bread or shelter from day to day. An Irishman sitting angling on the shore, with an alder-pole and a clothes line. At frequent intervals, the quiet of the scene is suddenly broken by a loud report, like thunder, rolling along the banks, echoing and reverberating afar. It is a blast of stone. Along the shore, sometimes sticks of timber made fast, either separately or several together; stones of some size, varying the pebbles and sand; the clayey spot, where a shallow brook runs into the river, not with a deep outlet, but finding its way across the bank in two or three separate streams. Looking upward into the deep glen whence it issues, you see its shady current. Elsewhere, a high bank, with the beach between it and the river; the bank broken and caved away; so that the earth looks fresh and yellow, and is penetrated by the nests of birds. Elsewhere an old shiny tree-trunk, half in and half out of the water. Perhaps an island of gravel, long and narrow, in the centre of the river. Chips, blocks of wood, slabs, and other scraps of lumber, strewed along the beach. Logs drifting down. The high bank covered with various trees and shrubbery; and in one place two or three Irish shanties looking down.

One of Bridge's sisters has been afflicted with a severe dysentery; and it is supposed to be caused by her having assisted to dress a dead man in his robe. The doctor told her that such was the general effect of contact with a person recently dead. This is ugly. . . .

Saturday, August 12th

Left Augusta a week ago this morning, for Thomaston. Nothing particular in our ride across the country. Fellow-passenger, Boston dry-goods dealer, travelling to collect bills; at many of the country-stores, he would get out and show his unwelcome visage. In the taverns, prints from Scripture, varnished and on rollers; such as the Judgement of Christ—also, a queer set of colored engravings of the story of the Prodigal Son, the figures being clad in modern costume—or at least not more than half a century back. The father, a grave clerical person, with a white wig and black broadcloth suit. The son with a cocked hat and laced clothes, drinking wine out of glasses, and embracing a whore in fashionable dress &c. At Thomaston, a nice, comfortable boarding-house tavern, without a bar, or any sort of wine or spirits. An old lady from Boston, with her three daughters, one of whom was teaching music and the other two schoolmistresses. A frank, free, mirthful daughter of the landlady, about twenty-four years old, between whom and myself there immediately sprung up a flirtation, which made us both feel rather solemncholy when we parted on Tuesday morning. She is capable, I know, of strong feelings; and her features expressed something of the kind, when we held out our hands for a parting grasp. Music in the evenings, with a song by a rather pretty, fantastic little devil of a brunette, about eighteen years old, who has married within a year, and spent the last summer in a trip to the Springs and elsewhere. Her manner of walking; by jerks, with a quiver as if she were made of calves-feet jelly. I talk with everybody—to Mrs. Trott, good sense—to Mary, good sense with a mixture of fun—to Mrs. Gleason, sentiment, romance, and nonsense.—Sunday, walked with Cilley to see General Knox's old mansion—a large rusty-looking edifice of wood, with some grandeur in the architecture, standing on the banks of the river, close by the site of an old burial ground, and near where an ancient fort had been erected for defence against the French and Indians. General Knox formerly owned a square of thirty miles in this part of the country; and he wished to settle it with a tenantry, after the fashion of English gentlemen. He would permit no edifices to be erected within a certain distance of his mansion. His patent covered, of course, the whole present town of Thomaston, together with Waldoboro' and divers other flourishing commercial and country villages; and would have been of incalculable value, could it have remained unbroken to the present time. But the General lived in grand style, and received throngs of visiters from foreign parts; and was obliged to part with large tracts of his possessions, till now there is little left but the ruinous mansion, and the ground immediately around it. His tomb stands near the house, a spacious receptacle, an iron door, at the end of a turf-covered mound, and surmounted by an obelisk of the Thomaston marble. There are inscriptions to the memory of several of his family; for he had many children, male and female, all of whom are now dead but one daughter, a widow of fifty, recently married to Hon. John Holmes. There is a stone fence around the monument. On the outside of this are the grave-stones and large flat tomb-stones of the ancient burial ground, the tomb-stones being of red-freestone, with vacant spaces, formerly inlaid with slate, on which were the inscriptions and perhaps coats of arms. One of these spaces was in the shape of a heart. The people of Thomaston were very wrathful that the General should have laid out his grounds over this old burial-place; and he dared never throw down the grave-stones, though his wife, a haughty English lady, often teazed him to do so. But when the old

General was dead, Lady Knox, as they called her, caused them to be prostrated, as they now lie. She was a woman of violent passions, fond of gallants, and so proud an aristocrat, that, as long as she lived, she would never enter any house in Thomaston except her own. When a married daughter was sick, she used to go in her carriage to the door, and send up to enquire how she did. The General was personally very popular, but his wife ruled him. The house and its vicinity, and the whole tract covered by Knox's patent, may be taken as an illustration of what must be the result of American schemes of aristocracy. It is not forty years since this house was built, and Knox was in his glory; but now the house is all in decay, while, within a stones throw of it, is a street of neat, smart, white edifices of one and two stories, occupied chiefly by thriving mechanics. But towns have grown up, where Knox probably meant to have forests and parks. On the banks of the river, where he meant to have only one wharf, for his own west-India vessels and yacht, there are our two wharves, with stores, and a lime-kiln. Little appertains to the mansion, except the tomb, and the old burial ground, and the old fort. The descendants are all poor; and the inheritance was merely sufficient to make a dissipated and drunken fellow of the one of the old General's sons, who survived to middle age. This man's habits were as bad as possible, as long as he had any money; but when quite ruined, he reformed. The daughter, the only survivor of Knox's children (herself childless) is a mild and amiable woman, therein totally differing from her mother. Knox, when he first visited his estate, arriving in a vessel, was visited by a deputation of the squatters, who had resolved to resist him to the death. He received them with great courtesy, made them dine with him aboard their vessel, and sent them back to their constituents in great love and admiration of him. He used to have a vessel running to Philadelphia, I think, and bringing him all sorts of delicacies. His way of raising money, was to give a mortgage on his estate, of a hundred thousand dollars at a time, and receive that nominal amount in goods, which he would immediately sell at auction for perhaps thirty thousand. Died by a chicken-bone. Near the house is the remains of a covered way, by which the french once attempted to gain admittance into the fort; but the work caved in and buried a good many of them, and the rest gave up the siege. There was recently an old inhabitant living, who remembered when the people used to reside in the fort.

Owl's-Head, a watering-place, terminating a point of land, six or seven miles from Thomaston. A long island shuts in the prospect of the sea; hither coasters &c and fishing-smacks run in, when a storm is anticipated. Two fat landlords, both young men. Something of a contrast in their dispositions; one of them being a brisk, lively, active, jesting fat man, the other more heavy and inert, making jests sluggishly if at all. Aboard the steam-boat, Professor Stuart of Andover, sitting on a sofa in the saloon, generally in conversation with some person, resolving their doubts on one point or other, speaking in a very audible voice; and strangers stand or sit around to hear him, as if her were an ancient apostle or philosopher. Himself a bulky man, with a large, massive face, particularly calm in its expression, and mild enough to be pleasing. When not otherwise occupied, reading without much notice of what is going on around him. Speaking without effort, yet thoughtfully.

Got lost in a fog, the morning after leaving Owls Head. Fired a brass cannon, rang bell, blew steam like a whale snorting. After one of the reports of the cannon, heard a horn blown at no great distance, the sound coming soon after the report. Doubtful whether it came from the shore or a vessel. Continued our ringing and snorting; and by and bye something was seen to mingle with the fog, that obscured everything beyond fifty yards from us; at first it seemed only like a deeper wreath of fog; deepened still more, till it took the aspects of sails; then the hull of a small schooner, beating down towards us; the wind laying her over towards us, so that her gunnel was almost in the water, and we could see the whole of her sloping deck. "Schooner ahoy," say we. "Halloo." "Have you seen Boston Light this morning?" "Yes; it bears North north-west, two miles distant!" "Very much obliged to you." cries our Captain. So the coaster vanishes into the mist behind; we get up our steam, and soon enter the harbor, meeting vessels of every rig; and the fog clearing away, shows a cloudy sky. Aboard, an old one-eyed sailor, who had lost one of his feet, and had walked on the stump from Eastport to Bangor, thereby making a shocking sore.

Penobscot bay is full of islands, close to which the steam-boat is continually passing. Some are large, with portions of forest and portions of cleared land; some are mere rocks, with a little green or none, and inhabited by sea-birds, which fly and flap about and cry hoarsely; their eggs may be gathered by the bushel, and are good to eat. Other islands have one house and barn on them, the sole family being lords and rulers of all the land which the sea girds. The owner of such an island must have a peculiar sense of property and lordship; he must feel more like his own master and own man, than other people can. [. . .] Other islands, perhaps, high precipitous black bluffs, are crowned with white light-houses, whence, as evening comes on, twinkles a star across the melancholy deep; seen from vessels coming on the coast, seen from the mainland, seen from island to island. Darkness descending, and looking down at the broad wake left by the wheels of the steam boat, we may see sparkles of sea-fire.

THEODORE WINTHROP
1828–1861

Born into a distinguished New England family, Theodore Winthrop was raised in New Haven, Conn., and educated at Yale. Over the next dozen years he held a variety of positions that allowed him to travel extensively in Europe, Panama, California, and the Northwest. For a time he practiced law in the Midwest, but he returned to New York to pursue a career as a writer. With the outbreak of the Civil War he enlisted and was killed two months later leading a charge at Great Bethel, Virginia. His novels—*Cecil Dreeme* (1861), *John Brent* (1862), and *Edwin Brothertoft* (1862)—were published posthumously and were immensely popular for the next forty years. The novels are melodramatic in plot and stilted in style, but the sketches of his journeys display great vitality. *The Canoe and the Saddle* (1863) describes his travels in the Northwest, and *Life in the Open Air* (1863) contains accounts of his impressions of Maine. Winthrop vacationed at Mt. Desert with a group of friends in 1855; he thoroughly enjoyed the trip and used the island as a setting for part of his first novel, *Mr. Waddy's Return* (not published until 1904). He returned to the Maine woods with the painter Frederick E. Church, and in 1856 he was a stump orator in parts of the state for the Fremont campaign.

Life in the Open Air

Off.

At five, P.M., we found ourselves—Iglesias, a party of friends, and myself—on board the Isaac Newton, a great, ugly, three-tiered box that walks the North River, like a laboratory of greasy odors.

In this stately cinder-mill were American citizens. Not to discuss spitting, which is for spittoons, not literature, our fellow-travellers on the deck of the "floating palace" were passably endurable people, in looks, style, and language. I dodge discrimination, and characterize them *en masse* by negations. The passengers of the Isaac Newton, on a certain evening of July, 18—, were not so intrusively green and so gasping as Britons, not so ill-dressed and pretentious as Gauls, not so ardently futile and so lubberly as Germans. Such were the negative virtues of our fellow-citizen travellers; and base would it be to exhibit their positive vices.

And so no more of passengers or passage. I will not describe our evening on the river. Alas for the duty of straightforwardness and dramatic unity! Episodes seem so often sweeter than plots! The wayside joys are better than the final successes. The flowers along the vista, brighter than the victor-wreaths at its close. I may not dally on my way, turning to the right and the left for beauty and caricature. I will balance on the strict edge of my narrative, as a seventh-heavenward Mahometan with wine-forbidden steadiness of poise treads Al Seràt, his bridge of a sword-blade.

Next morning, at Albany, divergent trains cleft our party into a better and a worser half. The beautiful girls, our better half, fled westward to ripen their pallid roses with richer summer-hues in mosquitoless inland dells. Iglesias and I were still northward bound.

At the Saratoga station we sipped a dreary, faded reminiscence of former joys and sparkling brilliancy long dead, in cups of Congress-water, brought by unattractive Ganymedes and sold in the train,—draughts flat, flabby, and utterly bubbleless, lukewarm heel-taps with a flavor of savorless salt.

Still northward journeying, and feeling the sea-side moisture evaporate from our blood under inland suns and sultry inland breezes, we came to Lake Champlain.

As before banquets, to excite appetite, one takes the gentle oyster, so we, before the serious pleasure of our journey, tasted the Adirondack region, paradise of Cockney sportsmen. . . .

The Adirondacks provide a compact, convenient, accessible little wilderness,—an excellent field for the experiments of tyros. When a tyro, whether shot, fisherman, or forester, has proved himself fully there, let him dislodge into some vaster wilderness, away from guides by the day and superintending hunters, away from the incursions of the Cockney tribe, and let out the caged savage within him for a tough struggle with Nature. It needs a struggle tough and resolute to force that Protean lady to observe at all her challenger.

It is well to go to the Adirondacks. They are shaggy, and shagginess is a valuable trait. The lakes are very well,—very well indeed. The objection to the region is not the mountains, which are reasonably shaggy,—not the lakes and rivers, which are water, a capital element. The real difficulty is the society: not the autochthonous society,—they are worthy people, and it is hardly to be mentioned as a fault that they are not a discriminating race, and will asseverate that all fish are trout, and the most arrant mutton is venison,—but the immigrant colonizing society. Cockneys are to be found at every turn, flaunting their banners of the awkward squad, proclaiming to the world with protuberant pride that they are the veritable backwoodsmen,—rather doing it, rather astonishing the natives, they think. And so they are. One squad of such neophytes might be entertaining; but when every square mile echoes with their hails, lost, poor babes, within a furlong of their camps, and when the woods become dim and the air civic with their cooking-smokes, and the subtle odor of fried pork overpowers methylic fragrance among the trees, then he who loves forests for their solitude leaves these brethren to their clumsy joys, and wanders elsewhere deeper into sylvan scenes.

Our visit to the Adirondacks was episodic; and as I have forsworn episodes, I turn away from them with this mild slander, and strike again our Maine track. With lips impurpled by the earliest huckleberries, we came out again upon Champlain. We crossed that water-logged valley in a steamboat, and hastened on, through a pleasant interlude of our rough journey, across Vermont and New Hampshire, two States not without interest to their residents, but of none to this narrative.

By coach and wagon, by highway and by-way, by horse-power and steam-power, we proceeded, until it chanced, one August afternoon, that we left railways and their regions at a way-side station, and let our lingering feet march us along the Valley of the Upper Connecticut. This lovely river, baptizer of Iglesia's childhood, was here shallow and musical, half river, half brook; it had passed the tinkling period, and plashed and rumbled voicefully over rock and shallow.

It was a fair and verdant valley where we walked, overlooked by hills of pleasant pastoral slope. All the land was gay and ripe with yellow harvest. Strolling along, as if the business of travel were forgotten, we placidly identified ourselves with the placid scenery. We became Arcadians both. Such is Arcadia, if I have read aright: a realm where sunshine never scorches, and yet shade is sweet; where simple pleasures please; where the blue sky and the bright water and the green fields satisfy forever. . . .

The weather now, as we drove on, seemed to think that Iglesias deserved better of it. Rain-globes strung upon branches, each globe the possible home of a sparkle, had waited long enough unillumined. Sunlight suddenly discovered this desponding patience and rewarded it. Every drop selected its own ray from the liberal bundle, and, crowding itself full of radiance, became a mirror of sky and cloud and forest. Also, by the searching sunbeams' store of regal purple, ripe raspberries were betrayed. On these, magnified by their convex lenses of water, we pounced. Showers shook playfully upon us from the vines, while we revelled in fruitiness. We ran before our gormers, they gormed by us while we plucked, we ran by, plucked again, and again were gormingly overtaken and overtook. Thus we ate our way luxuriously through the Dixville Notch, a capital cleft in a northern spur of the White Mountains.

Picturesque is a curiously convenient, undiscriminating epithet. I use it here. The Dixville Notch is, briefly, picturesque,—a fine gorge between a crumbling conical crag and a scarped precipice,—a pass easily defensible, except at the season when raspberries would distract sentinels.

Now we came upon our proper field of action. We entered the State of Maine at Township Letter B. A sharper harshness of articulation in stray passengers told us that we were approaching the vocal influence of the name Androscoggin. People talked as if, instead of ivory ring or coral rattle to develop their infantile teeth, they had bitten upon pine knots. Voices were resinous and astringent. An opera, with a chorus drummed up in those regions, could dispense with violins. . . .

Moosehead.

Moosehead Lake is a little bigger than the Lago di Guarda, and therefore, according to our American standard, rather more important. It is not very grand, not very picturesque, but considerably better than no lake,—a meritorious mean; not pretty and shadowy, like a thousand lakelets all over the land, nor tame, broad, and sham-oceanic, like the tanks of Niagara. On the west, near its southern end, is a well-intended blackness and roughness called Squaw Mountain. The rest on that side is undistinguished pine woods.

Mount Kinneo is midway up the lake, on the east. It is the showpiece of the region,—the best they can do for a precipice, and really admirably done. Kinneo is a solid mass of purple flint rising seven hundred feet upright from the water. By the aide of this block could some Archimedes appear, armed with a suitable *"pou stô"* and a mallet heavy enough, he might strike fire to the world. Since percussion-guns and friction cigar-lighters came in, flint has somewhat lost its value; and Kinneo is of no practical use at present. We cannot allow inutilities in this world. Where is the Archimedes? He could make a handsome thing of it by flashing us off with a spark into a new system of things.

Below this dangerous cliff on the lake-bank is the Kinneo House, where fishermen and sportsmen may dwell, and kill or catch, as skill or fortune favors. The historical success of all catchers and killers is well balanced, since men who cannot master facts are always men of imagination, and it is as easy for them to invent as for the other class to do. Boston men haunt Kinneo. For a hero who has not skill enough or imagination enough to kill a moose stands rather in Nowhere with Boston fashion. The tameness of that pleasant little capital makes its belles ardent for tales of wild adventure. New York women are less exacting; a few of them, indeed, like a dash of the adventurous in their lover; but most of them are business-women, fighting their way out of vulgarity into style, and romance is an interruption.

Kinneo was an old station of Iglesias's, in those days when he was probing New England for the picturesque. When the steamer landed, he acted as cicerone, and pointed out to me the main object of interest thereabouts,—the dinner-table. We dined with lumbermen and moose-hunters, scufflingly.

The moose is the lion of these regions. Near Greenville, a gigantic pair of moose-horns marks a fork in the road. Thenceforth moose-facts and moose-legends become the staple of conversation. Moose-meat, combining the flavor of beefsteak and the white of turtle, appears on the table. Moose-horns with full explanations, so that the buyer can play the part of hunter, are for sale. Tame mooselings are exhibited. Sportsmen at Kinneo can choose a *matinée* with the trout or a *soirée* with the moose.

The chief fact of a moose's person is that pair of strange excrescences, his horns. Like fronds of tree-fern, like great coral or sea-fans, these great palmated plates of bone lift themselves from his head, grand, useless, clumsy. A pair of moose-horns overlooks me as I write; they weigh twenty pounds, are nearly five feet in spread, on the right horn are nine developed and two undeveloped antlers, the plates are sixteen inches broad,—a doughty head-piece.

Every year the great, slow-witted animal must renew his head-gear. He must lose the deformity, his pride, and cultivate another. In spring, when the first anemone trembles to the vernal breeze, the moose nods welcome to the wind, and as he nods feels something rattle on his skull. He nods again, as Homer sometimes did. Lo! something drops. A horn has dropped, and he stands a bewildered unicorn. For a few days he steers wild; in this ill-balanced course his lone horn strikes every tree on this side as he dodges from that side. The unhappy creature is staggered, body and mind. In what Jericho of the forest can he hide his diminished head? He flies frantic. He runs amuck through the woods. Days pass by in gloom and then comes despair; another horn falls, and he becomes defenceless; and not till autumn does his brow bear again its full honors.

I make no apology for giving a few lines to the great event of a moose's life. He is the hero of those evergreen-woods,—a hero too little recognized, except by stealthy assassins, meeting him by midnight for massacre. No one seems to have viewed him in his dramatic character, as a forest-monarch enacting every year the tragicomedy of decoronation and recoronation.

The Kinneo House is head-quarters for moose-hunters. This summer the waters of Maine were diluvial, the feeding-grounds were swamped. Of this we took little note: we were in chase of something certain not to be drowned; and the higher the deluge, the easier we could float to Katahdin. After dinner we took the steamboat again for the upper end of the lake.

It was a day of days for sunny summer sailing. Purple haziness curtained the dark front of Kinneo,—a delicate haze purpled by this black promontory, but melting blue like a cloud-fall of cloudless sky upon loftier distant summits. The lake rippled pleasantly, flashing at every ripple.

Suddenly, "Katahdin!" said Iglesias.

Yes, there was a dim point, the object of our pilgrimage.

Katahdin,—the more I saw of it, the more grateful I was to the three powers who enabled me to see it: to Nature for building it, to Iglesias for guiding me to it, to myself for going.

We sat upon the deck and let Katahdin grow,—and sitting, talked of mountains, somewhat to this effect:—

Mountains are the best things to be seen. Within the keen outline of a great peak is packed more of distance, of detail, of light and shade, of color, of all the qualities of space, than vision can get in any other way. No one who has not seen mountains knows how far the eye can reach. Level horizons are within cannon-shot. Mountain horizons not only may be a hundred miles away, but they lift up a hundred miles at length, to be seen at a look. Mountains make a background against which blue sky can be seen; between them and the eye are so many miles of visible atmosphere, domesticated, brought down to the regions of earth, not resting overhead, a vagueness and a void. Air, blue in full daylight, rose and violet at sunset, gray like powdered starlight by night, is collected and isolated by a mountain, so that the eye can comprehend it in nearer acquaintance. There is nothing so refined as the outline of a distant mountain: even a rose-leaf is stiff-edged and harsh in comparison. Nothing else has that definite indefiniteness, that melting permanence, that evanescing changelessness. Clouds in vain strive to imitate it; they are made of slighter stuff; they can be blunt or ragged, but they cannot have that solid positiveness.

Mountains, too, are very stationary,—always at their post. They are characters of dignity, not without noble changes of mood; but these changes are not bewildering, capricious shifts. A mountain can be studied like a picture; its majesty, its grace can be got by heart. Purple precipice, blue pyramid, cone or dome of snow, it is a simple image and a positive thought. It is a delicate fact, first of beauty,—then, as you approach, a strong fact of majesty and power. But even in its cloudy, distant fairness there is a concise, emphatic reality altogether uncloud-like.

Manly men need the wilderness and the mountain. Katahdin is the best mountain in the wildest wild to be had on this side of the continent. He looked at us encouragingly over the hills. I saw that he was all that Iglesias, connoisseur of mountains, had promised, and was content to wait for the day of meeting.

The steamboat dumped us and our canoe on a wharf at the lake-head about four o'clock. A wharf promised a settlement, which, however, did not exist. There was population,—one man and one great ox. Following the inland-pointing nose of the ox, we saw, penetrating the forest, a wooden railroad. Ox-locomotive, and no other, befitted such rails. The train was one great go-cart. We packed our traps upon it, roofed them with our birch, and, without much ceremony of whistling, moved on. As we started, so did the steamboat. The link between us and the inhabited world grew more and more attenuated. Finally it snapped, and we were in the actual wilderness. . . .

Toward Katahdin.

Singularly enough, mill-dams are always found below mill-ponds. Analogously in the Maine rivers, below the lakes, rapids are. Rapids too often compel carries. While we breakfasted without steak of bear or cutlet of moose, Ripogenus gradually retracted itself, and became conscious again of what poetry there is in a lake's pause and a rapid's flow. Fog condensed into water, and water submitting to its destiny went cascading down through a wild defile where no birch could follow.

The Ripogenus carry is three miles long, a faint path through thickets.

"First half," said Cancut, "'s plain enough; but after that 't would take a philosopher with his spectacles on to find it."

This was discouraging. Philosophers twain we might deem ourselves; but what is a craftsman without tools? And never a goggle had we.

But the trappers of muskrats had become our fast friends. They insisted upon lightening our loads over the brambly league. This was kindly. Cancut's elongated head-piece, the birch, was his share of the burden; and a bag of bread, a firkin of various grub, damp blankets for three, and multitudinous traps, seemed more than two could carry at one trip over this longest and roughest of portages.

We paddled from the camp to the lake-foot, and there, while the others compacted the portables for portage, Iglesias and I, at cost of a ducking with mist-drops from the thickets, scrambled up a crag for a supreme view of the fair lake and the clear mountain. And we did well. Katahdin, from the hill guarding the exit of the Penobscot from Ripogenus, is eminent and emphatic, a signal and solitary pyramid, grander than any below the realms of the unchangeable, more distinctly mountainous than any mountain of those that stop short of the venerable honors of eternal snow.

We trod the trail, we others, easier than Cancut. He found it hard to thread the mazes of an overgrown path and navigate his canoe at the same time. "Better," thought he, as he staggered and plunged and bumped along, extricating his boat-bonnet now from a bower of raspberry-bushes, now from the branches of a brotherly birch-tree,—"better," thought he, "were I seated in what I bear, and bounding gayly over the billow. Peril is better than pother."

Bushwhacking thus for a league, we circumvented the peril, and came upon the river flowing fair and free. The trappers said adieu, and launched us. Back then they went to consult their traps and flay their fragrant captives, and we shot forward.

That was a day all poetry and all music. Mountain airs bent and blunted the noonday sunbeams. There was shade of delicate birches on either hand, whenever we loved to linger. Our feather-shallop went dancing on, fleet as the current, and whenever a passion for speed came after moments of luxurious sloth, we could change floating at the river's will into leaps and chasing, with a few strokes of the paddle. All was untouched, unvisited wilderness, and we from bend to bend the first discoverers. So we might fancy ourselves; for civilization had been here only to cut pines, not to plant houses. Yet these fair curves, and liberal reaches, and bright rapids of the birchen-bowered river were only solitary, not lonely. It is never lonely with Nature. Without unnatural men or unnatural beasts, she is capital society by herself. And so we found her,—a lovely being in perfect toilet, which I describe, in an indiscriminating, masculine way, by saying that it was a forest and a river and lakes and a mountain and doubtless sky, all made resplendent by her judicious disposition of a most becoming light. Iglesias and I, being old friends, were received into close intimacy. She smiled upon us unaffectedly, and had a thousand exquisite things to say. drawing us out also, with feminine tact, to say our best things, and teaching us to be conscious, in her presence, of more delicate possibilities of refinement and a tenderer poetic sense. So we voyaged through the sunny hours, and were happy.

Yet there was no monotony in our progress. We could not always drift and glide. Sometimes we must fight our way. Below the placid reaches were the inevitable "rips" and rapids: some we could shoot without hitting anything; some would hit us heavily, did we try to shoot. Whenever the rocks in the current were only as thick as the plums in a boarding-school pudding, we could venture to run the gauntlet; whenever they multiplied to a school-boy's ideal, we were arrested. Just at the brink of peril we would sweep in by an eddy into a shady pool by the shore. At such spots we found a path across the carry. Cancut at once proceeded to bonnet himself with the trickling birch. Iglesias and I took up the packs and hurried on with minds intent on berries. Berries were always found,— blueberries covered with a cloudy bloom, blueberries pulpy, saccharine, plenteous. . . .

Camp Katahdin.

Our camping-place was worthy of its view. On the bank, high and dry, a noble yellow birch had been strong enough to thrust back the forest, making a glade for its own private abode. Other travellers had already been received in this natural pavilion. We had had predecessors, and they had built them a hut, a half roof of hemlock bark, resting on a frame. Time had developed the wrinkles in this covering into cracks, and cracks only wait to be leaks. First, then, we must mend our mansion. Material was at hand; hemlocks, with a back-load of bark, stood ready to be disburdened. In August they have worn their garment so long that they yield it unwillingly. Cancut's axe, however, was insinuating, not to say peremptory. He peeled off and brought great scales of rough purple roofing, and we disposed them, according to the laws of forest architecture, upon our cabin. It became a good example of the *renaissance*. Storm, if such a traveller were approaching, was shut out at top and sides; our blankets could become curtains in front and completely hide us from that unwelcome vagrant, should he peer about seeking whom he might duck and what he might damage.

Our lodge, built, must be furnished. We need a luxurious carpet, couch, and bed; and if we have these, will be content without secondary articles. Here, too, material was ready, and only the artist wanting, to use it. While Cancut peeled the hemlocks, Iglesias and I stripped off armfuls of boughs and twigs from the spruces to "bough down" our camp. "Boughing down" is shingling the floor elaborately with evergreen foliage; and when it is done well, the result counts among the high luxuries of the globe. As the feathers of this bed are harsh stems covered with leafage, the process of bed-making must be systematic, the stems thoroughly covered, and the surface smooth and elastic. I have slept on the various beds of the world,—in a hammock, in a pew, on German feathers, on a bear-skin, on a mat, on a hide; all, all give but a feeble, restless, unrecreating slumber, compared to the spruce or hemlock bed in a forest of Maine. This is fragrant, springy, soft, well-fitting, better than any Sybarite's couch of uncrumpled rose-leaves. It sweetly rustles when you roll, and, by a gently titillation with the little javelin-leaves, keeps up a pleasant electricity over the cuticle. Rheumatism never, after nights on such a bed; agues never; vigor, ardor, fervor, always.

We despatched our camp-building and bed-making with speed, for we had a purpose. The Penobscot was a very beautiful river, and the Ayboljockameegus a very pretty stream; and if there is one place in the world where trout, at certain seasons, are likely to be found, it is in a beautiful river at the mouth of a pretty stream. Now we wanted trout; it was in the programme that something more delicate than salt-pork should grace our banquets before Katahdin. Cancut sustained our *a priori,* that trout were waiting for us over by the Aybol. By this time the tree-shadows, so stiff at noon, began to relax and drift down stream, cooling the surface. The trout could leave their shy lairs down in the chilly deeps, and come up without fear of being parboiled. Besides, as evening came, trout thought of their supper, as we did ours.

Hereupon I had a new sensation. We made ready our flies and our rods, and embarked, as I supposed, to be ferried across and fish from *terra firma.* But no, Cancut dropped anchor very quietly opposite the Aybol's mouth. Iglesias, the man of Maine experience, seemed nought surprised. We were to throw our lines, as it appeared, from the birch; we were to peril our lives on the unsteady basis of a roly-poly vessel,—to keep our places and ballast our bowl, during the excitement of hooking pounds. Self-poise is an acrobatic feat, when a person, not loaded at the heels, undertakes trout-fishing from a birch.

We threw our flies. Instantly at the lucky hackle something darted, seized it, and whirled to fly, with the unwholesome bit in its mouth, up the peaceful Ayboljockameegus. But the lucky man, and he happened to be the novice, forgot, while giving the capturing jerk of his hook, that his fulcrum was not solid rock. The slight shell tilted, turned—over not quite, over enough to give everybody a start. One lesson teaches the docile. Caution thereafter presided over our fishing. She told us to sit low, keep cool, cast gently, strike firmly, play lightly, and pull in steadily. So we did. As the spotted sparklers were rapidly translated from water to a lighter element, a well-fed cheerfulness developed in our trio. We could not speak, for fear of breaking the spell; we smiled at each other. Twenty-three times the smile went round. Twenty-three trout, and not a pigmy among them, lay at our feet. More fish for one dinner and breakfast would be waste and wanton self-indulgence. We stopped. And I must avow, not to claim too much heroism, that the fish had also stopped. So we paddled home contented.

Then, O Walton! O Davy! O Scrope! ye fishers hard by taverns! luxury was ours of which ye know no more than a Chinaman does of music. Under the noble yellow birch we cooked our own fish. We used our scanty kitchen-battery with skill. We cooked with the high art of simplicity. Where Nature has done her best, only fools rush in to improve: on the salmonids, fresh and salt, she has lavished her creative refinements; cookery should only ripen and develop. From our silver gleaming pile of pounders, we chose the larger and the smaller for appropriate experiments. Then we tested our experiments; we tasted our examples. Success. And the success in science proves knowledge and skill. We feasted. The delicacy of our food made each feaster a finer essence.

So we supped, reclined upon our couch of spruce-twigs. In our good cheer we pitied the Eft of Katahdin: he might sneer, but he was supperless. We were grateful to Nature for the grand mountain, for the fair and sylvan woods, for the lovely river and what it had yielded us.

By the time we had finished our flaky fare and sipped our chocolate from the Magdalena, Night announced herself,—Night, a jealous, dark lady, eclipsed and made invisible all her rivals, that she might solely possess us. Night's whispers lulled us. The rippling river, the rustling leaves, the hum of insects grew more audible; and these are gentle sounds that prove wide quietude in Nature, and tell man that the burr and buzz in his day-laboring brain have ceased, and he had better be breathing deep in harmony. So we disposed ourselves upon the fragrant couch of spruce-boughs, and sank slowly and deeper into sleep, as divers sink into the thick waters down below, into the dreamy waters far below the plunge of sunshine. . . .

Up Katahdin.

Next morning, when we awoke, just before the gray of dawn, the sky was clear and scintillating; but there was a white cotton night-cap on the head of Katahdin. As we inspected him, he drew his night-cap down farther, hinting that he did not wish to see the sun that day. When a mountain is thus in the sulks after a storm, it is well not to disturb him: he will not offer the prize of a view. Experience taught us this: but then experience is only an empiric at the best.

Besides, whether Katahdin were bare-headed or cloud-capped, it would be better to blunder upward than lounge all day in camp and eat Sybaritic dinners. We longed for the nervy climb. We must have it. "Up!" said tingling blood to brain. "Dash through the forest! Grasp the crag, and leap the cleft! Sweet flash forth the streamlets from granite fissures. To breathe the winds that smite the peaks is life."

As soon as dawn bloomed in the woods we breakfasted, and ferried the river before sunrise. The ascent subdivides itself into five zones. 1. A scantily wooded acclivity, where bears abound. 2. A dense, swampy forest region. 3. Steep, mossy mountain-side, heavily wooded. 4. A belt of dwarf spruces, nearly impenetrable. 5. Ragged rock.

Cancut was our leader to-day. There are by far too many blueberries in the first zone. No one, of course, intends to dally, but the purple beauties tempted, and too often we were seduced. Still such yielding spurred us on to hastier speed, when we looked up after delay and saw the self-denying far ahead.

To write an epic or climb a mountain is merely a dogged thing; the result is more interesting to most than the process. Mountains, being cloud-compellers, are rain-shedders, and the shed water will not always flow with decorous gayety in dell or glen. Sometimes it stays bewildered in a bog, and here the climber must plunge. In the moist places great trees grow, die, fall, rot, and barricade the way with their corpses. Katahdin has to endure all the ills of mountain being, and we had all the usual difficulties to fight through doggedly. When we were clumsy, we tumbled and rose up torn. Still we plodded on, following a path blazed by the Bostonians, Cancut's late charge, and we grumblingly thanked them.

Going up, we got higher and drier. The mountain-side became steeper than it could stay, and several land-avalanches, ancient or modern, crossed our path. It would be sad to think that all the eternal hills were crumbling thus, outwardly, unless we knew that they bubble up inwardly as fast. Posterity is thus cared for in regard to the picturesque. Cascading streams also shot by us, carrying light and music. From them we stole refreshment, and did not find the waters mineral and astringent, as Mr. Turner, the first climber, calumniously asserts.

The trees were still large and surprisingly parallel to the mountain wall. Deep soft moss covered whatever was beneath, and sometimes this would yield and let the foot measure a crevice. Perilous pitfalls; but we clambered unharmed. The moss, so rich, deep, soft, and earthily fragrant, was a springy stair-carpet of a steep stairway. And sometimes when the carpet slipped and the state of heels over head seemed imminent, we held to the baluster-trees, as one after wassail clings to the lamp-post.

Even on this minor mountain the law of diminishing vegetation can be studied. The great trees abandoned us, and stayed indolently down in shelter. Next the little wiry trees ceased to be the comrades of our climb. They were no longer to be seen planted upon jutting crags, and, bold as standard-bearers, inciting us to mount higher. Big spruces, knobby with balls of gum, dwindled away into little ugly dwarf spruces, hostile, as dwarfs are said to be always, to human comfort. They grew man-high, and hedged themselves together into a dense thicket. We could not go under, nor over, nor through. To traverse them at all, must recall the period when we were squirrels or cats, in some former state of being.

Somehow we pierced, as man does ever, whether he owes it to the beast or the man in him. From time to time, when in this struggle we came to an open point of rock, we would remember that we were on high, and turn to assure ourselves that nether earth was where we had left it. We always found it *in situ,* in belts green, white, and blue, a tricolor of woods, water, and sky. Lakes were there without number, forest without limit. We could not analyze yet, for there was work to do. Also, whenever we paused, there was the old temptation, blueberries. Every outcropping ledge offered store of tonic, ozone-fed blueberries, or of mountain-cranberries, crimson and of concentrated flavor, or of the white snowberry, most delicate of fruits that grow.

As we were creeping over the top of the dwarf wood, Cancut, who was in advance, suddenly disappeared; he seemed to fall through a gap in the spruces, and we heard his voice calling in cavernous tones. We crawled forward and looked over. It was the upper camp of the Bostonians. They had profited by a hole in the rocks, and chopped away the stunted scrubs to enlarge it into a snug artificial abyss. It was snug, and so to the eye is a cell at Sing-Sing. If they were very misshapen Bostonians, they may have succeeded in lying there comfortably. I looked down ten feet into the rough chasm, and I saw, *Corpo di Bacco!* I saw a cork.

To this station our predecessors had come in an easy day's walk from the river; here they had tossed through a night, and given a whole day to finish the ascent, returning hither again for a second night. As we purposed to put all this travel within one day, we could not stay and sympathize with the late tenants. A little more squirrel-like skipping and cat-like creeping over the spruces, and we were out among bulky boulders and rough *débris* on a shoulder of the mountain. Alas! the higher, the more hopeless. Katahdin, as he had taken pains to inform us, meant to wear the veil all day. He was drawing down the white drapery about his throat and letting it fall over his shoulders. Sun and wind struggled mightily with his sulky fit; sunshine rifted off bits of the veil, and wind seized, whirled them away, and, dragging them over the spruces below, tore them to rags. Evidently, if we wished to see the world, we must stop here and survey, before the growing vapor covered all. We climbed to the edge of Cloudland, and stood fronting the semicircle of southward view.

Katahdin's self is finer than what Katahdin sees. Katahdin is distinct, and its view is indistinct. It is a vague panorama, a mappy, unmethodic maze of water and woods, very roomy, very vast, very simple,—and these are capital qualities, but also quite monotonous. A lover of largeness and scope has the proper emotions stirred, but a lover of variety very soon finds himself counting the lakes. It is a wide view, and it is a proud thing for a man six feet or less high, to feel that he himself, standing on something he himself has climbed, and having Katahdin under his feet a mere convenience, can see all Maine. It does not make Maine less, but the spectator more, and that is a useful moral result. Maine's face, thus exposed, has almost no features: there are no great mountains visible, none that seem more than green hillocks in the distance. Besides sky, Katahdin's view contains only the two primal necessities of wood and water. Nowhere have I seen such breadth of solemn forest, gloomy, were it not for the cheerful interruption of many fair lakes, and bright ways of river linking them.

Far away on the southern horizon we detected the heights of Mount Desert, our old familiar haunt. All the northern semicircle was lost to us by the fog. We lost also the view of the mountain itself. All the bleak, lonely, barren, ancient waste of bare summit was shrouded in cold fog. The impressive gray ruin and Titanic havoc of a granite mountain-top, the heaped boulders, the crumbling crags, the crater-like depression, the long stern reaches of sierra, the dark curving slopes channelled and polished by the storms and fine drifting mists of æons, the down-right plunge of precipices, all the savageness of harsh rock, unsoftened by other vegetation than rusty moss and the dull green splashes of lichen, all this was hidden, except when the mist, white and delicate where we stood, but thick and black above, opened whimsically and delusively, as mountain mists will do, and gave us vistas into the upper desolation. After such momentary rifts the mist thickened again, and swooped forward as if to involve our station, but noon sunshine, reverberated from the plains and valleys and lakes below, was our ally; sunshine checked the overcoming mist, and it stayed overhead, an unwelcome parasol, making our August a chilly November. Besides what our eyes lost, our minds lost, unless they had imagination enough to create it, the sentiment of triumph and valiant energy that the man of body and soul feels upon the windy heights, the highest, whence he looks far and wide, like a master of realms, and knows that the world is his; and they lost the sentiment of solemn joy that the man of soul recognizes as one of the surest intimations of immortality, stirring within him, whenever he is in the unearthly regions, the higher world.

We stayed studying the pleasant solitude and dreamy breadth of Katahdin's panorama for a long time, and every moment the mystery of the mist above grew more enticing. Pride also was awakened. We turned from sunshine and Cosmos into fog and Chaos. We made ourselves quite miserable for nought. We clambered up into Nowhere into a great, white, ghostly void. We saw nothing but the rough surfaces we trod. We pressed along crater-like edges, and all below was filled with mist, troubled and rushing upward like the smoke of a volcano. Up we went,—nothing but granite and gray dimness. Where we arrived we know not. It was a top, certainly; that was proved by the fact that there was nothing within sight. We cannot claim that it was the topmost top; Kimchinjinga might have towered within pistol-shot; popgun-shot was our extremest range of vision, except for one instant, when a kind-hearted sunbeam gave us a vanishing glimpse of a white lake and breadth of forest far in the unknown North toward Canada. . . .

PART II:
ESSAYS AND SKETCHES

ELIJAH KELLOGG
1813–1901

Elijah Kellogg was born and raised in Portland. Before he entered Bowdoin College, he had spent one year "indentured" on his cousin's farm and three years at sea. While in college he befriended the people of neighboring Harpswell, and he returned to the town after his studies at Andover Theological Seminary. He served the parish in Harpswell for eleven years and then moved to the Mariner's Church in Boston. Kellogg's literary career had started in seminary with declamations written as a class exercise; he published his first long tale, a story of pioneer Maine entitled *Good Old Times,* in 1867, and followed this with nearly thirty works for juveniles over the next two decades. The stories stress the virtues of neighborliness and fair dealing, and many are set in Casco Bay and at Bowdoin College. Unfortunately, Kellogg's publisher failed and he lost the copyrights to nearly all his books. He returned to Harpswell in 1885 and lived with the support of the townspeople. Kellogg's declamations, which included "Spartacus to the Gladiators," "Regulus to the Carthaginians," "Hannibal at the Altar," and "Pericles to the People," were standard fare for schoolchildren of the nineteenth century.

Pericles to the People

Imagine yourself at Athens, among that strange people of feverish blood, who deify to-day the man they slaughtered but yesterday. The voice of the herald proclaims that Pericles is to be arraigned before the tribunal of the people. Borne along by the crowd, you enter the hall of justice. Not a sword rattles in its scabbard; not a mailed foot rings on the marble floor; one deep, intense, ominous silence pervades that dangerous assembly, as Pericles, rising, thus addresses them:—

"Ye men of Athens, I come not here to plead for life, though it be spent in exile; to entreat for a breath, though it be drawn in the damps of a dungeon; but to refute a vile slander; to show that he who invents and propagates a falsehood, like Sisyphus, rolls a stone to return and crush him. Cratinus accuses me of having embezzled the money raised for the defence of Greece, and of having expended it in adorning the city of Athens, as a proud and vain woman decketh herself with jewels.

"Have I not defended Greece, while Sparta and the allies were reposing in comfort by their own firesides? He avers that I was often at the House of Phidias to admire his statues, but insinuates that I had a softer motive. Suppose I had; rather let him show in what I have betrayed my country, when I have oppressed the poor, polluted myself with bribes, or turned back in the hour of battle. He accuses me of sacrificing the lives of brave men to my vaulting ambition and even affects to shed tears over those who fell, in the flower of their youth, at Samos.

"Sacrificing! Were they machines to move at my bidding? bullocks to be dragged up and offered at the altar of Mars? Were they Persian mercenaries, to be driven with whips to the conflict? or were they patriots defending their firesides, and I their elder brother? They were the descendants of those who fell at Marathon, —men whose youthful locks had been worn off by the helmet, and whose fingers grew to the sword-hilt.

"The parents of those brave men did not, with reddening cheeks, behold them lying on some feverish couch, like a sick girl, crying for cooling drinks; but they died with their wounds in front, the broken sword in their hand, and the shout of victory ringing in their ears. Oh, yes! one hour of glorious conflict—when the blood leaps and the muscles rally for the mastery, when the hero's soul wings its way through gaping wounds to Elysium—is worth a whole eternity of sitting in senates and dull debates, and private bickerings, and tame, common life.

"One day, as we were making forced marches across the isthmus in pursuit of the Lacedæmonians, a woman, following the camp as a sutler, with a child at her breast, fell and expired from fatigue. A soldier raised a spear to despatch the infant. Moved with compassion, I struck down his weapon; for I thought of my own little ones at home, whose kisses were scarcely yet cold on my lips, and even in the confusion of pursuit, I provided him with a nurse.

"On my return, he accompanied me, grew up with my children, fed at my table, slept in my tent, and fought behind my shield. As a reward for life, education, and a thousand anxious cares incurred, he has now, by false accusation, summoned me to the tribunal of my country, to plead for that life which has ever been held cheap in her service. What shall be done with such a wretch? I hear you exclaim: 'Send for the executioner! burn him to ashes! fling him from the Acropolis!'

"Cratinus, thou art that wretch; and yet methinks thou hast not altogether the noble bearing of the patriot who rejoices that he has been able to bring to justice the betrayer of his country; but thou hast rather the look of some timid shepherd, who, in chasing the stag, and pursuing the goat, has, all unwittingly, stumbled upon the lair of the lion, and, too terrified to flee, stands shivering before the glaring eyeball of the tawny brute.

"Thou small thing, I will not hurt thee; for, in the proud consciousness of right, I could even pity thee. And, when again thou liest among the slain at Megara, thy helmet cleft, the lance of the enemy at thy throat, and thou with not strength enough to parry it, then call for Pericles, and he will *again* come to thy rescue. Farewell, thou grateful child! thou faithful friend! thou manly enemy!"

HENRY DAVID THOREAU
1817–1862

Henry David Thoreau, a native of Concord, Mass., graduated from Harvard at the age of twenty in 1837. While in college he began his journals, a detailed chronicle of his thoughts and observations that formed the basis of all his books. Although he taught school for a few years, Thoreau never pursued a career in the ordinary sense; instead, he preferred to live simply and work as a handyman and surveyor. His approach to life reflected his strong individualism—spending two years in a house which he built himself on Walden Pond, refusing to pay a poll tax to a government that allowed slavery, and publicly praising John Brown after the Harper's Ferry raid. Thoreau visited Maine in 1846, 1853, and 1857, and his accounts were published posthumously as *The Maine Woods* (1864). The book is a collection of three essays rather than a unified volume, but it reveals his respect for the wilderness and the men who inhabited it. The following excerpt describes Thoreau's solitary ascent to the summit of Mt. Katahdin and his confrontation with untamed Nature.

From *The Maine Woods*

In the morning, after whetting our appetite on some raw pork, a wafer of hard bread, and a dipper of condensed cloud or waterspout, we all together began to make our way up the falls, which I have described; this time choosing the right hand, or highest peak, which was not the one I had approached before. But soon my companions were lost to my sight behind the mountain ridge in my rear, which still seemed ever retreating before me, and I climbed alone over huge rocks, loosely poised, a mile or more, still edging toward the clouds—for though the day was clear elsewhere, the summit was concealed by mist. The mountain seemed a vast aggregation of loose rocks, as if sometime it had rained rocks, and they lay as they fell on the mountain sides, nowhere fairly at rest, but leaning on each other, all rocking-stones, with cavities between, but scarcely any soil or smoother shelf. They were the raw materials of a planet dropped from an unseen quarry, which the vast chemistry of nature would anon work up, or work down, into the smiling and verdant plains and valleys of earth. This was an undone extremity of the globe; as in lignite we see coal in the process of formation.

At length I entered within the skirts of the cloud which seemed forever drifting over the summit, and yet would never be gone, but was generated out of that pure air as fast as it flowed away; and when, a quarter of a mile further, I reached the summit of the ridge, which those who have seen in clearer weather say is about five miles long, and contains a thousand acres of table-land, I was deep within the hostile ranks of clouds, and all objects were obscured by them. Now the wind would blow me out a yard of clear sunlight, wherein I stood; then a gray, dawning light was all it could accomplish, the cloud-line ever rising and falling with the wind's intensity. Sometimes it seemed as if the summit would be cleared in a few moments and smile in sunshine: but what was gained on one side was lost on another. It was like sitting in a chimney and waiting for the smoke to blow away. It was, in fact, a cloud-factory,—these were the cloud-works, and the wind turned them off done from the cool, bare rocks. Occasionally, when the windy columns broke in to me, I caught sight of a dark, damp crag to the right or left; the mist driving ceaselessly between it and me. It reminded me of the creations of the old epic and dramatic poets, of Atlas, Vulcan, the Cyclops, and Prometheus. Such was Caucasus and the rock where Prometheus was bound. Æschylus had no doubt visited such scenery as this. It was vast, Titanic, and such as man never inhabits. Some part of the beholder, even some vital part, seems to escape through the loose grating of his ribs as he ascends. He is more lone than you can imagine. There is less of substantial thought and fair understanding in him, than in the plains where men inhabit. His reason is dispersed and shadowy, more thin and subtile like the air. Vast, Titanic, inhuman Nature has got him at disadvantage, caught him alone, and pilfers him of some of his divine faculty. She does not smile on him as in the plains. She seems to say sternly, why came ye here before your time? This ground is not prepared for you. Is it enough that I smile in the valleys? I have never made this soil for thy feet, this air for thy breathing, these rocks for thy neighbors. I cannot pity nor fondle thee here, but forever relentlessly drive thee hence to where I *am* kind. Why seek me where I have not called thee, and then complain because you find me but a stepmother? Shouldst thou freeze or starve, or shudder thy life away, here is no shrine, nor altar, nor any access to my ear.

> "Chaos and ancient Night, I come no spy
> With purpose to explore or to disturb
> The secrets of your realm, but * * *
> * * * * * * * as my way
> Lies through your spacious empire up to light."

The tops of mountains are among the unfinished parts of the globe, whither it is a slight insult to the gods to climb and pry into their secrets, and try their effect on our humanity. Only daring and insolent men, perchance, go there. Simple races, as savages, do not climb mountains—their tops are sacred and mysterious tracts never visited by them. Pomola is always angry with those who climb to the summit of Ktaadn.

According to Jackson, who in his capacity of geological surveyor of the state, has accurately measured it—the altitude of Ktaadn is 5,300 feet, or a little more than one mile above the level of the sea—and he adds: "It is then evidently the highest point in the State of Maine, and is the most abrupt granite mountain in New England." The peculiarities of that spacious table-land on which I was standing, as well as the remarkable semicircular precipice or basin on the eastern side, were all concealed by the mist. I had brought my whole pack to the top, not knowing but I should have to make my descent to the river, and possibly to the settled portion of the state alone and by some other route, and wishing to have a complete outfit with me. But at length, fearing that my companions would be anxious to reach the river before night, and knowing that the clouds might rest on the mountain for days, I was compelled to descend. Occasionally, as I came down, the wind would blow me a vista open through which I could see the country eastward, boundless forests, and lakes, and streams, gleaming in the sun, some of them emptying into the East Branch. There were also new mountains in sight in that direction. Now and then some small bird of the sparrow family would flit away before me, unable to command its course, like a fragment of the gray rock blown off by the wind.

I found my companions where I had left them, on the side of the peak, gathering the mountain cranberries, which filled every crevice between the rocks, together with blue berries, which had a spicier flavor the higher up they grew, but were not the less agreeable to our palates. When the country is settled and roads are made, these cranberries will perhaps become an article of commerce. From this elevation, just on the skirts of the clouds, we could overlook the country west and south for a hundred miles. There it was, the State of Maine, which we had seen on the map, but not much like that. Immeasurable forest for the sun to shine on, that eastern *stuff* we hear of in Massachusetts. No clearing, no house. It did not look as if a solitary traveller had cut so much as a walking-stick there. Countless lakes,—Moosehead in the southwest, forty miles long by ten wide, like a gleaming silver platter at the end of the table; Chesuncook, eighteen long by three wide, without an island; Millinocket, on the south, with its hundred islands; and a hundred others without a name; and mountains also, whose names, for the most part, are known only to the Indians. The forest looked like a firm grass sward, and the effect of these lakes in its midst has been well compared by one who has since visited this same spot, to that of a "mirror broken into a thousand fragments, and wildly scattered over the grass, reflecting the full blaze of the sun." It was a large farm for somebody, when cleared. According to the Gazetteer, which was printed before the boundary question was settled, this single Penobscot county in which we were, was larger than the whole State of Vermont, with its fourteen counties; and this was only a part of the wild lands of Maine. We are concerned now, however, about natural, not political limits. We were about eighty miles, as the bird flies from Bangor, or one hundred and fifteen as we had ridden, and walked, and paddled. We had to console ourselves with the reflection that this view was probably as good as that from the peak, as far as it went, and what were a mountain without its attendant clouds and mists? Like ourselves, neither Bailey nor Jackson had obtained a clear view from the summit.

Setting out on our return to the river, still at an early hour in the day, we decided to follow the course of the torrent, which we supposed to be Murch Brook, as long as it would not lead us too far out of our way. We thus travelled about four miles in the very torrent itself, continually crossing and recrossing it, leaping from rock to rock, and jumping with the stream down falls of seven or eight feet, or sometimes sliding down on our backs in a thin sheet of water. This ravine had been the scene of an extraordinary freshet in the spring, apparently accompanied by a slide from the mountain. It must have been filled with a stream of stones and water, at least twenty feet above the present level of the torrent. For a rod or two on either side of its channel, the trees were barked and splintered up to their tops, the birches bent over, twisted, and sometimes finely split like a stable-broom; some a foot in diameter snapped off, and whole clumps of trees bent over with the weight of rocks piled on them. In one place we noticed a rock two or three feet in diameter, lodged nearly twenty feet high in the crotch of a tree. For the whole four miles, we saw but one rill emptying in, and the volume of water did not seem to be increased from the first. We travelled thus very rapidly with a downward impetus, and grew remarkably expert at leaping from rock to rock, for leap we must, and leap we did, whether there was any rock at the right distance or not. It was a pleasant picture when the foremost turned about and looked up the winding ravine, walled in with rocks and the green forest, to see at intervals of a rod or two, a red-shirted or green-jacketed mountaineer against the white torrent, leaping down the channel with his pack on his back, or pausing upon a convenient rock in the midst of the torrent to mend a rent in his clothes, or unstrap the dipper at his belt to take a draught of the water. At one place we were startled by seeing, on a little sandy shelf by the side of the stream, the fresh print of a man's foot, and for a moment realized how Robinson Crusoe felt in a similar case; but at last we remembered that we had struck this stream on our way up, though we could not have told where, and one had descended into the ravine for a drink. The cool air above, and the continual bathing of our bodies in mountain water, alternate foot, sitz, douche, and plunge baths, made this walk exceedingly refreshing, and we had travelled only a mile or two after leaving the torrent, before every thread of our clothes was as dry as usual, owing perhaps to a peculiar quality in the atmosphere.

After leaving the torrent, being in doubt about our course, Tom threw down his pack at the foot of the loftiest spruce tree at hand, and shinned up the bare trunk some twenty feet, and then climbed through the green tower, lost to our sight, until he held the topmost spray in his hand. McCauslin, in his younger days, had marched through the wilderness with a body of troops, under General Somebody, and with one other man did all the scouting and spying service. The General's word was: "Throw down the top of that tree," and there was no tree in the Maine woods so high that it did not lose its top in such a case. I have heard a story of two men being lost once in these woods, nearer to the settlements than this, who climbed the loftiest pine they could find, some six feet in diameter at the ground, from whose top they discovered a solitary clearing and its smoke. When at this height, some two hundred feet from the ground, one of them became dizzy, and fainted in his companion's arms, and the latter had to accomplish the descent with him, alternately fainting and reviving, as best he could. To Tom we cried, where away does the summit bear? where the burnt lands? The last he could only conjecture; he descried, however, a little meadow and pond, lying probably in our course, which we concluded to steer for. On reaching this secluded meadow, we found fresh tracks of moose on the shore of the pond, and the water was still unsettled as if they had fled before us. A little further, in a dense thicket, we seemed to be still on their trail. It was a small meadow, of a few acres, on the mountain side, concealed by the forest, and perhaps never seen by a white man before, where one would think that the moose might browse and bathe, and rest in peace. Pursuing this course, we soon reached the open land, which went sloping down some miles toward the Penobscot.

Perhaps I most fully realized that this was primeval, untamed, and forever untameable *Nature,* or whatever else men call it, while coming down this part of the mountain. We were passing over "Burnt Lands," burnt by lightning, perchance, though they showed no recent marks of fire, hardly so much as a charred stump, but looked rather like a natural pasture for the moose and deer, exceedingly wild and desolate, with occasional strips of timber crossing them, and low poplars springing up, and patches of blueberries here and there. I found myself traversing them familiarly, like some pasture run to waste, or partially reclaimed by man; but when I reflected what man, what brother or sister or kinsman of our race made it and claimed it, I expected the proprietor to rise up and dispute my passage. It is difficult to conceive of a region uninhabited by man. We habitually presume his presence and influence everywhere. And yet we have not seen pure Nature, unless we have seen her thus vast, and drear, and inhuman, though in the midst of cities. Nature was here something savage and awful, though beautiful. I looked with awe at the ground I trod on, to see what the Powers had made there, the form and fashion and material of their work. This was that Earth of which we have heard, made out of Chaos and Old Night. Here was no man's garden, but the unhandselled globe. It was not lawn, nor pasture, nor mead, nor woodland, nor lea, nor arable, nor waste-land. It was the fresh and natural surface of the planet Earth, as it was made forever and ever,—to be the dwelling of man, we say,—so Nature made it, and man may use it if he can. Man was not to be associated with it. It was Matter, vast, terrific,—not his Mother Earth that we have heard of, not for him to tread on, or be buried in,—no, it were being too familiar even to let his bones lie there—the home this of Necessity and Fate. There was there felt the presence of a force not bound to be kind to man. It was a place for heathenism and superstitious rites,—to be inhabited by men nearer of kin to the rocks and to wild animals than we. We walked over it with a certain awe, stopping from time to time to pick the blueberries which grew there, and had a smart and spicy taste. Perchance where *our* wild pines stand, and leaves lie on their forest floor in Concord, there were once reapers, and husbandmen planted grain; but here not even the surface had been scarred by man, but it was a specimen of what God saw fit to make this world. What is it to be admitted to a museum, to see a myriad of particular things, compared with being shown some star's surface, some hard matter in its home! I stand in awe of my body, this matter to which I am bound has become so strange to me. I fear not spirits, ghosts, of which I am one,—*that* my body might,—but I fear bodies, I tremble to meet them. What is this Titan that has possession of me? Talk of mysteries!—Think of our life in nature,—daily to be shown matter, to come in contact with it,—rocks, trees, wind on our cheeks! the *solid* earth! the *actual* world! the *common sense! Contact! Contact! Who* are we? *where* are we?

Ere long we recognized some rocks and other features in the landscape which we had purposely impressed on our memories, and quickening our pace, by two o'clock we reached the batteau. . . .

HOLMAN DAY
1865–1935

Holman (Francis) Day was born in Vassalboro and educated at Colby College. He did editorial work on newspapers in Bangor, Dexter, and Lewiston for several years, and in 1900 he published his first book, *Up in Maine: Stories of Yankee Life Told in Verse.* This and other popular collections of verse, *Pine Tree Ballads* (1902) and *Kin o' Ktaadn* (1904), utilized the straightforward rhyming of storytelling speech. Day's novels combined broad humor and melodrama and were widely read; several — *Squire Phin* (1905), *King Spruce* (1908), *The Ramrodders* (1910), and *The Rider of the King Log* (1919) — also drew upon Maine manners and customs. Day spent his later years in California writing scenarios for films. As a journalist Day was one of Maine's respected spokesmen; in "The Queer Folk of the Maine Coast" he expresses the resentment felt by many natives toward those from "outside."

The Queer Folk of the Maine Coast

Of old, muskets drove the Abnakis off the coast of Maine. Today, money is driving away another race.

Between Kittery Point and Quoddy Head "resorters" have acquired hundreds of headlands and thousands of islands. A phalanx of cottages fronts the sea. More than half the States in the Union are represented in these summer colonies. Cove and cape, the coast is pretty well monopolized by nonresidents; "no-trespass" signs are so thickly set that they form a blazed trail. The man from the city resents intrusion. For that matter, the queer squatter people who have been dispossessed find little relish in being stared at as human curiosities. Therefore they have hidden themselves in the deep gashes of the coast cliffs; their little huts are now at the head of crooked coves where pleasure craft do not venture; or they have located on little nubbins of islands that city people do not buy, for these islands may be approached only at flood-tide. And in their retreats the "queer folk" resent intrusion as heartily as do the rich folk on their reserves.

So the "queer folk" live alone— and it is said that isolation develops eccentricity. The ocean creeps to the doors of their huts, and the winter waves thunder in their ears—and there are those who say that the din of the sea beats curious ideas into the head.

Even the Maine "native" himself, the thrifty farmer who sells his produce to the city "sojourner" or takes summer boarders, does not understand the queer folk of the lonely coves very well. The nooks that they have chosen for hiding-places have no roads leading to them. The islands that they have pre-empted have been "set off" by act of the Legislature from the nearest coast towns, in order that the towns may not have the unfortunates on their hands as paupers. These people who have been abandoned dwell in a sort of "no man's land." They do not pay taxes, they do not vote. Fashion is close to many of them, just over that ridge of coast ledge or down that stretch of water—for fashion has picked most of the choice spots on the Maine coast for its sojourn. But the queer folk are not interested in any display that fashion may make. They are not envious, they do not want to beg. Where penury and pride meet in the cities there are heartburnings. But the man tossing in the battered dory in the swash of the millionaire's yacht neither sighs nor glares, provided he be one of the queer folk. For the queer folk are queer in one respect especially: they dwell content in their own world, which is often a world of illusion—for solitariness and the sea breed strange thoughts.

Ossian Dustin, of Newcastle, would not change places with a millionaire, so he says. Yet Uncle Ossian, at eighty, lives alone in a little hut with a dirt floor, and earns about fifty dollars a year by sawing fire-wood and doing odd jobs. But fifty dollars supply his frugal needs, and he has the most of his time to devote to hunting for Cap'n Kidd's treasure, in the buried existence of which he implicity believes.

The case of Uncle Ossian illustrates the type of that content that relieves these hidden human tragedies of the Maine coast of some of their pitifulness. During most of his long life, as often as he has found opportunity, Uncle Ossian has hunted and dug along the ragged Lincoln coast. He has toiled nights, for the most part, believing that in the night a treasure-seeker can best circumvent the enchantments laid on buried pirate spoils. He has kept vigil oftenest in the region of Cod Lead Nubble. He searches with a treasure-rod made by his own hands. He has the tip of a cow's horn, plugged with wood and containing various metals. In the wooden plug are stuck parallel strips of whalebone, and he clutches these strips, one in each hand, and walks along, balancing the tip of horn. When he passes over the famous iron pot the tip, thus is his belief, will turn down and point at the buried treasure. There is nothing remarkable in Uncle Ossian's quest, for other men in Maine have hunted for Kidd's treasure. But his radiant courage and his unfailing optimism are striking. He believes that he "is always right on the edge" of finding the gold. He says his spade has struck against the iron pot several times, but that enchantment has whisked away the treasure. He expects that eventually his own charms will prevail over the powers of evil. He believes that the long waiting and the disappointments have been merely a test of his courage and good faith—remarkable philosophy in a man who is eighty years old and has not succeeded. He is reanimated occasionally by the sight of a figure all of shining gold that comes rowing up the reach from the sea, and he is confident that this is a good spirit sent to guide him to the treasure, and that the spirit will sometime prevail over the imps who watch the iron pot.

Uncle Ossian affirms that he has passed as happy a life as any man he knows; he says that the money will "come in handy" in his old age, and that he shall first buy a stone for his mother's grave, and then a house with a floor in it for himself. It can scarcely be said that Uncle Ossian's unfailing cheerfulness springs from any philosophy of life that he has evolved. But after our talk I came out of his dingy hut with the feeling that probably some of the proud folk in the cottages down the bay needed pity more than he.

On Little Spruce Island I found three old men, brothers—William, Daniel and Nehemiah Shanks. They have lived there all their lives in a tumble-down little shelter. They are melancholy old men. They are contented, but the sea has brought to them a strange, brooding, wistful solemnity. William and Daniel never married. Nehemiah has had a poor little romance that broke his heart. When he was young he used to go with his father to Portland to sell their fare of fish. The only woman to whom he had ever spoken was his mother—for no one except the Shanks family has ever lived on Little Spruce. A woman of the waterside in Portland made him her prey for the sake of his little hoard of savings, married him, induced him to forge his father's name and draw the family savings from the bank—and then deserted him. He went home with his confession of wrong-doing.

"Then you must look out for the boys after I'm dead," said his father, forgiving him. Nehemiah has spent his life "looking out for the boys," who are now infirm old men. "It is my duty in return for my father's pardon of my wrongdoing," he told me, "and I have tried to do my best. I am the youngest, and I am best able to work."

For more than twenty years William has never come out of the hut into the sunshine. He told me that he feared the sun might heat his brains and interfere with his life-work, which is the composition of poetry. There is a blanket hung across one end of the hut. William sits behind this blanket and fixes his eyes on the sunlight that enters through a knothole and "composes." He states that now he is the author of a thousand pieces of poetry. He has committed nothing to paper. He has memorized all of them, he says.

While William idles, Nehemiah tills the little garden, catches fish, digs clams, and cooks. He is cheerfully the burden-bearer, and with some pride says that he is the head of the family; for when his father imposed the trust on him he did so with a ceremony truly patriarchal: he gave into Nehemiah's hands the staff on which he had leaned for many years, saying that it should be the badge of Nehemiah's authority. Nehemiah described the scene to me, tears trickling down his wrinkled cheeks. Memory was only a partial spur to this grief.

Daniel, after more than sixty years of obedience, had become a most amazing rebel. He had declared that another flood had been prophesied to him in a vision, and that he had been ordered to build an ark on Little Spruce. Little Spruce is owned by a lady in Boston, as part of an extensive holding of islands. The Shanks brothers have been permitted to remain as squatters on condition that they do not disturb the standing timber. Nehemiah gave this promise to the manager of the estate.

Daniel, though threescore and ten, took the family axe, handsaw, and hammer and proceeded to his labors on his ark. Nehemiah stood in front of the lordly spruce that Daniel was about to attack with the axe, and in the name of the Shanks family forbade him to chop. Daniel had the zeal of monomania and insisted. Then Nehemiah brandished the family staff and threatened to chastise the disobedient son of their father. Daniel, in a frenzy, made at his brother with the axe, routed him, captured the staff, chopped it up, and then began on the tree. He laid waste quite a section of woodland before Nehemiah got word to the agent. Then in high dudgeon Daniel built a shack of his own. He lives in it and refuses to speak to his brothers. Nehemiah, tall, grave, dignified, with the flowing white beard of a patriarch, stood upon a knoll and pointed over to Daniel's hut and told me of the unfortunate affair, sorrowfully, without anger. Daniel, realizing that his misdeeds were exposed to a stranger, shook his fists from afar and leaped up and down in what was apparently ecstasy of rage. He waylaid me before I had left Little Spruce, and informed me that after being bossed by his brother for more than sixty years he proposed to run his own affairs for the rest of his life. Nehemiah came in his turn to the shore after Daniel had trudged away to his hut, cracking his hard little fists above his head in his temper.

"I still hope to be able to meet father at the door of heaven and tell him that I kept the Shanks family together and kept it decent, as he would have liked to have me keep it," said Nehemiah, sadly. "Daniel was always hard to manage; father found him so. But

I think he will come back to his home, for I am the only one in the family who can cook things as mother used to cook them."

Bushy Island, to which I came when a poor little human drama was at its climax, is a bare handful of earth without a tree on it. Quarter of a century ago Henry Tripp, after roving along the coast, settled there. He was an old man even then, bent at his hips into almost a right angle. Fourteen years ago a woman, as old as he, came from the main and dwelt with him in his little house. In fourteen years she was off that patch of island only twice.

"Hermit Tripp," as he was called, believed that Kidd had buried his treasure on Bushy. Old and decrepit as he was, he began to dig the island. He wore out shovel after shovel at his task. When he died he had shovelled nearly half the island off into the sea, cleaning the earth down to bed-rock.

He died in August, 1908. On the night of his death a summer gale swept the coast, wrecking cottages and flattening acres of trees on the main near Bushy. When the old woman realized that Tripp was dying she took a big hand-bell and, though so weak and old that she could walk only with difficulty, she went out on the high land of the island and rang the bell with all her strength, hoping that in some lull of the gale the sound would be heard on the main.

At midnight she went to the hut to minister to the old man, and found him dead. Then she resumed her vigil on the shore, ringing the bell, blinded by the lightning, drenched by the rains, and blown about by the gale.

People heard and came off to the island the next day. But Bushy Island is one of those "set-off" places, a no man's land so far as the law goes. Three towns at first disclaimed responsibility for the burial expenses of a pauper. The old woman stayed alone with her dead a second night. Then came men and dug his grave, a pebble-toss from his hut, and laid him there. Some one read a bit from the tattered old Bible that was found in the house. Those who had buried the old man went away and left the old woman alone. Chance and idle curiosity brought me to Bushy one day. I had supposed that charity had provided a home elsewhere for the lonely tenant. But she was still there. She was ill, she was hungry, she had not sufficient strength to walk or to build a fire. There is no fresh water on Bushy. She had a scanty supply in a jug.

It is not necessary to go into the details of the measures promptly taken for her relief. At first she concealed her name. We discovered what it was from some old letters that were flying about the little yard. She "had been some one" once on a time. She has a brother living, a worthy and prominent man in an inland town. He came promptly when I communicated with him, and went with me to visit his sister in the hut on Bushy Island. He had not seen her, had not heard from her, for many years. He had sought for her, but she had disappeared. He and she are the only ones left of a well-known family.

One can imagine how fiction would have handled this reunion. But real life has its own grim methods. It was high tide and the launch swung close to the corner of the hut, under which the waves were lapping. The brother hesitated, misery on his countenance.

"Go in first, please!" he implored.

She gave him only a careless glance when he sat down in the unspeakable shelter.

"For God's sake, take me out!" he gasped. "I can't stand this!"

We were not in the place ten seconds. He had not heart or strength to make this forlorn creature know him for what he was. He hurried into the launch and left the island. This is how fact tersely dismissed a situation that fiction would have lingered over.

It is proper in this connection to state that later the brother appointed me his agent and almoner, and before the fall grew late the woman was removed from the island to a comfortable home, where she is now cared for. Her mental faculties that had been impaired by her privations have been regained in a measure, but she has never made any inquiries regarding her family. On our visits to her we find her reading her Bible and, to use her words, "preparing my soul for the great change."

This case also brought to my attention a character who ought to be interesting from a sociological point of view. He is an addition to the varied army of vagrants—he is a water tramp. While search for some honest persons who would take the old woman as a boarder was in progress, those interested in the case carried cooked food each day and plenty of dainties. She declared that she felt perfectly safe to stay alone nights—and, in fact, the hut was too wretched a place to serve as a lodging for any person except the poor old creature who had become accustomed to it.

Now appears a human derelict in a barnacled old dory! He seemed to sniff those food delicacies from afar. He billeted himself on the poor old woman, coming in the edge of the evening, remaining the night, and departing before charity came again with heaped hands.

This especial water tramp has been a peregrinator in Casco waters for many years, a stolid, weather-beaten man, and even the gulls of the bay take more thought as to where they may perch for the night. There are a dozen or more of his ilk scattered alongshore. The city man who comes down to his cottage in the spring and finds a window forced, the left-overs of his larder devoured, and his summer clothes gone, has this gentry of the coast to thank. The water tramp steals only what he can eat and what he can wear. He dwells in a cottage as long as it suits his taste or convenience, or until the crackers, canned goods, and firewood are gone. Then he moves to the next. He is not a good housekeeper, and the cottager who finds his débris in the spring has a bad quarter of an hour and a lively desire for vengeance. If he will keep sharp watch he will find his old coat on the back of a "dory vagabond." But it doesn't trouble the water tramp if he is sent to jail. He goes up-country stoically, and returns to seek his living in the same old way.

But there is one who stands forth from among these petty thieves with almost the proportions of a modern Viking. He came coasting along from Nova Scotia in a gray and seamed old Hampton boat, leisurely seeking adventures and three meals a day, and arrived in the Pemaquid region.

He lingered there for some weeks. His name was MacTush, he had the swagger of a border chieftain, and his hair was the hair of a Norseman, and he found favor in the eyes of a wife whose husband was away upon the Grand Banks on a "mack'rel-chancin' " trip. So the stranger stole the wife, four children, and such furniture from the house as could be stowed in the Hampton boat. He sailed back to Nova Scotia.

As time went on the wife regretted. But it was not regret for the abandoned husband. Here once more fact differs from fiction. She was sorry that she had not been able to take more of her belongings. The Viking's hut in Nova Scotia was but scantily furnished. She kept remembering certain choice things that had been left behind in the hurry of departure and on account of lack of room in the Hampton boat. She urged her new lord to go back and get another load. The story of how she urged came out later in the Lincoln County court. The Viking went back a few months after his first foray. The wife told him that the house would be locked up and the husband away to the Banks once more. The freebooter was removing the rest of the furniture—finding the house untenanted, as the wife had prophesied; but he was apprehended by friends of the absent husband. The judge in imposing sentence stated that a thief who would steal a man's wife, four children, and half his furniture, and then come back after the rest of the household goods, was too much of a rogue to expect mercy, and MacTush is in jail for a number of years.

Louds Island, off the coast of Bristol, occupies perhaps a more anomalous position than any other land along the Atlantic seaboard. It has a considerable population of thrifty fishermen and farmers; they live in good houses and are intelligent. They and their ancestors have dwelt there for more than one hundred and fifty years. But the men of the island have never voted in any election, town or State or national. They have never paid any State, town, or county taxes. They resisted the draft at the time of the Civil War and drove the officers off the island with clubs and rocks. They say that they do not need the protecting arm of State or national government. They raise money for schools and roads, elect municipal officers to administer affairs, and seem to get along very comfortably as an independent principality. Flattering overtures have been made by Bristol; by coming into the fold the islanders would receive State school money, have an opportunity to vote, and obtain other advantages. But Louds Island will not affiliate. There has never been a crime committed on the island, no one ever locks his door, and almost every one is a relation of some one else.

While Louds Island is genially beckoned into the family by Bristol, Malaga Island is getting the cold shoulder from Phippsburg —the town that contains the site of ancient "Augusta," pioneer of all New England settlements.

As a "no man's land" Malaga has more striking peculiarities than any other island alongshore. There are about fifty persons on it, of all grades of negro blood, and most of them descendants of a runaway slave who came and hid there more years ago than any man about there remembers. These people form a strange clan. They have married and intermarried until the trespass on consanguinity has produced its usual lamentable effects. They are as near to being children of nature as possible for people to be who are only a stone's throw from the mainland and civilization. They lack entirely the spirit of thrift and of providing for future emergencies. Winter after winter, through all the years, they have shivered and starved, but never does November find a wood-pile on Malaga, nor a week's supply of food in reserve. To counsel on economy and to preachment on thrift they are as inattentive as little children would be. A coast missionary took in hand one especially improvident family of six—father, mother, and four children well grown. Spurred by him, they fished, dug clams, sold bait to trawlers, and at the end of the summer had saved about seventy dollars among them. Then the missionary went away, confident that at least one Malaga family would reach "March Hill" in comparative comfort. When his back was turned they used for kindlings the shingles that he had given them for the repair of their miserable hut, bought six dogs in order that each member of the family could have his own pet, and spent the rest of the money for sweets, pickles, jellies, and fancy groceries.

Charity, after a few experiences with the "Malagaites," as they are called by their indifferent neighbors on the main, grows a bit discouraged. Donations of money bring more harm to them than otherwise. Old clothes and a doling of something to eat form charity's only resource. A State agent who looks after paupers in unorganized places goes over to Malaga occasionally, thins out the dogs, travels about to see whether medical attendance is required by any one, gives those actually hungry an order on the nearest grocery-store, and does not trouble himself to give good advice; it was discovered a great many years ago that good advice is wasted in

Malaga. A while ago the agent took along a notary and had marriages performed between six couples whose naïve ideas of wedlock had not reached out to the fact that a ceremony was necessary.

In summer all the people of the colony work as best they are able, but the scope of what they can do is so limited and the returns in money so small that it is not surprising that winter finds them with hands empty.

Women put on trousers and boots and dig clams with the men. Occasionally farmers on the main hire the women to work in the fields. The men are too lazy. The woman who earns the most money is one who lives in what was once the cabin of a schooner. She takes in washings from the main. As she cannot stand upright in her house, she climbs upon the roof and there toils at her tub.

Certain amateur sociologists have been wondering and planning what to do with Malaga and the Malagaites. Popular subscription has erected a neat little schoolhouse, in which a teacher, paid by the State, began her work in November, 1908. The children will be taught how to read and write, and the women will take lessons in sewing and darning and patching. There have been few needles on Malaga in the past.

The people of the island are singularly susceptible to religious influence, and most of them row to the main on Sundays to attend church. With the exception that their ideas of the social code of morals are primitive, they are blameless so far as their relations with the world go; they are not vicious, they show none of that sullenness that marks similar strata of society, and they extend the rude hospitality of their island with touching warmth and sincerity.

The rude gashes in the coast of Maine afford good hiding-places for those who desire to leave the world behind. One day a youth dropped off a coaster and looked about a Maine fishing-village. He stayed long enough to fall desperately in love with a girl whose father owned a Grand Banks smack and was accordingly in the upper ranks of village society. The young man, poorly clad and a stranger, was repulsed, naturally. When he undertook to explain that he was a runaway from a wealthy English family he was looked upon with still greater suspicion.

He set at work digging clams for a living and feeding his soul on occasional fleeting glimpses of the girl he loved. His story had been scoffed at with so great unanimity that he did not make any more revelations regarding his prospects. But one day he appeared at the office of a lawyer in the shire town of the county, and produced papers just received from England that required only his signature and his oath to yield him $15,000 from an estate in his native country. He got the money, put it into a bank, bought out the general store in the fishing-village, married the girl, and from the butt became the boss of the place. It would be pleasing to state that he remained the boss and lived happily ever after, but again does grim fact tip over fiction's apple-cart—as life is lived in the cracks o' the coast!

That young man was instructed by the lawyer in the use of a check-book, and it did not seem like spending real money when he wrote a check. He bought all the fishing-boats for sale along that part of the coast. Every one who had anything to sell hurried up from cove, island, and far inlet and sold it to this young man, who had become drunken with flattery and adulation after having been despised so long. Travelling salesmen heard of him, and descended and filled his store to bursting with goods—goods that he tossed out on credit to the throng that hung around him.

When, at the end of eight months or so, he got notice from the bank stating that he had overdrawn his account he did not understand, and went to the lawyer to have the matter explained. When it was explained he was dazed. He had not thought that fifteen thousand dollars could ever be cleaned out by writing on little slips of paper!

His affairs were so mixed that he was obliged to assign, and it is easy to understand what an assignment would do to a man who did not know that fifteen thousand dollars do not make an inexhaustible treasure. I am afraid that what I have heard is true: that he is digging clams again.

But while he lasted he was the most talked-about young man along a good bit of coast. Even old "Six-fingered Simpson" of the Crumples heard of him—and the Crumples is at the end of the world! Simpson pawed over his scanty possessions, found something to sell, and came up and sold it. He had not been to the mainland before in twenty years. The list of things that Simpson had never seen comprised all of man's inventions between locomotives and phonographs. The new Midas of the coast had a phonograph, and he was willing to amaze Simpson. But Simpson was not amazed. He listened, walked around the contrivance, and declared that some one hidden down-cellar was making the noise that came through the horn. He listened to the parlor organ without comment. But when he rejoined his son, who had been waiting for him at the shore, afraid to venture among those devil gimcracks, he said:

"The most of it didn't amount to much. But you ought to have seen the critter in the parlor. His woman set down 'side of it, and it showed its teeth to her, and she cuffed along them teeth and trod on its tail, and it growled and whined away savage enough, now, I tell ye!"

So we turned at the Crumples and came home from our exploring, for it is plain that the Crumples is at the end of the world!

FANNIE HARDY ECKSTORM
1865–1946

Fannie Hardy Eckstorm was born and raised in Brewer, and she became intimately acquainted with the Maine wilderness by accompanying her fur trader father in his travels. After graduating from Smith College, Fannie served as Brewer's superintendent of schools and then worked in Boston as a reader of scientific manuscripts for the publisher D.C. Heath. In 1893 she married the Rev. Jacob Eckstorm; the couple lived in Oregon, Eastport, Maine, and Providence, R.I. After Eckstorm's death in 1899, she returned to Brewer with her two children. During the next five decades Mrs. Eckstorm was active in civic affairs and devoted herself to studying various aspects of Maine's heritage. Her investigations resulted in significant writings on ornithological subjects, the lumbering industry, ballads of Maine, and Indian history, language and legend. The excerpt chosen from *The Penobscot Man* (1904) illustrates Mrs. Eckstorm's success in preserving the near-legendary exploits of Maine's river drivers through her vigorous prose and painstaking research.

A Clump of Posies

I never met the lady face to face, and none of the men ever told me whether they thought her plain or pretty, though they gave out that she was "all right," and that they were *Amici usque ad aras,* or its woods equivalent. However, there can be no question about the truth of the story: for we were in the woods that year and had the same guide, Wilbur Webster, who was drowned that winter in the lake behind Kineo. Were he alive, he would vouch for all I say; but I heard enough of it from others. On the whole it is a pretty story.

Down on Ripogenus, where the little knoll springs in the road to give you a view over the treetops of that rounded mountain with the shining patches of ledge near its summit, from which all hunters long have called it the Squaw's Bosom,—just about halfway across the carry, a natural resting-place, and delightful withal because it is so cosy and yet so open, is the Putting-in Place, where in spring the river-drivers launch their boats for the adventurous passage of the other mile and a half of Ripogenus. It is delightful there in springtime, hedged with birches, carpeted with bracken, murmuring with the hum of bees and of the rushing river many rods below.

There the batteaus are laid out bottom up; there the fire smokes under the searing-irons and the keg of pitch is kept hot, while the old batteau-pitcher, deft and wise at his trade, goes over the sides and bottom of each one, and daubs and smears and sears with his irons until he has made ready each boat for her ordeal by water, soon to be undergone. Here he sings to himself and smokes, runs his left hand lightly but searchingly over the smooth surface, scanning it with close-bent head, before he lifts himself with hands on hips to straighten his bowed back. He is an old man, used to the River; he likes his calling, but he does not meddle much with young and little things, either to notice or to molest. The brown hare thumps up and sniffs at him and thumps off again; the vireos and redstarts carol to him without his hearing; and the little flowers grow bravely, unpicked and perhaps unseen. Even the coy lady's-slipper,[1] that wanton, wayward flower, who spreads her skirts and flutters her ribbons, curtsying and coquetting, playing fast-and-loose with all her lovers; who hides herself in the forest and turns invisible and every year seeks a new home,—even she did not try to fascinate the old man by her capriciousness, but grew boldly out in the sunshine, in a great clump, as thickset as a garden plant, and almost within the cart-track of the carry road. These, however, were the demurest little flowers, not blushing pinkish like their coquettish sisters, but immaculately white and as staid as Quakeresses; they raised their eleven little heads—a very large family for their tribe—and lifted their great waxen lips and spread their fluttering pennons in purest innocence and childlikeness. There was never a prettier bunch of lady's-slippers, and yet of the almost two hundred men who passed there several times a day, not one seemed to have any more eyes than the old batteau-pitcher, not one had ever given them the compliment of a glance. It took something very like a miracle to make those men see what one would have supposed that they could not help seeing; for the little clump of posies is the beginning and the middle and the ending of this story.

A miracle is, literally, something which excites astonishment. The cause may be decried as commonplace, but there was certainly no deficiency in the effect when the men came dragging in at dusk from their outposts to the camp at the upper end of Ripogenus, and found a new tent there pitched among their own, and in it a Woman.

"Well, that does beat all hell!" was their frank comment, and there followed interrogations very much to the point, in satisfaction of which those who were lucky enough to have been at the upper end

[1]*Cypripedium acaule,* the stemless lady's-slipper, our only common species here.

of the carry that afternoon, and therefore possessed of the news, announced that though she wa'n't quite a pullet, she wa'n't no old hen neither.

"Schoolma'am?"

"Naw! Not a bittee!"

"Glasses an' short hair?"

"Naw!" (more viciously). "All right, I tell ye, all right, an' Wilbur Webster backs the deal. Friends of Joe Francis's an' Steve's, an' come up the Lake[2] with the Old Man, who's comin' down to-morrer. Stands to the West Branch Drive to do the pretty thing by 'em."

Up in the carpenter shop, which was built on an extravagant scale, with the sky for a roof and the whole earth for a floor, and nothing else in it but a litter of shavings and a tall horse for making poles and peavey handles, some of the older men discussed the incident without approval.

The grumbler, who was not young, swore about the folly of bringing a woman on the drive where men had to work and didn't want to be side-stepping, and where they mebbe might like to talk some to their blame selves all on the quiet when the blank logs was contrairy, 'thout havin' to stop and think who was by.

One of the others suggested that at the worst she couldn't be everywhere to once,—which was axiomatic,—and as there was a hunderd an' seventy-five of them against her alone, they could gamble on a least a hunderd and seventy-four chances in their favor, which was long odds.

Still the grumbler allowed that it was rank inconsiderate to come their way at all; that the drive wa'n't no place for a woman anyways, and folks that knowed when they was well off stayed to home and let men work; and if the women took to comin' there so thick, they'd be just 'bliged to leave the logs in the woods to rot all by their blank selves. He was right, too. Tourists have no more business on the drive than Sunday-school picnics have between firing-lines, and if anything unpleasant happens, they may blame themselves.

There was no rejoicing among the old men over the advent of a woman. Down the hill, in the two long rows of open-fronted tents, with the fires between, the younger fellows also sat in gloom. It did seem a little homey, perhaps, to have a girl around, especially to know that there was a *nice* girl around, whom one could look at without speaking to, and who would be as much above the reek of their daily life as if living on the top of Katahdin. (She had on a red dress? Well, just like a red-bird in a glass case, to be looked at

[2]"The Lake" always meant Moosehead.

respectfully without touching.) Ripogenus was hard enough to get logs and boats over; and the life was monotonous in spite of its dangers. This would be something different, something like going to church, thought one or two. Maybe she might speak to some of them, to a few of them, to one or two of them anyway.

Then they looked across the fire at the fellows on the other side of it. And they saw themselves! Such a set of tatterdemalions never graced a corn-field. They looked from man to man and saw hardly a whole garment apiece. They saw rags, and they saw holes, and they saw scriptural patches of new cloth upon old garments, producing the prophesied rents. There were men with trousers abbreviated to a sort of trunks, or cut off just below the knee to prevent "calking," and some sensitive souls, who abhorred setness of design, wore their nether garments with one leg cut below and the other above the knee. There were some without coat, vest, or trousers, or any part of them, but attired in full suits of underwear. This economical and attractive costume sometimes white, but oftener originally a vivid scarlet, reduced by rains and perspiration to a whitish red, once whole perhaps, but now pinned together with huge horse safety-pins and variously adorned with patches of old mittens, was an ultra style which would have attracted attention in the most exclusive circles. There were men in rigs in which they would not have let their own mothers see them, and men who, tired and hungry as they were would not have come down the carry-path till after dark, had they known beforehand that there was a woman on the carry. Oh, the dove-cote of the West Branch Drive got fluttered that time!

But what cause had they to look for such a calamity? It was thunder out of a clear sky,—everything all right in the morning when they left, and then the thunderbolt! No human foresight could have warded off the stroke, for never within the memory of the oldest man, not of the log-maker, nor the carpenter, nor the batteau-pitcher, not of the men who had almost outlived their usefulness, had there ever been a woman on the drive.

"And to have my broadcloth suit to home!" lamented one of the most out at elbows, breaking the gloom.

"And that Chinyman ain't sent back my shiny collars yet this week," said another, the joke being that there was not a Celestial within a hundred miles as the crow flew, nor a starched collar within two days' woods journey.

"Well, you'd ort to see me in my paytent leathers and high dickey and rambeaver," put in a third; "I reckon I'm just scrum when I *do* get fixed up; but it hain't no use; this here toney underwear that I'm a-sportin' is too far ahead o' the spring styles for this northern climate; makes me look like a last year's bird's nest."

"I count a old swamp robin's nest[3] a heap tidier lookin' set o' tatters 'n them clo'es what you have on, Bill. It don't look quite so all fallin' to pieces; but the wangan bills on this drive's goin' to be somthin' hijjus. I was hopesin' to come out with a dollar or two to the good, time we got into boom, but I guess I sh'll blow it all in for wangan, and come out in the Comp'ny's debt same's ush'al."

The man next to him was looking at his feet stretched out to the fire. There were neither heels nor toes to the socks he had on, but still he accounted them presentable; anything is that has an inch or two of the top left.

"Guess I sh'll hev to give 'em their time, boys; they'll do for patches anyhow. If there was more pairs of 'em, it would be easier to shingle 'em on over the wust o' the holes. Say, can't I swap my jack-knife for a pair of old mittens?"

Thereupon the price of old mittens and stockings went up by jumps, till the market in worn-out socks was the firmest ever known on the drive. No danger of its being suddenly beared by some one with a reserve of foot and hand gear. That year there wasn't a cast-off garment left upon the end of the carry, and every one knows that usually the path of the drive is littered with old clothes and old shoes. The demand for thread and needles was lively also, and had any one been playing Peeping Polly that night, long after their usual hour for turning in, the West Branch Drive might have been seen bending over their work, patching by firelight, in weariness of soul, but with the honest intention of being presentable on the morrow.

But when they got a chance at the wangan chest and could endow themselves in its glories, what a brave array of aniline they did present! Even Solomon might have studied their attire to the profitable neglect of the lily of the field. To attempt to describe the styles at Ripogenus that year would beggar the describer. Full suits of underwear went out of fashion with a bound, and a kaleidoscope of cut and color followed,—red, blue, green, yellow, stripes, plaids, patches. The Girl had known a little of the rainbow attractions of Epstein's and of Pretto's, but such cheerful combinations of color were wholly new; she wondered where is the Zeitgeist's shop and the roaring loom which wove such clothes. Some no doubt they brought into the woods with them; some they purchased from the wangan chest; but some must have come straight from Tom a Bedlam's. It would have turned the head of any girl who thought that so much was done on her account. This one never dreamed of that, —I have thought since then that she was rather stupid, for a girl.

[3]"Swamp robin" is the vernacular name for the hermit thrush and also for the olive-backed, the two not being distinguished by woodsmen; but as the former nests on the ground, this man must have meant the olive-backed thrush's or even the catbird's nest.

She was pleased with the fantastic costumes and with their picturesqueness against the green background, she found O'Connor a good comrade, and she forgot that she was either part of the show herself—or the sole spectator. Least of all did she imagine that she and the gentlemen of the extraordinary clothes were taking parts in a little comedy of courtesy, chivalry, and sentiment as pretty as it was light. Something of it she perceived while she was with them; a part she did not learn till after she had left them; and the prettiest part of all she would never have known anything about, had not the clump of posies at the Putting-in Place stopped her to tell a dolorous tale.

When the Girl went up to visit O'Connor on the drive, it was in the face of some friendly expostulation. O'Connor is known to be a noisy lad, and quiet folk are sometimes aghast at his performances.

"You could hear him when he started from the Rapogenus Chutes,
You could hear the cronching-cranching of his swashing, spike-
sole boots,
You could even hear the colors in the flannel shirt he wore,
And the forest fairly shivered at the way O'Connor swore.
'Twas averred that in the city, full a hundred miles away,
They felt a little tremor when O'Connor drew his pay.

****

"O'Connor reached the city and he reached it with a jar,
He had piled up all the cushions in the centre of the car.
—Had set them all on fire, and around the blazing pile
He was dancing 'dingle breakdowns' in a very jovial style.
And before they got him cornered they had rung in three alarms,
And it took the whole department to tie his legs and arms."[4]

Of course the drive is not all O'Connor; no one estimates, at the highest figure, that it will yield more than nine hundred and twenty-five one thousandths pure O'Connor, the remainder being an alloy of the virtues. Even Bangor is philistine to this extent; for the wisdom of Bangor about woodsmen is largely the fruit plucked from the tree of police-court knowledge. So Bangor had said, and said seriously: "Why do you take your daughter up there? How *dare* you do it—among all those rough men? Do you really think it is—?" But he thought it *was*. Bangor does not realize that, next to his courage, what most distinguishes O'Connor is his respectful behavior to women. He may be drunk, but he is never insolent to a lady, never affronts her by look or comment, never makes it unpleasant for her to pass through the streets that he frequents.

[4]"O'Connor from the Drive," in Mr. Holman F. Day's *Pine Tree Ballads*.

When in the woods and lacking all the temptations which make city life so briefly but uproariously happy, O'Connor shows his more attractive side, and the Girl was pleased to see how charming it was. The men on that drive were probably not selected for their good clothes or their superior morals, but with an eye solely to their ability to get the logs along. They were officially classified as "white men, Irishmen, Province men, Bluenoses, Prince Edward Islanders,[5] Canadian French, St. Francis, Micmac, Penobscot, and Passamaquoddy Indians;" but among all this mixed crew, in almost a week of familiar intercourse, not a man failed to be honest, orderly, and civil. Not a man was heard to swear, and the only impropriety of any sort was unwitting, and was promptly rebuked by several who could see, what the speaker did not, that it must be overheard. Boxes of camera plates, which would have been unbribable tell-tales to any meddling with the tent during long hours of absence, showed that not even an innocent curiosity ever went so far as to look at what was left in their keeping. In all ways they proved their good-will.

The Girl was charmed with other evidences of their kindliness. They were kind always to their great horses, which that year for the first time were used to draw the boats across the carry. The squirrels frisked about the wangan tents almost within arm's length of the cook. The little birds were tame and numerous. The wild hares seemed to know no fear. One day the men found a fawn too young to walk. They petted and talked to it, brought it out to be seen, and then carefully left it where the mother would find it again. A hermit thrush had built a nest close beside the carry road, within the campground limits. She had selected that spot before she knew that men and horses and dynamite and millions of logs, thundering down over the falls, were to shake the earth itself and break the sylvan stillness. She had not dreamed that twenty-six great boats, drawn by heavy-footed horses, clanking stout harness and straining at the sledge whose runners clung to the bare earth, were to be dragged past her little house under the broken cherry-sprout overarched with last year's bracken. Yet she stoutly held her ground and stayed upon her eggs, though only a rod away passed the bustle of the drive. The nest was pointed out to the men that they might not accidentally crush it, and often they would stand in the road and watch the little bright-eyed mother, but not one of them ever startled her in order to see the eggs. When they were all gone and the carry was quiet again, she was still there under her little house, bright-eyed and confident.

The men were fond of flowers, too. Later in the season, when flowers are more abundant, the drivers will often be seen picking

---

[5]The last three were called P.I.'s, though strictly speaking, a P.I. is a Prince Edward Islander.

the harebells that grow upon the ledges, or a sprig of cardinal flower from the water's edge. If there is a pond lily to be had, it will be found twined into some driver's hat-band, or looped about his neck by its twisted stem. For some reason they had not noticed that clump of lady's-slippers at the Putting-in Place. There they lifted their heads in brave array, thick-set and green as to leaf, waxen and pure white as to petal. Perhaps the men avoided trampling on them, possibly they admired and left them on their stalks, but for some reason, neglect or conservation, no one disturbed them.

Up, down, and across that carry for almost a week flitted the Girl and her attendants, chatting, observing, photographing, fishing, idling in unalloyed delight through the longest and brightest of summer days, the guests of everybody. At any moment and at any point between Chesuncook Pond and Ambajemackomas, they were likely to appear, she with her camera, Wilbur with his rifle, and there was always some one right there ready to be of service. Big Oliver, the cook, had beans and biscuit to spare in any quantity,—and they were good. The men wanted to give her a chance to see how a jam is picked, and twenty of them picking off on the Little Arches insisted on standing still, that she might have a good chance to take their picture, while she as unweariedly waited for them to get into action. The men on the stations were always ready for a visit. There was an Indian boy, tribe and name unknown, who had plenty of time to spend a little hunting for a partridge's nest, which they never found, though they had some fun in hunting. There was a Province lad watching on the Little Arches when she came to wait there for the men to come down and pick a jam. He was on an island, to be reached only by walking a log across to the shore; but he must go ashore and hunt up the butt end of a log to make her a seat. Then because there was a cold wind drawing down the gorge, in spite of the warm June sunshine, he must go ashore several times to get wood to build a fire for her, by which they sat and chatted until she saw just what is that homesickness which takes a man engaged at dangerous work far off from home. Evenings, Joe Francis and Steve Stanislaus would come dragging wearily up the hill to eat a little supper at the tent, or to drink tea out of tin dippers as they lay about the fire and told stories, such stories that the echoes of their laughter may be heard yet hanging about the bluffs on Ripogenus. The morning after their arrival the Old Man came down,—he was not at all old, being the youngest of the three contractors of the drive that year; the name was a mere courtesy title. Out of his short time with his men he took almost half a day showing points of interest, explaining the technicalities of the work, telling old stories, acting as guide himself all the way across to the Big Eddy, three miles below, that nothing worth seeing should be missed.

Such a perfect excursion in the woods never was, and yet, although it did not trouble her, the Girl had noticed something strange. Wherever she appeared the men, if not too busy, seemed to be a little watchful; they were very careful of her; they treated her regardfully. She had the strictest orders never to go out of sight of her companions, and Wilbur always carried his heavy Winchester, which she knew was loaded. Is there danger in the house of one's friends? What possible harm could threaten a girl so protected by a universal good-will? She knew that she did not even need attendants on that carry, much less a rifle to defend her. There was nothing to shoot at that season. If there had been, they did not wish to shoot it. Moreover, it had been specially arranged not to bring a gun on the excursion. The Girl was puzzled by this little cloud of apprehension which every one seemed to see except herself. It is the custom in the woods to obey orders and ask no questions: one who is keen arrives at conclusions in other ways, and "other ways" is precisely the woman's way.

The afternoon was hot, and it is a long trip down to Ambajemackomas and back to Ripogenus Lake. "What's the use, Wilbur, to carry that big forty-four seventy?" said she. "The camera and plates are load enough; it's six miles down there and not a step less back again, and we've been down to the Big Eddy and back this morning. Better leave the rifle behind, hadn't we?"

There is no wile feminine so hard to fend against as a little friendly interest; Wilbur was caught unprepared.

"There's nothing to shoot anyway at this season," said she, helping him out, as one does a trout with a landing-net.

"There's bears," said he rather desperately; "you know June's just the season for bears to be running about."

She was entirely satisfied that it was not bears. She was not afraid of bears anyway; yet she did not know what was the real reason for carrying the rifle, not knowing as much as everybody else did.

For Wilbur Webster, when he arrived at the carry, had brought down news; Mr. Murphy had verified it, and rumor therewith picked up the report and ran with it as only rumor can run, spreading everywhere that the Sunday before, this being Thursday, one Jack Russell had sworn openly in the 'Suncook House that if certain people came into the country where he was, he would shoot them on sight. Two days after that they appeared on the very spot where he uttered his threat, and it remained to be seen whether he would back down. The situation was not without interest at any time, but with a woman figuring in the title role, it was unique; certainly it appealed to the West Branch Drive. To have a scoundrel like Jack Russell threaten to shoot a lady who was their guest passed the limit. They were no longer critical spectators; the game was their own, and they played it with zeal.

Thereafter Wilbur became the centre of innumerable conferences, all semi-private.

"Do they know it?" was always the first question.

"I told *him* first off," was Wilbur's stereotyped answer. "We didn't want to spoil *her* good time, so he said to take my rifle, and we'd see whether the woods was a free country."

"S'pose she suspects anything?"

"Shouldn't be so much surprised," replied Wilbur. "When she asked me why I lugged that big forty-four, I just floundered around in my mind for a minute; you can't lie to her quite as easy as you can to a sport, so I struck bears. 'Yes, there's bears,' says she, kind of cool and twinkling. She knows as well as I do about how much bears are going to be bothering around this whole West Branch Drive."

"What's he got agin *her?*" was another question.

Then Wilbur explained the origin of the grudge.

"Say, that so? Can she prove it on him?"

"I ruther guess she holds a full house on facts," modestly responded Wilbur, not stating that he was the man who had supplied most of them, at some personal risk.

"Oh, it will stand law all right," said Wilbur. They were waiting at the Putting-in Place among the men gathered to meet the luncheon boy. That was why so many men had leisure to stand and talk. It is one of the sights to see the luncheon boy come trotting along with his firkin of salt beef and baking-powder biscuit in one hand, and in the other an immense coffee-pot, carried by a bail, while down his back hang a double row of pint dippers strung together by the handles, reminding one of Jack Mann's saying that the worst load he ever carried was five hundred pint dippers without handles against a head wind. The Girl could very easily amuse herself questing about after birds and flowers, while she waited for a chance to get a photograph of the luncheon boy.

"The law," went on Wilbur, the Girl just now being out of range, "is just the thing Jack Russell got too much of out in the States; it's more for his health to stay up here to 'Suncook where he ain't reminded of jails. Your Old Man has got a warrant out agin him for assault, and the sheriff could have both hands full of papers if the complaints all came in to once. Jack Russell takes his settlements out of court, now you'd better believe. Maybe what he said to me wa'n't nothing but guff, but maybe I ain't going to keep my eyes peeled for things moving the bushes t' other side the river!"

"Oh, he ain't looking for trouble; don't you worry, Wilbur," said one.

"No, I ain't worrying any; I'm keeping my sights up for eighty yards *and* a few extry cartridges in my right-hand pocket."

A hunter's voice is always high-pitched, and a little excitement, which makes him forget his usual caution, will cause it to carry far. The Girl heard this last remark. She was some distance off one side, looking at some flowers.

"Oh, come here, Wilbur," she called; "just look at this bunch of lady's-slippers! Aren't they the prettiest ones you ever saw?"

So Wilbur had to come and admire. It seemed to the Girl that there had been enough of a conversation which carried a man's voice up so high and made him forget his proper caution. What he was saying was very likely only "talk for P.I.'s" (which is a sort of buncombe), but that remark about the rifle-sights she bore in mind. She sat down and thought it all out at the next opportunity. She knew the butt end from the muzzle of a rifle, and knew that a hunter would not be likely to have the slide of his sights up for any such range; but what he had said seemed to have the ring of substantial truth about it, that he was prepared for a long shot. There are no long shots in the woods in June; one cannot see eighty yards then, unless there is open ground; here there was no open except along the river. One doesn't go prepared to shoot bears across a raging river with inaccessible bluffs and no means of crossing. Besides, bears would never account for that stringent order never to get out of sight. She was beginning to perceive that here was some mystery.

What was it which Wilbur had told and Mr. Murphy had corroborated? That the Sunday before at the 'Suncook House, Jack Russell, "as mad as Mike," had spit forth his spite against certain people.

What was it about? Oh, about his killing rising twenty moose last summer for their hides; she had written something about it, and had sent him one of the papers with it in, so as to be fair.

"And if either of them ever puts foot into this country again I'm going to shoot 'em!" said Jack Russell.

"Well," spoke up Wilbur, who was among the crowd, "guess you won't have to wait long for your chance, Jack."

"How's that?" asked several.

"Oh, I hear," went on Wilbur as nonchalantly as if the letter announcing it were not in his pocket, "that they are coming up the Lake to-morrow, both of 'em."

"Where to?" asked Jack, wavering.

"Ri' down *here,* Jack." And the steel in Wilbur's voice must have rung clear.

"Who's goin' guide for 'em?" inquired Russell.

"*I* be, Jack!" retorted Wilbur. Blades were out then. Wilbur was a proved man, and there was no mistaking what he meant.

This was too much for Jack Russell. He found it was just the right time to set some bear-traps up Harrington Lake way, which was miles out of the road of all tourists, far back in the woods. The whole of Chesuncook rippled with laughter at the performance, and then all subsided to a calm. What disturbed Wilbur was that Harrington lies on the further side of Ripogenus, quite a convenient distance for any one who wanted to stroll down for the day and, in some warm and mossy nook, to lie across an impassable chasm and take pot-shots at photographing tourists scrambling over the rocks on the other side.

Meantime the Girl knew next to nothing of what was going on. Here and there she caught some shred of conversation which, when raveled out, always gave the name of Jack Russell, and she wondered into what sort of stuff it had been woven, and especially what kind of goods could bear Jack Russell's name on every yard; it was considered no guarantee of quality at that time and place, for he came as near being a desperado as any one there in the woods. She did not think anything about Jack Russell, least of all would she have suspected that the drive was taking his threat seriously. It was enough that everybody was so kind, and that no one except once ever did anything which displeased her. That time she was angry—and then she wasn't.

It was one noon coming back from the Big Eddy; it was hot, and to save time they were returning by the carry road instead of by the river-bank. At the Putting-in Place she looked for her clump of posies. They were missing. Not one was left.

A flame of anger burst forth at seeing them so despoiled. "It's a shame!" she cried; "I wouldn't touch one of them, they were so pretty, the prettiest moccasin-flowers that ever were, and now some one has gone and picked all that great bunch! Can't people ever learn to leave a pretty thing alone!"

Her anger had not cooled before there came the dappled dawn of a new idea, and she ceased to blame the spoilers until she should be sure.

Men are fickle creatures, and those she had seen here were about to be fed. If they had picked the flowers to look at, they would gaze at the waxy blooms a moment, then roll them in their fingers and, when the flowers hung limp and their hands were full of meat and drink, they would drop them where they stood. There she would find the wilted, yellowing blossoms, with flabby, hanging pouch and draggled, twisted pennons, telling the world-old story of thoughtless ravage. She looked all about. There were no flowers there.

Then she looked at the plants again, more carefully. Their poor little denuded stems stood up tall and stiff, full length; every flower must have been nipped off just beneath its little chin, it was not done hastily, nor ruthlessly with the whole hand, but deliberately, with thumb and finger.

Then she blushed, neck and ears, redder than her hat. The doubtful dawn of her idea was full day now; she knew what had happened. For there came to her some chaffer on the way up from the Big Eddy. She had stepped in a muddy spot in the road, and they had told her, Wilbur and her father, that of the men who saw that track not one would ever efface it with his own; that sentiment still was dear to woodsmen. She had laughed and thereafter avoided the muddy places; one would not wish to put too great a strain upon sentiment. But now she remembered that when she had called to Wilbur, she had touched the flowers, lifting their heavy heads as she praised their beauty. That had sealed their doom. In eleven different pockets, pressed in the folds of a home letter or crumpled in the corner of a greasy pocketbook, the eleven little lady's-slippers were carried as keepsakes.

It is many years since that occurred, and yet she can never help feeling guilty for compassing the destruction of those pretty flowers; though glad that she can give to them a more enduring life.

That was not all, though she did not know it till long afterwards, when the clerk of the drive told the story. Wilbur's rifle was really not of the slightest consequence; it might just as well have been left in camp. For the West Branch Drive had taken upon itself to settle everything in its own thoroughgoing way. It decided—that is, enough of it decided, and there was no call for contrary-minded—that it objected to having Jack Russell interfering with its company. Then they discussed the matter of ways and means.

"Send him word," said one, and who so apt to be the man as the very one who had grumbled loudest about having women on the drive, "send him word to leave our company alone. If he don't, tell him we've got men enough and we've got rope enough"—

The message was somewhat pointed. It is quite a distance from Ripogenus up to Harrington, all woods, and P.L.D. runs no post-office department; but it was delivered with dispatch. When Jack Russell ran into us on the upper end of Chesuncook Carry, a sort of head-on collision, before the Smiths of Chesuncook as outside witnesses, and it was fight, run, or be friends, he was entirely civil. Although too much must not be inferred from such a statement, we parted quite as cordial as when we met. However, Chesuncook shook with inextinguishable laughter; its merriment was both loud and long-continued, and it became so disturbing to Jack Russell's ears that by the time the leaves were falling, he turned his canoe prow northward, and was last seen going down the Allegash in search of a climate more congenial to his health.

HENRY BESTON

1888–1968

Henry Beston (Sheahan) was born in Quincy, Mass., and educated at Harvard. During the course of his life he taught at the University of Lyons and Harvard, edited *Living Age,* and served on the editorial board of *The Atlantic.* Beston married the author Elizabeth Coatsworth; the pair traveled and eventually settled at "Chimney Farm" in Nobleboro, Maine. A sensitive craftsman, Beston is noted for his lucid and balanced prose and for his deep reverence and respect for the natural world. His works include *The Outermost House* (1928), a Thoreau-like account of a year spent alone on Cape Cod; *Northern Farm, a Chronicle of Maine* (1948); and *The St. Lawrence* (1942), part of the Rivers of America series. Beston also wrote children's books and compiled a state of Maine reader entitled *White Pine and Blue Water* (1950).

From *Northern Farm*

II

Our house stands above a pond, a rolling slope of old fields leading down to the tumble and jumble of rocks which make the shore. We do not see the whole pond but only a kind of comfortable bay some two miles long and perhaps a mile or so across. To the south lies a country road, a wooded vale, and a great farm above on a hill; across and to the east are woods again and then a more rural scene of farms and open land. It is the north, and as I set down these words the whole country lies quiescent in the cup of winter's hand.

Last night, coming in from the barn, I stood awhile in the moonlight looking down towards the pond in winter solitude. Because this year winds have swept the surface clean of early snows, the light of the high and wintry moon glowed palely upwards again from a sombre, even a black fixity of ice. Nothing could have seemed more frozen to stone, more a part of universal silence.

All about me, too, seemed still, field and faraway stand of pine lying frozen in the motionless air to the same moonlit absence of all sound. Had I paused but a moment and then closed the door behind me, I probably would have spoken of the silence of the night. But I lingered a longish while, and lingering found that the seeming stillness was but the interval between the shuddering, the mysterious outcrying of the frozen pond. For the pond was hollow with sound, as it is sometimes when the nights are bitter and the ice free from snow.

It is the voice of solid ice one hears and not the wail and crash and goblin sighing of moving ice floes such as one hears on the wintry St. Lawrence below the Isle of Orleans. The sounds made by the pond are sounds of power moving in bondage, of force constrained within a force and going where it can. The ice is taking up, settling, expanding, and cracking across though there is not a sign of all this either from the hill above or from the shore.

What I first heard was a kind of abrupt, disembodied groan. It came from the pond . . . and from nowhere. An interval of silence followed, perhaps a half note or a full note long. Then across, again from below, again disembodied, a long, booming, and hollow utterance, and then again a groan.

Again and again came the sounds; the night was still yet never still. Curiously enough, I had heard nothing while busy in the barn. Now, I heard. Neither faint nor heavy-loud, yet each one distinct and audible, the murmurs rose and ended and began again in the night. Sometimes there was a sort of hollow oboe sound, and sometimes a groan with a delicate undertone of thunder.

As I stood listening to the ice below, I became aware that I was really listening to the whole pond. There are miles of ice to the north and a shore of coves and bays, and all this ice was eloquent under the moon. Now east, now west, now from some far inlet, now from the cove hidden in the pines, the pond cried out in its strange and hollow tongue.

The nearer sounds were, of course, the louder, but even those in the distance were strangely clear. And save for this sound of ice, there seemed no other sound in all the world.

Just as I turned to go in, there came from below one curious and sinister crack which ran off into a sound like the whine of a giant whip of steel lashed through the moonlit air.

My old friends and neighbors, Howard and Agnes Rollins, used to tell me that the ice often spoke and groaned before a big storm. I must watch the glass and the wind and the northeast.

Farm Diary

Somebody in a red suit of mackinaw cloth and a wool hat is on the pond, fishing through the ice for pickerel. In winter pickerel tend to lose their somewhat muddy taste. / Cold, dark and windless night, and the windows of farms across the pond throw paths of light upon the ice, paths blurred in outline and motionless, having none of the life of the living water. / The last three nights having been rather arctic, I have been getting up at 3 A.M. to replenish the coal fire. The living room has been comfortably warm, and the outlying dependencies warmish, the core of heat fortifying the life of the sleeping house. / Elizabeth returns from a neighbor's with a present, a jar of mincemeat made from deer meat, a colonial recipe treasured on the farms.

The farm country is now a winter splendor of heavy woolens, a good, healthy-spirited display of mackinaws in bright colors, cheerful plaid shirts, and heavy woolen caps of plaided red, green, or royal blue. The pageant is at its best when snow has fallen, and the bright colors move about against a universal white.

Some scholar has said, and very wisely, that the songs of a people are an excellent token of their character. The student of human nature would do well to add their clothes! Let him meditate on the fact that in peasant countries where the earth is the real wealth, and the farm lives by its own farm prides and farm traditions, the costumes worn are the most vital, beautiful, and gay that have ever been seen in western civilization.

Conversely, the clothes of an industrial world are the most dreary, ugly, muddy clothes that a way of living has ever put on human backs. Look at them as they are worn by any average urban crowd. There is no sense of hope in them, nothing of life in any mood of pride. Sartorially, this is a new thing in human history. From the noble savage onward, man has been something of a gay dog.

I am glad that the north country goes in for clothes with life and color. It is an excellent sign. Which reminds me that if the neighbors see me wearing a particularly gorgeous new pair of hand-knitted yellow socks, they can recognize a Christmas present arranged for by Elizabeth.

XI

Every once in a while, and in good snowshoeing weather, I go down into my woods to look at the tracks of the wild creatures and see what we have for neighbors. We live on a kind of mitten-shaped peninsula in a pond, and our woods begin at the stony, overgrown backbone of the area, and grow down a rather steep slope to the secluded cove which gives us a shoreline to the west.

The woods are at once farm country and the old forest of the north. White pines and hemlocks predominate and make it an evergreen country, some of our bigger pines being miraculous survivors of the great primeval growth. I imagine that these would have been "mast pines" in the old ship building days, for they tower green above the other tree-tops, straight as the "sticks" of a full-rigged ship.

I have hardwood, too, rock maple, yellow birch, red oak, and beech, which we cut for our winter fires. In one secluded nook stands a superb primeval ash, beautiful as the tree of Odin, Yggdrasil, which held the worlds together.

The last time I visited the woods, the snow lay deep. All winter long, new snow had fallen on old, mingling the surfaces into one heavier depth and mass of white. Entering the region, I took the farm track whose beginning is a natural arch of pine boughs through which one sees a mild slope leading down into woods. The snow deepened, the light changed, and something more hushed took the place of the open light and the larger sound.

To each side, beyond the trunks of the bordering trees, the beautiful, delicately-shadowed snow lay with a surface but a few days old and still light because of the low temperatures. Far and near, the wind and snow had scattered it over with a dust of bark and tiniest fallen twigs, with broken-off tufts of needles from the white pines, and with a green and universal rain of the terminal twigs of hemlocks. At one place a familiar spring had welled up through the white and was flowing across the wood road and downhill in a vein of living water and uncovered earth.

As I "mushed" on into a little clearing, walking towards the sun, I had a glimpse of a winter effect I always like to see. On the tops of the trees the wind was blowing, and just ahead of me there suddenly fell from a hemlock branch a quantity of snow which disintegrated to powder in the sunlit air. As it thus dissolved, the snow dust turned to a mist of rainbow brilliance, a certain coppery, bronzy glow seeming to hang for a moment against the sun.

There were tracks everywhere, the most common being those of the "snowshoe rabbit"—really the varying hare, and the fox. This northern and arctic hare has its familiar name from the tracks its huge forefeet leave in the snow, and very like the prints of small snowshoes they are, even to an occasional comic suggestion of the pattern of the weave. His arch enemy the fox, too, had been everywhere about, that direct, purposeful single line now crossing the road, now following it awhile, now leading off into the more open growth.

Animals use our human roads almost as much as we do. I came upon hardwood trees with a woodsy litter beneath them, and marked where various grey squirrels had drawn upon their reserves of food; but saw squirrel tracks most often near the old stone-walls. A porcupine had followed a lesser wood-road a good half mile—taking all the shortcuts!—and a small deer had gone down the side of a hill, the divided hoof mark very clearly imprinted where the snow lay windswept and thin.

Of the makers of the tracks, I saw nothing. Calling to each other like school children, I heard chickadees in a kind of sunlit glen, and when I came out of the woods, one watched me from a young hemlock and sang his greeting.

Farm Diary

"Did you catch anything?" I asked a friend who had returned from pickerel fishing through the ice. "Yes, four and a cold." / The owls are beginning to hoot in the woods. The great horned owl winters here, and in the depth of winter hoots before a thaw; it is almost a sure sign. When spring draws near, the owls hoot, thaw or no thaw. / There is an old expression in use here for a snow-storm which comes after the spring robins return: we call it a "robin storm." I was amused the other night to hear the participle "suppering" —"You can get Bill while he's suppering over to his brother's." / Elizabeth has gone on a week-end visit to her sister's, leaving the house well-stocked and everything comfortable, but the little dog and I both think that the whistle of next Monday's arriving train will be a very pleasant sound.

A few days before the Vernal Equinox we have a kind of special celebration in the farm kitchen and at breakfast time. The kitchen, as I have said, is in the ell of the house, and because on one side the windows face due east, we have for the greater part of the year the awakening and refreshing presence of the morning sun. As October draws near, the great disk, moving south, with every sunrise draws nearer a corner of the main house extended beyond the ell and cutting off our view to the southeast.

Nearer and nearer to the fated corner moves the great lamp, nearer and nearer, turns it, and the kitchen does not have morning sunlight till long months have worn away.

If we were people of the Golden Age and the Golden Bough, we would get our pipes and timbrels, our long trumpets of bronze, and our other musical what-have-yous ready for March fifteenth. On that morning the sun, which has been steadily approaching the corner, turns it, the golden round rising clear of all obstruction and flooding the kitchen with the first spring light. It is for us an occasion of real joy. We may not belong to the Golden Age or the years of the Golden Bough, but we can observe and rejoice, and in such natural joy and natural response lies one of the profoundest secrets of human happiness.

E.B. WHITE

1899–

Born in Mount Vernon, N.Y., E(lwyn) B(rooks) White received his A.B. from Cornell. After working in Seattle and Alaska for a year, he returned to Manhattan as an advertising copy writer; in 1927 he joined the staff of the *New Yorker.* White was active in many different areas of the magazine's operation, but he became particularly known for his urbane "Talk of the Town" column. In the late thirties White moved to Maine with his wife and small son and settled in a saltwater farmhouse in North Brooklin. He wrote "One Man's Meat" for *Harper's* between 1938-43 and then rejoined the *New Yorker,* continuing to live much of the year in Maine. As one of America's foremost essayists, White has been awarded numerous honorary degrees, a gold medal from the National Institute of Arts and Letters, and the Presidential Medal of Freedom. White's essays, which are written in graceful prose, display both wit and seriousness; his acute observations on the local situation can also encompass the larger problems faced by the human race. Among his collections are *Is Sex Necessary?* (1929, with James Thurber), *One Man's Meat* (1942), *The Second Tree from the Corner* (1953), and *Two Points of My Compass* (1962). In addition, White has been acclaimed for his children's literature (*Charlotte's Web* and *Stuart Little*) and for his revision of William Strunk, Jr.'s *The Elements of Style* (1959).

The Winter of the Great Snows

Allen Cove, March 27, 1971

Somebody told me the other day that a seagull won't eat a smelt. Even if the gull takes the smelt by mistake, he will disgorge it. I find this hard to believe, but I haven't had a chance to experiment with a smelt and a live gull. I've always supposed a gull would eat anything. If Herbert Tapley were alive, I would put the question to him and be sure of a straight answer. But Herbert is dead, and I find people quite evasive when I ask them if a gull will eat a smelt. I raised a gull chick once, and it never refused anything I handed it. And once, years ago, when I worked in a ship, I used to empty garbage into a chute that discharged overboard. Gulls attended this rite in great numbers, screaming their appreciation. I can't recall ever seeing a gull reject anything that came out of that chute. There were never any smelts in the garbage, though, and this leaves the question wide open. A smelt has rather a sweet taste—there seems to be nothing of the salt sea in its flesh. Perhaps that's why a gull won't eat a smelt, if indeed it is true.

This has not been an ideal winter for pure experimentation here in the East—to see if a gull will eat a smelt. It has been more a time of simple survival, to see if a man can stay alive in the cold. The snows arrived early, before the ground froze. Storm followed storm, each depositing its load and rousing the plowman in the night. And then the cold set in, steady and hard. The ponds froze, then the saltwater coves and harbors, then the bay itself. As far as I know, the ground, despite the deep cold, remains unfrozen: snow is a buffer against the frost, an almost perfect insulating material. A fellow recently reported driving a stake into a snowbank, and when the point of the stake reached ground level it kept right on going. I haven't tested this—it's like the gull and the smelt, a matter of hearsay. But I would have to have a pretty long stake, so remote is the ground.

When snow accumulates week after week, month after month, it works curious miracles. Familiar objects simply disappear, like my pig house and the welltop near the barn door, and one tends to forget that they are there. Our cedar hedge (about five feet high) disappeared months ago, along with the pink snow fences that are set to hold the drifts. My two small guard dogs, Jones and Susy, enjoy the change in elevation and the excitement of patrol duty along the crusted top of the hedge, where they had never been before. They have lookout posts made of snow that the plow has thrown high in the air, giving them a chance to take the long view of things. For a while, the barnyard fence was buried under a magnificent drift. This delighted the geese, who promptly walked to freedom on their orange-colored snowshoes. They then took off into the air, snowshoes and all, freedom having gone to their heads, and visited the trout pond, where they spent an enjoyable morning on the ice. On several occasions this winter, we had to shovel a path for the geese, to make it possible for them to get from their pen in the barn to their favorite loitering spot in the barn cellar. Imagine a man's shovelling a path for a goose! So the goose can loiter!

The door of the woodshed hasn't been open since early in December, the snows having sealed it shut. The house, which always gets banked with spruce brush against the winter never got banked. The flower beds never got covered. We were simply caught short: the snow arrived ahead of schedule and in large amounts. (I think we've had something like one hundred inches, all told.) We did manage to give the rosebushes decent burial; they are not only out of sight but almost out of mind. It takes an effort of the imagination to conjure up a rose. Only an inch or two of the tall stakes that mark the grave is visible. For most of the winter, the highway has resembled an enormous bobsled run: the passage of the plow builds towering walls of snow higher than the roof of your car, so that you travel through a great white trough, sealed against disaster. (Last summer, my car went off the road and I hit a pole and broke it. The accident was six months too soon—I should have waited till January, when a soft cushion of snow surrounded all poles. I passed my pole the other day and noticed that it had recovered fully from the blow, but I haven't.)

Maine towns take winter seriously. They are ready with money and trucks and men and sand and salt. Derring-do is in good supply, and the roads stay open, no matter what. The things that do *not* stay open are the driveways of the people. Every new swipe of the plow hurls a gift of snow into the mouth of a driveway, so that, in effect, the plowmen, often working while we sleep snug in our beds, create a magnificent smooth, broad highway to which nobody can gain access with his automobile until he has passed a private miracle of snow removal. It is tantalizing to see a fine stretch of well-plowed public road just the other side of a six-foot barricade of private snow. My scheme for town plowing would be to have each big plow attended by a small plow, as a big fish is sometimes attended by a small fish. There would be a pause at each driveway while the little plow removes the snow that the big plow has deposited. But I am just a dreamer. I have two plows of my own—a big V on the pickup and a lift-blade on the little Cub tractor. Even with this equipment, we were licked a lot of the time this winter and had to call for help. It got so there was no place to put the snow even if you were able to push it around. On the day before Christmas, the storm was so great, the wind so high, people were marooned in my house and had to spend the night. And a couple of days later I had to hire a loader to lift the snow from the mouth of the driveway, scurry across the road with it, and drop it into the swamp.

Except for winter's causing me to become housebound, I like the cold. I like snow. I like the descent to the dark, cold kitchen at six in the morning, to put a fire in the wood stove and listen to weather from Boston. My movements at that hour are ritualistic—they vary hardly at all from morning to morning. I steal down in my wrapper carrying a pair of corduroy pants under one arm and balancing a small tray (by de Miskey) that holds the empty glasses from the night before. The night nurse has preceded me into the living room and has hooked up the thermostat—too high. I nudge it down. As I enter the kitchen, my left hand shoots out and snaps on the largest burner on the electric stove. Then I set the glasses in the sink, snap on the pantry light, start the cold water in the tap, and fill the kettle with fresh spring water, which I then set atop the now red burner. Then comes the real warmup: with a poker I clear the grate in the big black Home Crawford 8-20, roll up two sheets of yesterday's Bangor *Daily News,* and lay them in the firebox along with a few sticks of cedar kindling and two sticks of stovewood on top of that. (I always put on my glasses before stuffing the *News* in, to see who is dead and to find out what's been going on in the world, because I seldom have time in these twilight years to read newspapers—too many other things to tend to. I always check on "Dear Abby" at this dawn hour, finding it a comfort to read about people whose problems are even greater than mine, like the man yesterday who sought Abby's advice because his wife would sleep with him only on Thursday nights, which was all right until his bowling club changed *its* night to Thursday, and by the time the man got home his wife was far gone in shut-eye.) I drop the match, open the flue to "Kindle," open the bottom draft, and wait a few seconds to catch the first reassuring sound of snap-and-crackle. (That's the phrase around here for a wood fire—always "snap-and-crackle.") As the first light of day filters into the kitchen, I set out the juicer, set out the coffeepot and coffee, set out the pitchers for milk and cream, and, if it's a Tuesday or a Thursday or a Saturday, solemnly mark the milk order blank and tuck it in the milk box in the entryway while the subzero draft creeps in around my ankles. A good beginning for the day. Then I pull my trousers on over my pajama bottoms, pull on my barn boots, drape myself in a wool shirt and a down jacket, and pay a call in the barn, where the geese give me a tumultuous reception, one of them imitating Bert Lahr's vibrato gargle.

The guard changes here at seven: the night nurse goes off (if her car will start) and the housekeeper comes on (if her brother-in-law's truck has started). I observe all this from an upstairs window. It is less splendid than the change at Buckingham Palace but somehow more impressive, the palace guard never having been dependent on the vagaries of the internal-combustion engine in a subzero wintertime.

The chief topics of conversation this winter have been the weather, the schools, and the shadow of oil. Quarreling over the schools has split the town wide open, as it has neighboring towns here on the mainland and over on Deer Isle. Feeling ran so high some people stopped speaking to each other—which is one form of discourse. Forty years ago, when I landed here, we had five one-room or two-room schoolhouses scattered at strategic points. The scholars walked to school. We also had our high school, which was a cultural monument in the town along with the two stores, the Baptist church, the Beth-Eden chapel, and the Rockbound chapel. Times have changed. All through New England, the little red schoolhouse is on the skids, and the small high school that graduates only four or five seniors in June, in a gymnasium decked with lilac and apple blossoms, is doomed. The State Board of Education withholds its blessing from high schools that enroll fewer than three hundred students. Under mounting pressure from the state, the towns organized a school administrative district, usually referred to as SAD. Sad is the word for it. A plan was drawn for an area schoolhouse at a central point near the Deer Isle Bridge, but it was voted down. Too much money and too many frills. Another plan was drawn and failed. Meanwhile, schoolchildren were shuttled around, here and there, in an attempt to close the gap. We no longer have a high school in town; the building is used for the junior-high grades. Most of the children in the ninth, tenth, eleventh, and twelfth grades are carried by bus across to the high school in the town of Deer Isle. A few travel in the opposite direction to a nearby academy. Sending their children over to an island irritated a lot of parents; some disapproved of the building, some had a deep feeling that when you leave the mainland and head for an island in the sea you are headed in the wrong direction—back toward primitivism. Other parents were violently opposed to dispatching their offspring to the academy town, on the score that the place was a citadel of evil, just one step short of Gomorrah. (There was also an ancient athletic rivalry, which left scars that have never healed.) The closing of our high school caused an acute pain in the hearts of most of the townsfolk, to whom the building was a symbol of their own cultural life and a place where one's loyalty was real, lasting, and sustaining. All in all, the schools are a mess.

Feeling about oil is now running high, but it lacks the acute pain of nostalgia that characterizes the school controversy. Oil is the pain of the future. A company called Maine Clean Fuels wants to build a refinery on Sears Island, at the head of Penobscot Bay, bringing barges and 200,000-ton tankers slithering through the fog-draped, ledge-encrusted, tide-ripped waters of one of the most beautiful bodies of water in Maine or anywhere. The proposal sticks in all our crops. Battle lines have been drawn, public meetings have been held. On one side, or in one corner, are Maine's Department of Economic Development, the executives of the oil company (full of joyous promises and glad tidings of a better life and cheaper fuel), and some people in Searsport who hope that oil will bring jobs and elevate the economy of the town. On the other side, or in the other corner, are Ossie Beal and his Maine Lobstermen's Association, the Audubon Society, the Sierra Club, various conservation groups, the *Maine Times,* several action groups hastily formed for the purpose of beating oil, and thousands of property owners (usually described as "rich" property owners) who just have a feeling in their bones that oil is bad news any way you look at it. A

200,000-ton tanker makes an aircraft carrier look like a dory, and if there were to be a bad spill, it could mean the end of marine life and bird life in the bay.

Searsport was host to a public meeting last week to give the oilmen a chance to present their case. It must have been a barrel of fun. The constabulary was out in full force, CBS News turned up with its cameras, and a carefully selected group of concerned citizens was admitted. The meeting was set up in such a way as to prevent the anti-oil people from releasing their wrath when they rose to speak. It was a powder-keg meeting that failed to explode. Week after next, a hearing is scheduled at which the state's Environmental Improvement Commission will listen to testimony. This body, I believe, now has kingmaking authority and can turn thumbs down on an industrial newcomer if he looks and smells like a pollutant.

Pollution stirred our town a couple of years ago when our harbor became filthy as a result of sewage discharged from a school of theology that had magically turned up in our midst. The school had inherited a big old pipe when it bought the property; at low water the pipe lay on the stinking flats, exposed, broken in three places, and discharging. The town was powerless to act, having no ordinance on the books covering any nuisance of the sort. So the Environmental people were called and came over from Augusta. Testimony was offered by clamdiggers, boat owners, the health officer of the town, and concerned citizens. It took a long while, but the nuisance was finally abated and theology acquired a long-overdue septic tank. (The waste had been backing up into the school's swimming pool, it turned out, making the pool probably the largest and most spectacular tank in the whole county—a real tomato surprise.) Anyway, the water of the harbor is clear again, a classic case of cleanliness next to godliness. Clamming is still restricted.

Town Meeting came early this year—March 1st. I wasn't able to attend but have studied the report. One birth was reported in 1970, and twelve deaths. It would appear from this that although the population explosion is still an issue worldwide, we have it licked locally. The town appropriated $7,000 for snow removal and sanding, in addition to $3,000 from unappropriated surplus—a total of $10,000 to get the snow removed. There was no argument. If there's one thing people are agreed on, it's this: the snow must get removed. A century ago in New England, the approach to snow was quite different. When snow began to fly, people switched to runners. Roads were not plowed out, they were rolled down. A giant roller pulled by horses packed the surface to a fine, smooth glaze. Then the sleighs came out, with their bells. And sleds, to haul wood out from the woodlots. Wheels were laid away for the season. The old pleasure in runners hasn't died, though. The snowmobile is the big new thing

—life on runners. It pollutes in two ways: with its exhaust fumes and with its noise.

The town voted to enact an ordinance regulating the taking of shellfish. It is now illegal for a nonresident to dig clams, except that he may dig not more than a peck in any one day for the use of himself and his family. A year ago, the town voted to enact an ordinance regulating the use of the town dump. At that meeting, I suggested an ordinance prohibiting the discharge of human waste into ponds and salt water, but it got laid to rest. The selectmen investigated the matter and reported that such an ordinance would be "very complex, extremely difficult to enforce, and possibly declared to be unconstitutional." It seems sad that the town can regulate the taking of shellfish but can't regulate the discharge of the waste that makes the shellfish inedible. But that's the way it is. Years ago, I was sized up as a man who was amiable, honest, and impractical, and I've always agreed with that estimate. Now, I'm not just impractical, I'm unconstitutional.

And I still don't know whether a gull will eat a smelt.

LOUISE DICKINSON RICH
1903–

Louise Dickinson Rich was born in Huntington, Mass., and has pursued careers in both teaching and writing. In 1934 she married Ralph Eugene Rich, a Bostonian who had retired to the Rangeley Lake region. Mrs. Rich thus renounced civilization to raise a family in the wilderness. She vividly conveys the pleasures and drawbacks of such a life in *We Took to the Woods* (1942), which was a nonfiction best-seller. She continued the family chronicle in *Happy the Land* (1946), *My Neck of the Woods* (1950), and *Only Parent* (1953). In addition to her years in the deep woods, Mrs. Rich has lived on Gouldsboro Peninsula and has written about the coast of Maine. She is also the author of several books for juvenile readers.

But You Don't Live Here All the Year 'Round?

What people really mean when they ask if we live here the year 'round, is "But good Lord! Certainly you don't stay in here during the winter? You must be crazy!" Well, all right, we're crazy. I would have thought so myself, before I tried it.

I used to hate winter, too. When I was a child it was because winter meant school, and although I got along reasonably well there, school was something to be considered with nausea. Along about February I used to think of the stretch of time until June and freedom with such a hopeless depression as I have never known since. It just didn't seem possible that I could live that long. The only time in my whole scholastic career that I ever liked school was one spell when I was in the eighth grade; and the reason for my change of heart then had nothing to do with my studies. I fell in love with the boy who sat in front of me, and since he lived over on the other side of town, the only time I got to see him was during school hours. It made a difference in my attitude, but it didn't last very long. In spite of all the sentences I diagrammed for him, and the arithmetic answers I slipped under my desk into his eager palm, come Valentine's Day, he spent all his pocket money on a big lace and ribbon heart for a blonde who sat over in the dumb section, and who didn't know a verb from a common denominator. It soured me on the male for a time, but it taught me a lesson that has been valuable ever since: to wit, men may admire and use brains in a woman, but they don't love them. I reverted to my hatred of winter.

After I grew up, I still hated it, and I think that now I know the reason why. In civilization we try to combat winter. We try to modify it so we can continue to live the same sort of life that we live in summer. We plow the sidewalks so we can wear low shoes, and the roads so we can use cars. We heat every enclosed space and then, inadequately clad, dash quickly from one little pocket of hot air through a bitter no-man's land of cold to another. We fool around with sun lamps, trying to convince our skins that it is really August, and we eat travel-worn spinach in an attempt to sell the same idea to our stomachs. Naturally, it doesn't work very well. You can neither remodel nor ignore a thing as big as winter.

In the woods we don't try to. We just let winter be winter, and any adjustments that have to be made, we make in ourselves and our way of living. We have to. The skin between outdoors and indoors here is so much thinner than it is even in a small town, that it's sometimes hard to tell where one stops and the other begins. We can't dress, for example, for a day in the house. Such a thing doesn't exist. We have to go outdoors continually—to get in wood, to go to the john, to run down to the other house and put wood on the kitchen fire, to get water, to hack a piece of steak off the frozen deer hanging in the woodshed, or for any one of a dozen other reasons. Outdoors is just another, bigger, colder room. When we get up in the morning we dress with the idea that we'll be using this other room all day. When we step into it we make the concession of putting on mittens—if we're really going to be there long enough.

Everyone in here dresses more or less alike, until it comes to foot gear. We all, male and female, wear plaid wool shirts—two of them sometimes—and wool pants, ski or riding. We wear wool caps and home-made mittens, with leather mittens, called choppers, over them. The choppers don't keep the hands warm, but they keep the mittens dry and prevent their wearing out. We all wear wool socks. And there the great woods schism begins. Everyone has his own pet ideas of the proper footwear for below zero weather. No one will listen to any one else's opinion on the subject. Everyone knows he is right, and no one will dabble with experiments. Feet freeze too easily and frozen feet are too painful and serious to be courted deliberately.

Ralph belongs to the great gum-boot school of thought. Gumboots have high leather tops sewed on rubber feet. They are loose and roomy, and their addicts wear two or three pairs of heavy wool socks inside them. I guess they're all right, if you like them. Larry Parsons swears by laced, all-rubber knee boots and two pairs of socks. He claims that the leather tops of gum-boots get soaked when there is wet snow, and then where are you? The answer to that is that healthy feet perspire a little, and there is no chance for evaporation through rubber. So by night your socks are going to be wet anyhow, and what difference does it make how you get them wet? The Finnish lumberjacks who brought their equipment from the old country—and there are quite a number of them around here—have a good foot gear, consisting of heavy felt boots, knee high and about an inch thick—too thick to wet through, and much too thick to chill through. They look as though they'd be wonderful, but you can't get them in this country. Some of the native lumberjacks try to achieve the same effect by buying old-fashioned black buckled galoshes, about four sizes too big, and wearing four or five pairs of socks in them. They keep the feet warm, but it's like wearing a bucket on each foot. A few people wear high leather boots, but almost everyone else agrees that they are cold damn things. Nobody would be caught dead in a pair of ski boots. They're too stiff and heavy. Let the city folks have them. They don't know any better.

Myself, I wear one pair of wool socks, and the lightest, cheapest pair of sneakers I can buy, and nobody can convince me that this isn't the answer. Everyone else is working on the wrong principle, that of getting more and more layers between their feet and the cold. That's wrong. What they gain in insulation they sacrifice in foot flexibility. Their feet are just two petrified lumps wrapped in wool. According to my system, articulation isn't interfered with, and the blood circulates freely, bringing heat from the body to the feet as a hot water heating system brings heat to the radiators. I haven't been able to win any disciples to my belief, but that's all right. Neither have I ever had my feet frost-bitten.

I seem to have devoted a lot of space to what we wear on our feet in winter, but it's quite in proportion to the amount of time spent talking and thinking about it. It's a very vital matter.

Outside, life takes on pace with the approach of winter. It is the gay season, the season of parties and theatres and all the other things that will help people forget that outdoors something that they can't cope with is going on. Here life slows down, just as the world around us slows down. The leaves fall from the hardwood trees. Spruce and fir and pine stop growing and stand, dormant and black and thick, on mountain side and lake-shore, their slim tips pointing monotonously to the gray sky. Of course they don't move, but they seem to draw silently in around us. We realize suddenly what we have forgotten: that after all, there are only three families of us—only a dozen puny human souls strung out along the lake and river—against all the forces of nature. To the people Outside, "the forces of nature" is a convenient phrase out of a textbook. To us they are a reality. We know we haven't a Chinaman's chance of controlling them. We only hope we can out-maneuver them.

I always feel like a renegade when the first little powder snow comes. It never lasts long, and it isn't serious, but the proper attitude is the long face, the foreboding shake of the head, and the grim comment that it won't be long now. I would like to act as Kyak does, and go tearing around in circles, scooping up mouthfuls of snow as a fast train scoops up water, and leaping crazily and prodigiously over little snow-covered trees. I don't, partly because any tree I could leap over wouldn't be worth bothering with and I'd probably fall flat on my fanny anyhow, but mostly because I'd simply be too unpopular if anyone suspected my anti-social liking of winter. So I try to remember that in February, when the snow is four feet or more deep on the level and I'm flopping inexpertly around on snowshoes, I'll be cursing the day the stuff was invented and offering my hope of Heaven for a good long look at a patch of bare ground. I turn my attention to the first piece of outmaneuvering that we have to attend to.

That is the circumventing of the freeze-up, our official beginning of winter. That's the fall in-between period, when the lake is just frozen and the ice is too thick to put a boat through and too thin to support a man or a horse or a car. We never know when the freeze-up is going to start or how long it's going to last. The only thing we do know is that while it's going on, we are completely bottled up. The nearest A&P is some forty miles away, but it might as well be in Egypt. Whatever we are going to need over a period of two or three weeks, we have to bring in before the Arm starts to freeze over. Tea, coffee, sugar, flour—I go over the list in my sleep. Oatmeal, canned meat and fish, fruit, and vegetables. And canned milk! Good Lord, if I'd forgotten that again! One year we forgot it and the Parsons forgot it, and the Millers didn't buy any because they keep a cow and didn't have to. So the cow chose that time, of all times, to go dry. We all learned, the hard way, to like black coffee and tea. I still like it, but I don't like to remember how oatmeal tastes without milk on it.

The real problem, though, is fresh meat and eggs and butter. If we bring them in too early and the weather warms up, we have the most horrible phenomena known to the thrifty Yankee heart and soul—good food, slowly spoiling. If we cut the margin too fine, we wake up some morning and find a half an inch of ice—a futile and infuriating amount—on the lakes. So we watch the barometer and thermometer and stars and the thickness of Kyak's pelt and listen to the weather broadcasts on the radio and rush out at all hours of the day and night to hold a wet finger to the wind. And sometimes we guess right and sometimes we don't. So far we've managed to survive the consequences of errors in our computations, but it's a pretty harassing period to go through, all the same. . . .

LEW DIETZ
1907–

A resident of Rockport, Lew Dietz was born in Pittsburgh, Pa., and attended New York University. He has worked as a copy writer for Crowell Publishing Co. in New York, as an editor of the *Camden Herald,* and as an assistant editor of *Maine Coast Fisherman* and *Outdoor Maine.* His works—reflecting his interests in hunting, fishing, natural history, and the State of Maine—include an informal history of the Camden area, books for juvenile readers, *Wilderness River* (1961), *The Allagash* (1968), *Touch of Wildness* (1970), *Night Train at Wiscasset Station* (1977), *The Story of Andre* (1979), and numerous contributions to periodicals.

Wild Animals I Have Known—And Vice Versa

No one can deny that the primate known as man has come a long way since his lowly beginnings in the shallow Cambrian seas. It may well be that we have come too far too fast, and, much like the parvenu who made it big in a hurry, are all too anxious to dis-associate ourselves from our humble past.

Not satisfied with simply playing down the biological connection, we have for centuries attempted to shore up our egos by attributing to animals characteristics we find unbecoming in ourselves.

The other day I read in the paper where a judge had termed a man who beat his wife regularly a beast. I've been running the ridges of my home state of Maine for some forty years, and I have yet to come across a beast that beat his wife. Years ago, my mother reprimanded me for eating like a wild animal. It didn't occur to me until decades later that that should have been taken as a compliment. I've met few animals that eat more than they need and can comfortably assimilate.

Consider man's rather childish habit of rating animals according to their conformity with human behavior. Crowds gather and applaud when a seal balances an Indian club on his nose. They are beguiled by the notion that the seal is acting like a vaudeville juggler. The seal is simply acting like a seal: it's the juggler who is the mimic. A seal was balancing things on his nose long before man was endowed with prehensile fingers.

Scientists are just now beginning to discover that the birds and the beasts have a lot more going for them than we poor environment-trapped humans have ever realized. Dr. John Lilly, the dolphin man, after long electronic conversations with his charges, concluded not long ago that "man's position at the top of the hierarchy begins to be questioned."

At the risk of appearing to put myself above the ruck of purblind human kind, I wish to state that I have questioned man's top-dog position for some time. Perhaps it's only that I've had more opportunity to meet birds and beasts personally than most. And I mean *personally*. I believe it was Winston Churchill who, when informed that one of his advisers was a modest man, remarked, "He has a great deal to be modest about." My associations with creatures of feather and fur have built up my modesty to an awesome degree. To put it bluntly: animals are too smart for me. Moreover, they seem to delight in letting me know it.

One of the first rude shocks I sustained on the long, hard road to humility was the discovery that few animals feel any great compulsion to behave according to the book. As a child I was given to understand that a horse was a horse, and a cat a cat, and the behavior of each was more or less predictable. Of course, to many upstanding Americans all Pullman porters are Georges and all Chinese laundrymen Charlies. It never occurred to me, though, that some little old bird with a thimbleful of brains could put Jim Farley to shame in that business of remembering faces.

Not only did Butch know me, he took a personal and passionate dislike to me. Butch was a Canada jay I met on a hunting trip in the Maine woods. It was Butch who first opened my eyes to the truth that you just can't generalize about birds. Some birds, like some people, simply refuse to forgive and forget.

My partner and I, by dint of great effort, had jeeped twenty miles over a mountain with the hope of hunting alone. We decided to move into an abandoned logging cookshack, only to find that a jay had had the same idea. In the process of evicting him, I inadvertently plucked a few of his tail feathers.

Now, a bird's tail acts as sort of a keel. A bird, *sans* tail, looks in flight a bit like the town drunk on Saturday night. Butch discovered his handicap soon enough. To say that he was annoyed would be a pallid understatement: he was outraged. He began coursing around outside the camp giving me a large and vociferous piece of his mind. I said I was sorry. There didn't seem to be much else I could do about it. I didn't think there was anything the bird could do about it, either. I was dead wrong.

I found this out the first thing in the morning when I set forth with my rifle. The tailless and ireful jay was waiting for me. At first he didn't say too much, which should have been portentous. All he did as I started still-hunting up a mountain was to fly from tree to tree at my side and give me an occasional blast. This was irritating enough, naturally, but it wasn't until along about sundown that I realized the dark depth of his rascally intent.

I'd found a nice fresh game trail and was preparing myself to take a stand and wait for an unsuspecting deer when my fine-feathered friend found a comfortable perch overhead and began his filibuster. It was evident at once that no self-respecting deer would come within a half-mile of such a fuss (deer are curious, but not *that* curious). I tried to give my tormentor the slip. I Indian-footed off and found another stand. It was a waste of time. There was my avenging shadow in the neighboring jack spruce. He commenced to make the day hideous with his fishwife maledictions.

Suffice it to say, my rout was complete. I am still extremely fond of Canada jays, mind you. I would no more think of denigrating this avian species because of my experience with Butch than I would condemn all red squirrels because of my contretemps with Nosey. The idea that one can deal with individual members of these so-called lower species on any other than a person-to-person basis is part and parcel of the great anthropocentric delusion.

I'd made camp in the Rangeley region in Maine a few days before the deer season opened, with the idea of cruising out the country and bagging a few partridge for supper. It was a good beechnut year, and I'd found a nice ridge where the partridge were feeding on nuts.

That's where I met Nosey. He too was collecting nuts and hiding them under a stump of a tree. Seeking to make it perfectly clear that I would mind my business if he would mind his, I pretended not to notice where he was secreting his nuts.

A partridge seldom lights in where he intends to feed. He will roost in a tree some thirty or more yards away, case everything very carefully, drop to the ground, and then sneak in on foot. As I said, *I* knew what I was doing. Nosey couldn't quite figure it out. His curiosity about my operation began interfering with his own. Finally, he chucked his nut-hiding job entirely and came on over. This was all right with me, so long as he merely watched and kept his big mouth shut. But no, he had to offer criticism and a few chattered suggestions.

Then I heard a bird light into a thicket to my right. Nosey heard him too. He began skinning up and down a birch tree, jumping from limb to limb like a hysterical old maid trapped in a Turkish bath.

I was the very soul of patience. Even after I heard my supper fly off, I controlled my temper. I contented myself with issuing a few dark warnings, suggesting ominously that he had better go gather his beechnuts while he may. Much like some leather-lunged bleacher fan gets on an outfielder who had dropped a few easy fly balls, Nosey clearly was determined not to let up until he had a reaction. After the second and then the third partridge flew off, I reacted.

I am sure there are those who might consider my action childish, spiteful, and unbecoming a human being. I say that Nosey's behavior was unbecoming a red squirrel and reprisals were definitely in order. I simply walked over to where he had cached his beechnuts and ate them every one.

This was small solace for a ruined afternoon, I admit. The scorer would say that with animals I was still batting 0 for 2. That bear, Gus, failed to improve this average. Ever since Androcles took the thorn from that lion's paw there has been a myth going around that animals are grateful. Here again, I'm not saying there is no such thing as a grateful bear: I do insist that with this particular bruin kindness got you nowhere.

I will take no responsibility for starting Gus on his downward path. The case of beer I brought into camp near Spencer Lake was for my own use. It was, at least, until Gus discovered where I cooled it in the lake shallows. Without a by-your-leave, he smashed a bottle on a rock and lapped up the contents.

I can take beer or leave it alone. Gus just wasn't the temperate type. He came back every night, and, needless to say, we ran out of beer. In fact, so badly hooked was Gus that once we'd killed the case he came back and checked the empties I set out in the back. Gus simply lay on his back, supported the base of the bottle in his rear paws, steadied the neck at his mouth with his forepaws, then rocked back and forth until the last drop rolled down his parched throat.

And after he'd squeezed every last drop out of every last bottle, do you think he was grateful for my bounty and good fellowship? Not a bit of it! Not only did my fair-weather friend smash every bottle in his rage, he busted up a rustic table, an upturned canoe, and before going off in a huff, took one raking swipe at the door of the camp.

By the time I met Maggie I was pretty much reconciled to being cast in the role of chump in any relationship I might have with my feral cousins. Maggie liked to play golf. This was fine with me, except that Maggie insisted on playing with my golf balls.

I am primarily a solitary golfer, for the simple reason that I enjoy my own company and my own unorthodox shots off the first dog-legged tee. There was no problem rules. I couldn't imagine what was happening to my tee with my weak drives, but just let me lay one out beyond the bend and that was the last I'd ever see of that ball. It was only after I'd invested in the services of a caddy that the case of the missing golf balls was cracked. Bug-eyed, my caddy reported that no sooner had my ball hit the fairway than out would romp a fox with a troop of her pups. She'd snatch the bounding ball in her chaps, and off she'd head for the woods, the little ones at her heels.

My first reaction was to take a narrow, man's-eye view of this antisocial behavior. Then I realized that I couldn't even defend the position that I paid dues and Maggie didn't. I daresay there is not a golf club in America which would liberalize its bylaws to the extent of accepting a fox, no matter how well recommended. That left me with the alternative of accepting her right to fun and games and accommodating myself to her needs.

But then came the day I was invited to play in a foursome with the chairman of the greens committee. You can imagine the reaction when I explained I always hit two balls off the first tee, one for me and one for a fox, and that the fox's ball didn't count. As a matter of fact, I gave up golf shortly after that. I can only assume that Maggie has returned to the more productive and sensible game of stealing chickens.

I could go on like this, citing experience after sorry experience in which I was mismatched with my betters in the animal kingdom. I knew a porcupine that persisted in eating the insulation off my car wiring, a raccoon that stole doorknobs. I'm convinced there was nothing personal in these depredations. With Ragazzo, though, it was a different story.

A man's home is his castle. Perhaps there are some cats you can convince of this. Ragazzo, a great black cretin of a cat, alley-cum-Siamese, feared neither man nor the devil. He had come with my wife, a sort of package deal. For years I'd endured his vast disdain. I was convinced that that cat would stop at nothing to perpetuate his power. It wasn't until Rain, my beagle pup, joined the ménage that I realized the dark depths of his Iago mind.

Ragazzo had *his* way of doing things. His eating habits were particularly personal and rigid. He liked his food set on the floor first thing in the morning and left there so he could consume it at his leisure in the course of the day. The pup cleaned up his own with no such nonsense and, quite naturally, mistook Ragazzo's recesses as invitations to share. A few healthy swats quickly straightened her out on that point. But instead of knuckling under, Rain merely changed tactics. She learned to hide under the stove and wait for a propitious moment.

These hit-and-run forays brought her increasing punishment; but it also got her a deal of extra vitamins. I knew Ragazzo too well to think for a moment that he would take this threat to his monarchy lying down. Ragazzo had a sphinxlike face, but I could fairly see some dark plot developing in his crafty mind. That morning in September when he took even less than his usual sampling from his morning dish and departed without even a sidelong glance at the still shape under the kitchen stove, I was sure of it.

The screen door banged behind the cat. Rain, belly down, inched out from under the stove. She took one uneasy glance about her, then made cautiously for the dish. She took one gulp. That was all she had time for. There was a black flash, a hiss, and a flailing paw sent the luckless pup yelping and tumbling across the kitchen floor.

It was a moment before I could grasp the nature of the fiendish plot. Ragazzo *had* departed. But he had quickly circled the house, slipped in the back door, and secreted himself behind the washing machine to wait in ambush.

A man more secure in his position at the top of the hierarchy would have laid down an ultimatum. Bullied and outsmarted as I had been in my joustings with my furred and feathered coinhabiters of this pellet, I lacked the courage to trot out that one-of-us-must-go gambit. I would dearly love to say that it was with deliberate cunning and malice that I brought home that dead bobcat from a hunt in the North Woods.

Only the cat was home when I arrived. Naturally he didn't even bother to get out of my easy chair. In a bit of a huff I just tossed the bobcat in the corner by the kitchen stove. And there he was, forty pounds of crouched and frozen malevolence, when Ragazzo sashayed in to check his supper dish.

I am only assuming that this is what happened. I was cleaning up when I heard a chilling, primordial scream. I got down just in time to see Ragazzo depart through the cellar door. And he never did return.

It was a hollow victory. I'd rid myself of my black nemesis, but nothing I could say could quite rid my wife of the ugly notion that I was somehow implicated in her cat's desertion. The cat, for his part, stepped into a bed of roses. I soon learned that he had adopted an old maid down the street who thought nothing of walking to town in the depth of winter to buy him fresh fish.

Only once in all my years as a member of the species *Homo sapiens* have I had occasion to feel heartened. I met Yogi in the great salt marshes of Louisiana. An ornithologist I'd met was trying without success to get some film footage of the great blue heron's nuptials. He would sneak out into the marsh and make a blind. The cover being no more than waist-high, the heron would see him coming, and feeling that courtship was a private affair, refuse to cooperate.

One day, after repeated failures, the bird man said he had an idea and asked me to go with him. No sooner had we arrived at the blind than he asked me to go back to the road. More confused than annoyed, I did as he said. Imagine my amazement when he came out with his mission accomplished.

Had I at long last found something that I as a human could stand up and cheer about? Two men had come out on the marsh. One man had departed. Would you believe it, a great blue heron can't add or subtract worth a darn!

The fine, preening glow warmed me for no more than a few short months. That fall I saw a great blue heron fishing in the shallows of a northern lake. I watched as he waited with quiet dignity and lordly patience. It occurred to me, suddenly, that in the matter of being accepted or not being accepted as a peer of the human species, he couldn't care less.

PART III:
HUMOR

SEBA SMITH
1792–1868

Born in Buckfield, Maine, Seba Smith worked at various trades and taught school in the Bridgton area until he obtained a loan which enabled him to attend Bowdoin College. After graduating in 1818, Smith taught for another year, traveled, and returned to Maine to settle in Portland. In 1823 he married Elizabeth Oakes Prince (1806–1893), and the couple had five sons. Smith founded Maine's first daily newspaper, the *Portland Courier,* and introduced the humorous Downing letters to boost its circulation. At first Smith satirized the people and politics of Maine, but he soon sent his character to Washington to comment upon the policies of President Andrew Jackson. The homespun, non-partisan Downing and his innate shrewdness spawned a host of imitators, many of whom pirated the Downing name. To counteract this, Smith gathered a collection of authentic Downing letters and published them in 1833 as *The Life and Writings of Major Jack Downing of Downingville.* Smith was forced to sell the *Courier* as a result of heavy losses in land speculation. After a brief and unsuccessful business venture in the South, the Smiths settled in New York City, where they both engaged in literary activities. At the time Mrs. Oakes Smith's fame far surpassed her husband's, but today she is mainly of historical interest. She wrote poems, articles for popular magazines, plays, novels, and children's books; and during the 1850's she lectured extensively on the subject of women's rights. Smith contributed to periodicals, worked as an editor, and published books ranging from a dissertation on geometry to a metrical romance. One of his more popular works of this period was *'Way Down East* (1854), a collection of local color tales about Yankee customs and characters. Ill health forced Smith to retire to Long Island in 1860, but he left a prototype that inspired future generations of homely philosophers to continue to poke fun at the foibles of the social and political structures of American society.

From ***The Life and Writings of Major Jack Downing of Downingville***

LETTER LIV.

In which Major Downing goes up top the Congress house and listens to see if he can hear the guns in South Carolina, and also has a talk with the President, about the slander of the newspapers.

Washington City, Feb. 1, 1833.

[Note: The first of February, 1833, was the day appointed by South Carolina for putting in force her nullifying Ordinance.]

To the editor of the Portland Courier, in Mariners' Church Building, second story, eastern end, Fore Street away down east, in the State of Maine.

My Dear Friend.—This is nullification day, and it's most night, and I aint dead yet, and hant been shot at once to-day. I got up this morning as soon as it was light, and went out and looked away towards South Carolina, and listened as hard as I could to see if I could hear the guns crackin and the cannons roarin. But it was all still as a mouse. And I've been up top the Congress house five or six times to-day, and listened and listened, but all the firing I could hear was inside the Congress house itself, where the members were shooting their speeches at each other. I had my company all ready this morning with their dinners in their napsacks, to start as quick as we heard a single gun. We shant go till we hear something from these nullifiers, for the President says he aint agoing to begin the scrape, but if the nullifiers begin it, then the hardest must fend off.

Yesterday a friend handed me a couple of papers printed at Hallowell away down pretty near to Augusta in the State of Maine, called the American Advocate, and I found something in 'em that made me as mad as a March hair. The first one mentioned that Capt. Dow was chosen Mayor of Portland, and then said, he is the reputed author of the Jack Downing letters that have been published in the Portland Courier. The other paper that was printed two or three days afterwards, said Mr Dow the new mayor of Portland is not the author of Jack Downing's letters; they are written by Mr Seba Smith, the Editor of the Portland Courier. Now, Mr Editor, my good friend, is n't this too bad? I have n't come acrost any thing that made me feel so wamble-cropt this good while. Jest as if Major Jack Downing could n't write his own letters.

I've been to school, put it altogether, off and on, more than six months; and though I say it myself, I always used to be called the best scholar among all the boys in Downingville, and most always used to stand at the head of my class. I'd been through Webster's spelling book before I was fifteen, and before I was twenty I could cypher to the rule of three. And now to have it said that I dont write my own letters, is too bad. It's what I call a rascally shame. I was so boiling over with it last night, that I could n't hold in; and so I took the papers and went in and showed them to the President. I always go to the President when I have any difficulty, and when he has any he comes to me; so we help one another along as well as we can. When the President had read it, says he, Major Downing, it's strange to see how this world is given to lying. The public papers are beginning to slander you jest as they always do me. I have n't written scarcely a public document since I've been President, but what it's been laid off to Mr Van Buren, or Mr McLane, or Mr Livingston, or Mr Taney, or somebody or other. And how to help this slanderous business I dont know. But it's too provoking, Major, that's certain. Sometimes I've a good mind to make Congress pass a law that every editor who says I dont write my proclamations and messages, or that you dont write your letters, shall forfeit his press and types; and if that dont stop him, that he shall be strung up by the neck without Judge or Jury.

And now, Mr Editor, I wish you would jest give that Hallowell man a hint to mind his own p's and q's in future, and look out for his neck. And as you know very well that I do write my own letters, I would thank you jest to tell the public so.

I remain your sincere and loving friend,

Major Jack Downing.

LETTER LV.

In which Cousin Ephraim explains the science of Land-speculation.

Augusta, State of Maine, March 4, 1833.

To Major Jack Downing, at President Jackson's house in Washington City.

Dear Cousin Jack,—The Legislater folks have all cleared out to-day one arter t'other jest like a flock of sheep; and some of 'em have left me in the lurch tu, for they cleared out without paying me for my apples. Some of 'em went off in my debt as much as twenty cents, and some ninepence, and a shilling, and so on. They all kept telling me when they got paid off, they'd settle up with me. And so I waited with patience till they adjourned and thought I was as sure of my money as though it was in the Bank.

But, my patience, when they did adjourn, such a hubbub I guess you never see. They were flying about from one room to another, like so many pigeons shot in the head. They run into Mr Harris' room and clawed the money off of his table, hand over fist. I brustled up to some of 'em, and tried to settle. I come to one man that owed me twelve cents, and he had a ninepence in change, but he wouldn't let me have that, because he should lose a half cent. So, while we were bothering about it, trying to get it changed, the first I knew the rest of 'em had got their money in their pockets and were off like a shot, some of 'em in stages, and some in sleighs, and some footing it. I out and followed after 'em, but 'twas no use; I couldn't catch one of 'em. And as for my money, and apples tu, I guess I shall have to whistle for 'em now. Its pesky hard, for I owe four and sixpence here yet for my board, and I've paid away every cent I've got for my apples, and dont know but I shall have to come down with another load to clear out my expenses. Howsomever, you know uncle Joshua always told us never to cry for spilt milk, so I mean to hold my head up yet.

I dont know but I shall have to give up retailing apples, I meet with so many head-flaws about it. It was thinking that, soon as the Legislater adjourned, I'd take a load of apples and apple-sass, and a few sassages, and come on to Washington and go long with your company to South Carolina. But they say Mr Clay has put a stopper on that nullification business, so that its ten chances to one you wont have to go.

I dont care so much about the apple business after all; for I've found out a way to get rich forty times as fast as I can by retailing apples, or as you can by hunting after an office. And I advise you to come right home, as quick as you can come. Here's a business going on here that you can get rich by, ten times as quick as you can in any office, even if you should get to be President. The President dont have but twenty-five thousand dollars a year; but in this ere business that's going on here, a man can make twenty-five thousand dollars in a week if he's a mind to, and not work hard neither.

I spose by this time you begin to feel rather in a pucker to know what this business is. I'll tell you: but you must keep it to yourself, for if all them are Washington folks and Congress folks should come on here and go to dipping into it, I'm afraid they'd cut us all out. But between you and me, its only jest buying and selling land. Why, Jack, its forty times more profitable than money digging, or any other business that you ever see. I knew a man here t'other day from Bangor, that made ten thousand dollars, and I guess he want more than an hour about it. Most all the folks here and down to Portland and Bangor have got their fortunes made, and now we are beginning to take hold of it up in the country.

They've got a slice up in Downingville, and I missed it by being down here selling apples, or I should had a finger in the pie. Uncle Joshua Downing, you know he's an old fox, and always knows where to jump; well, he see how every body was getting rich, so he went and bought a piece of a township up back of Downingville, and give his note for a thousand dollars for it. And then he sold it to uncle Jacob and took his note for two thousand dollars; and uncle Jacob sold it to uncle Zackary and took his note for three thousand dollars; and uncle Zackary sold it to uncle Jim, and took his note for four thousand dollars; and uncle Jim sold it to cousin Sam, and took his note for five thousand dollars; and cousin Sam sold it to Bill Johnson, and took his note for six thousand dollars. So you see there's five of 'em that want worth ninepence apiece before, have now got a thousand dollars apiece clear, when their notes are paid.

And Bill Johnson's going to logging off of it, and they say he'll make more than any of 'em.

Come home, Jack, come home by all means, if you want to get rich. Give up your commission, and think no more about being President, or any thing else, but come home and buy land before its all gone.

Your loving cousin,

Ephraim Downing.

P.S. Didn't Mr Holmes and Mr Sprague look rather blue when they got the resolutions that our Legislater passed, giving them such a mortal whipping?

ARTEMUS WARD
1834–1867

Charles Farrar Browne was born in Waterford and attended a local country school until the age of thirteen, when his father died. Browne worked for newspapers in Norway and Skowhegan and then became a wandering journeyman. Eventually he landed in Cleveland and served as editor for the *Plain Dealer.* In 1858 he published his first article under the pseudonym of "Artemus Ward" and quickly gained his reputation. He moved to New York to work for *Vanity Fair,* and in 1861 he began his immensely popular lecture tours. Internationally renowned, Browne was invited to England, where he had great success as a lecturer and contributor to *Punch.* Browne died of tuberculosis in England at the height of his fame, and in accordance with his wishes he was buried at his birthplace in Maine. The character of Artemus Ward was a blend of shrewdness and illiteracy; his letters were filled with comic misspellings, puns, bad grammar, and exaggerations. His ideas were often absurd, but he managed to debunk many of the hypocritical and overly sentimental aspects of his society. Elements of Browne's style are now somewhat dated, but the Yankee philosopher Artemus Ward could count Samuel Clemens, Queen Victoria, and President Lincoln among his many admirers.

Interview with President Lincoln

I hav no politics. Not a one. I'm not in the bisness. If I was I spose I should holler versiffrusly in the streets at nite and go home to Betsy Jane smellin of coal ile and gin, in the mornin. I should go to the Poles arly. I should stay there all day. I should see to it that my nabers was thar. I should git carriges to take the kripples, the infirm and the indignant thar. I should be on guard agin frauds and sich. I should be on the look out for the infamus lise of the enemy, got up jest be4 elecshun for perlitical effeck. When all was over and my candydate was elected, I should move heving & erth—so to speak—until I got orfice, which if I didn't git a orfice I should turn round and abooze the Administration with all my mite and maine. But I'm not in the bizniss. I'm in a far more respectful bizniss nor what pollertics is. I wouldn't giv two cents to be a Congresser. The wuss insult I ever received was when sertin citizens of Baldinsville axed me to run fur the Legislater. Sez I, "My frends, dostest think I'd stoop to that there?" They turned as white as a sheet. I spoke in my most orfullest tones & they knowed I wasn't to be trifled with. They slunked out of site to onct.

There4, havin no politics, I made bold to visit Old Abe at his humstid in Springfield. I found the old feller in his parler, surrounded by a perfeck swarm of orfice seekers. Knowin he had been capting of a flat boat on the roarin Mississippy I thought I'd address him in sailor lingo, so sez I, "Old Abe, ahoy! Let out yer main-suls, reef hum the forecastle & throw yer jib-poop over-board! Shiver my timbers, my harty!" [N.B. This is ginuine mariner langwidge. I know, becawz I've seen sailor plays acted out by them New York theater fellers.] Old Abe lookt up quite cross & sez, "Send in yer petition by & by. I can't possibly look at it now. Indeed, I can't. It's on-possible, sir!"

"Mr. Linkin, who do you spect I air?" sed I.

"A orfice-seeker, to be sure," sed he.

"Wall, sir," sed I, "you's never more mistaken in your life. You hain't gut a orfiss I'd take under no circumstances. I'm A. Ward. Wax figgers is my perfeshun. I'm the father of Twins, and they look like me—*both of them*. I cum to pay a friendly visit to the President eleck of the United States. If so be you wants to see me, say so, if not, say so & I'm orf like a jug handle."

"Mr. Ward, sit down. I am glad to see you, Sir."

"Repose in Abraham's Buzzum!" sed one of the orfice seekers, his idee bein to git orf a goak at my expense.

"Wall," sez I, "ef all you fellers repose in that there Buzzum thar'll be mity poor nussin for sum of you!" whereupon Old Abe buttoned his weskit clear up and blusht like a maidin of sweet 16. Jest at this pint of the conversation another swarm of orfice-seekers arrove & cum pilin into the parler. Sum wanted post offices, sum wanted collectorships, sum wantid furrin missions, and all wanted sumthin. I thought Old Abe would go crazy. He hadn't more than had time to shake hands with 'em, before another tremenjis crowd cum porein onto his premises. His house and dooryard was now perfeckly overflowed with orfice seekers, all clameruss for a immejit interview with Old Abe. One man from Ohio, who had about seven inches of corn whiskey into him, mistook me for Old Abe and addrest me as "The Pra-hayrie Flower of the West!" Thinks I *you* want a offiss putty bad. Another man with a gold-heded cane and a red nose told Old Abe he was "a seckind Washington & the Pride of the Boundliss West."

Sez I, "Square, you wouldn't take a small post-offiss if you could git it, would you?"

Sez he, "A patrit is abuv them things, sir!"

"There's a putty big crop of patrits this season, ain't there, Squire?" sez I, when *another* crowd of offiss seekers pored in. The house, dooryard, barngs, woodshed was now all full, and when *another* crowd cum I told 'em not to go away for want of room as the hog-pen was still empty. One patrit from a small town in Michygan went up on top the house, got into the chimney and slid into the parler where Old Abe was endeverin to keep the hungry pack of orfice-seekers from chawin him up alive without benefit of clergy. The minit he reached the fireplace he jumpt up, brusht the soot out of his eyes, and yelled: "Don't make eny pintment at the Spunkville postoffiss till you've read my papers. All the respectful men in our town is signers to that there dockyment!"

"Good God!" cried Old Abe, "they cum upon me from the skize—down the chimneys, and from the bowels of the yerth!" He hadn't more'n got them words out of his delikit mouth before two fat offiss-seekers from Winconsin, in endeverin to crawl atween his legs for the purpuss of applyin for the tollgateship at Milwawky, upsot the President eleck, & he would hev gone sprawlin into the fireplace if I hadn't caught him in these arms. But I hadn't more'n stood him up strate before another man cum crashing down the chimney, his head strikin me viliently again the inards and prostratin my voluptoous form onto the floor. "Mr. Linkin," shoutid the infatooated being, "my papers is signed by every clergyman in our town, and likewise the skoolmaster!"

Sez I, "You egrejis ass," gittin up & brushin the dust from my eyes. "I'll sign your papers with this bunch of bones, if you don't be a little more keerful how you make my bread basket a depot in the futur. How do you like that air perfumery?" sez I, shuving my fist under his nose. "Them's the kind of papers I'll giv you! Them's the papers *you* want!"

"But I workt hard for the ticket; I toiled night and day! The patrit should be rewarded!"

"Virtoo," sed I, holdin' the infatooated man by the coat-collar, "virtoo, sir, is its own reward. Look at me!" He did look at me, and qualed be4 my gase. "The fact is," I continued, lookin' round on the hungry crowd, "there is scarcely a offiss for every ile lamp carrid round durin' this campane. I wish thare was. I wish thare was furrin missions to be filled on varis lonely Islands where eprydemics rage incessantly, and if I was in Old Abe's place I'd send every mother's son of you to them. What air you here for?" I continnered, warmin up considerable, "can't you giv Abe a minit's peace? Don't you see he's worrid most to death? Go home, you miserable men, go home & till the sile! Go to peddlin tinware—go to choppin wood—go to bilin' sope—stuff sassengers—black boots—git a clerkship on sum respectable manure cart—go round as original Swiss Bell Ringers—becum 'origenal and only' Campbell Minstrels—go to lecturin at 50 dollars a nite—imbark in the peanut bizniss—*write for the Ledger*—saw off your legs and go round givin concerts, with tuchin appeals to a charitable public, printed on your handbills—anything for a honest living, but don't come round here driving Old Abe crazy by your outrajis cuttings up! Go home. Stand not upon the order of your goin,' but go to onct! Ef in five minits from this time," sez I, pullin' out my new sixteen dollar hunt-in cased watch and brandishin' it before their eyes, "Ef in five minits from this time a single sole of you remains on these here premises, I'll go out to my cage near by, and let my Boy Constructor loose! & ef he gits amung you, you'll think old Solferino has cum again and no mistake!" You ought to hev seen them scamper, Mr. Fair. They run as tho Satun hisself was arter them with a red hot ten pronged pitchfork. In five minits the premises was clear.

"How kin I ever repay you, Mr. Ward, for your kindness?" sed Old Abe, advancin and shakin me warmly by the hand. "How kin I ever repay you, sir?"

"By givin the whole country a good, sound administration. By poerin' ile upon the troubled waturs, North and South. By pursooin' a patriotic, firm, and just course, and then if any State wants to secede, let 'em Sesesh!"

"How 'bout my Cabinit, Mister Ward?" sed Abe.

"Fill it up with Showmen, sir! Showmen, is devoid of politics. They hain't got any principles. They know how to cater for the public. They know what the public wants, North & South. Showmen, sir, is honest men. Ef you doubt their literary ability, look at their posters, and see small bills! Ef you want a Cabinit as is a Cabinit fill it up with showmen, but don't call on me. The moral wax figger perfeshun mustn't be permitted to go down while there's a drop of blood in these veins! A. Linkin, I wish you well! Ef Powers or Walcutt wus to pick out a model for a beautiful man, I scarcely think they'd sculp you; but ef you do the fair thing by your country you'll make as putty a angel as any of us! A. Linkin, use the talents which Nature has put into you judishusly and firmly, and all will be well! A. Linkin, adoo!"

He shook me cordyully by the hand—we exchanged picters, so we could gaze upon each others' liniments, when far away from one another—he at the hellum of the ship of State, and I at the hellum of the show bizniss—admittance only 15 cents.

BILL NYE
1850–1896

Bill Nye's many residences and occupations provided him with much material for his humorous writings. Edgar Wilson Nye was born in Shirley, Maine, raised in Wisconsin, and lived as an adult in Wyoming, New York City, and North Carolina. At various times in his life he worked as a farmer, lawyer, justice of the peace, legislator, educator, postmaster, newspaperman, and playwright. In 1881 he founded the Laramie *Boomerang,* which he edited until 1885. The humorous sketches that he contributed to this paper established his reputation and were frequently reprinted. He became a national celebrity by writing for the New York *World* and by conducting a series of lecture tours with James Whitcomb Riley throughout the country. Unlike other humorists of the time who continued to imitate the style of Artemus Ward, Nye did not pose as an outlandish character or depend upon slang or misspellings in his work. As "Farming in Maine" illustrates, though, Nye was not adverse to utilizing exaggeration in offering his insights into the American scene.

Farming in Maine

The State of Maine is a good place in which to experiment with prohibition, but it is not a good place to farm it in very largely.

In the first place, the season is generally a little reluctant. When I was up near Moosehead Lake, a short time ago, people were driving across that body of water on the ice with perfect impunity. That is one thing that interferes with the farming business in Maine. If a young man is sleigh-riding every night till midnight, he don't feel like hoeing corn the following day. Any man who has ever had his feet frost-bitten while bugging potatoes, will agree with me that it takes away the charm of pastoral pursuits. It is this desire to amalgamate dog days and Santa Claus, that has injured Maine as an agricultural hot-bed.

Another reason that might be assigned for refraining from agricultural pursuits in Maine, is that the agitator of the soil finds when it is too late that soil itself, which is essential to the successful propagation of crops has not been in use in Maine for years. While all over the State there is a magnificent stone foundation on which a farm might safely rest, the superstructure, or farm proper, has not been secured.

If I had known when I passed through Minnesota and Illinois what a soil famine there was in Maine, I would have brought some with me. The stone crop this year in Maine will be very great. If they do not crack open during the dry weather, there will be a great many. The stone bruise is also looking unusually well for this season of the year, and chilblains were in full bloom when I was there.

In the neighborhood of Pittsfield, the country seems to run largely to cold water and chattel mortgages. Some think that rum has always kept Maine back, but I claim that it has been wet feet. In another article I refer to the matter of rum in Maine more fully.

The agricultural resources of Pittsfield and vicinity are not great, the principal exports being spruce gum and Christmas trees. Here also the huckleberry hath her home. But the country seems to run largely to Christmas trees. They were not yet in bloom when I visited the State, so it was too early to gather popcorn balls and Christmas presents.

Here, near Pittsfield, is the birthplace of the only original wormless dried apple pie, with which we generally insult our gastric economy when we lunch along the railroad. These pies, when properly kiln-dried and rivetted, with German silver monogram on top, if fitted out with Yale time lock, make the best fire and burglar-proof wormless pies of commerce. They take the place of civil war, and as a promoter of intestine strife they have no equal.

The farms in Maine are fenced in with stone walls. I do not know why this is done, for I did not see anything on these farms that anyone would naturally yearn to carry away with him.

I saw some sheep in one of these enclosures. Their steel-pointed bills were lying on the wall near them, and they were resting their jaws in the crisp, frosty morning air. In another enclosure a farmer was planting clover seed with a hypodermic syringe, and covering it with a mustard plaster. He said that last year his clover was a complete failure because his mustard plasters were no good. He had tried to save money by using second-hand mustard plasters, and of course the clover seed, missing the warm stimulus, neglected to rally, and the crop was a failure.

Here may be noticed the canvas-back moose and a strong antipathy to good rum. I do not wonder that the people of Maine are hostile to rum—if they judge all rum by Maine rum. The moose is one of the most gamey of the finny tribe. He is caught in the fall of the year with a double-barrel shotgun and a pair of snow-shoes. He does not bite unless irritated, but little boys should not go near the female moose while she is on her nest. The masculine moose wears a harelip, and a hat rack on his head to which is attached a placard on which is printed:

PLEASE KEEP OFF THE GRASS.

This shows that the moose is a humorist.

JOHN GOULD

1908–

Born in Brighton, Mass., John (Thomas) Gould has spent much of his life in such Maine towns as Freeport, Lisbon Falls, and Friendship. A Bowdoin graduate, Gould has worked as a broadcaster, guide, farmer, and editor of the *Lisbon Enterprise.* He has been a columnist for the *Christian Science Monitor* and a feature writer for the *Boston Sunday Post, Baltimore Evening Sun,* and *Brunswick Record.* Gould's first humorous book, *Pre-Natal Care for Fathers,* appeared in 1941, and he has been chronicling the customs of Maine's inhabitants ever since.

How to Buy Wood

Old Henry had been a clerk in the Osgood Store for years, and one day a man came in and asked for Old Henry. Mr. Osgood said, "Why, Henry died last week."

"I'm sorry to hear that," said the man. And, after a pause, "Then there must be a vacancy?"

"No," said Mr. Osgood, "Henry didn't leave no vacancy."

A farm housewife known for her stingy portions at dinner, whenever she couldn't avoid feeding somebody, was occasionally twitted about it in sly remarks by those at her table. Once, with hot biscuits, she served a guest a remarkably small portion of comb honey. He surveyed it and said, "Aha! I see you keep a bee."

In Washington County Superior Court some terms ago, the justice was asking a few questions of the defendant in a divorce action. He said, "Have you been faithful to your wife?"

The gentleman replied, "Oh, yes—frequently."

Roland Baker had guided in the Rangeley Lakes region for years, and one of his regular "sports" was a wealthy New Yorker who always said farewell with, "And if you get down to New York this winter, be sure and look me up!" So one winter Roland was in New York for the sportsmen's show, and he looked the man up. He found the place, sounded the gong, and was royally received. Hospitality was complete and Roland had one of the best times of his life. After he got back to Rangeley he liked to tell about it, and a portion of his story went like this:

". . . and then before we went in to eat supper, they come around with some horse's doovers—that's French for eating between meals."

Flint Johnson's wife tells about the little girl from St. Come, up in Quebec, who came down to Maine to work in a summer camp. She spoke no English, and nobody in camp spoke any French, so Mrs. Johnson surmised the young lady might be lonesome. But then she heard the girl was making out fine, as the guides had undertaken to teach her some English. Soon afterwards Mrs. Johnson saw the girl in Riddle's Drug Store, so she spoke to her and said, "How's your English coming along?"

The girl said, "Goddam good!"

Roy Davis tells about the farmer in Newry who built a new shed, and he put a small and untrustworthy padlock on the door. "That lock won't do any good," somebody said to him.

"Well, it'll keep honest people from stealing."

The town of Harmony once claimed the biggest skinflint in the state. He came into Benoit's store one day with an egg in his hand and said, "My wife needs a new darning needle—will you swap me one for this egg?"

Benoit well knew the old fellow's reputation so, amused, he said, "Oh, I suppose so," and they went to the dry goods section in the rear of the store to select the needle. As they walked back to the front of the store Benoit had the egg in his hand, and the skinflint said, "Oh, I see you've put in a new sody fountain!"

Benoit said, "Yes, they're becoming popular, and I thought I'd give one a whirl."

"Well," said the old fellow, "don't that call for a drink on the house?"

"Sure," said Benoit. "What'll you have?"

"Anything with an egg in it."

So Benoit broke the egg in a glass, and it turned out to be a double-yolker.

"Aha!' said the skinflint. "You owe me another needle!"

A.W. Plummer, M.D., used to tell about the time he was driving out in the country to make a call, and he noticed the roof on a farmhouse had burst into flame around the chimney. He turned his horse into the driveway, pounded on the door, and when a woman stuck her head out he said, "Your house is on fire!"

Whether she was preoccupied or stupid, or perhaps didn't understand, the doctor never knew, but she said, "Is that all?"

Dr. Plummer said, "Well, that's all I happen to think of at the moment."

In Kennebec County Court they once had a case of accidental shooting—a hunting affair which may or may not have been quite that accidental. As in most cases of this kind arising out of the fall demises, both state and defense were moving cautiously, the one not caring to accuse where the other was loath to defend, and vice versa, and inferences were heaped on implications until the story got very interesting. At one point the defendant was telling his version of what happened, and he said that he mistook the victim for a deer.

Absorbed in the tale, His Honor leaned down over the bench and said, "Buck or doe?"

Elected to the city council in Lewiston, a man of low social order, no education, and nothing else to qualify him except that he got the most votes, was eager to take part in his first session. So when the city treasurer reported a deficit he cried out, "Let's spend it!"

Virgil Rodney lost an arm in some engagement in the Spanish-American War and had a lot of fun over it the rest of his life. Somebody was always coming up to sympathize and inquire as to how he lost it. Rodney would say, "Now, a good many people ask me that, and the truth is that it always embarrasses me. So I have made a rule, and I'll tell you how I lost my arm if you'll promise not to ask me any more questions about it."

"Certainly."

"Well," says Virgil, "it was bit off."

In town meeting at Freeport the citizens were voting on the school budget, and came to "Physical Training." In those days this was a new idea, and it had been voted through the year before on a trial basis. Most of the objection was in this vein: "I'll give my young-uns exercise enough splittin' wood, they don't need no teacher for working up a sweat." But the educators deemed the subject important, and the citizens went along. A graduate of Sargent School, a young lady, was hired to conduct the classes—she coached girls' basketball, and otherwise instructed in the care of the teeth, keeping the scalp clean, and related delicate topics. Now, after a year's trial, most citizens seemed to be "agin" it, but surprisingly one old farmer took the floor and supported the idea.

"I'm in favor of it," he said, "and I'll tell you why. We got a bunch of kids at our place, and while we try to bring them up right and be decent parents, I got to admit there are times when we fall short. Like, you take, brushing teeth. We keep after them, and we do what we can, but it ain't the same. We never had no luck keeping them faithful at it. But they've had a year of this here physical training, and they like the teacher first-rate, and now when they get up in the morning they fight for the toothbrush."

Judge William R. Pattangall once defended a man accused of arson. This fellow closed his home in Machias and started for Florida to spend the winter. Police intercepted him somewhere in

South Carolina, told him his house had burned down, and held him for the Maine authorities. The state contended he had lighted a candle in a basket of shavings, and when it burned down it set his house afire. Judge Pattangall, who had not been elevated at that time and was merely a practicing attorney, made his usual dramatic and effective appearance, and rather easily got the man acquitted.

The next day the man came to Pattangall's office to pay his fee, and with his departing handshake he said, "Now, Bill, if there's ever anything I can do for you, don't hesitate to call on."

"Well," said Pattangall. "There is something you can do for me. I wish you'd tell me where in hell you got a candle that would burn for three days."

Although Pattangall is better remembered for his trials, his career as a judge was not without the Pattangall touch. A juror, one time, asked to be excused and for his reason said, "My wife is about to become pregnant."

"Excused!" said the judge, instantly.

At this, one of the lawyers said, "I'm sure the court understands that the man means that his wife is about to be delivered of a child."

"Still excused," said Judge Pattangall. "This court recognizes both emergencies."

Del Bates tells about the fellow who came down from Patten to represent that town in the state legislature, and he was so horrified at the runaway tendencies that he began voting no on every appropriation. Early in the session this didn't matter, but later his vote became critical on a number of issues and quite an effort was made to switch him. But he remained adamant, so the party leaders finally asked the governor to intervene.

The fellow was impressed to be invited into the "front office" and he found the governor affable. But even with this high-quality coaxing he refused to change his vote. "I'm sure," said the governor at last, "that there must be a good many men in Patten more sensible than you are that the good people there could have sent down to represent them."

"There are," he said. "Any number of them. But I'm the only one who had a suit of clothes."

And now: how to buy wood. When the old Pejepscot Paper Company decided to liquidate its upriver pulp mill, it was soon picked up by the U.S. Gypsum Company, who began making wood-pulp insulation board. It was a good item and has proved a popular and profitable product. This is the only mill that widespread company has in Maine, and the sudden confrontation of Chicago management and Maine operation created some exciting times. For one thing, somebody had to come from the home office to inspect all departments and operations, so the directors would be informed as they programmed this new mill. When this vice-president arrived, full of big ideas, he had the best intentions in the world, but he was a nuisance. Everybody was polite, but nobody knew just how to deal with him. He was referred to as "The Snoop," and his questions were courteously answered even if they were sometimes foolish. In time he had inspected everything except the buying of wood.

Wood buying is difficult to explain. No forest based mill can operate without wood, and since U.S. Gypsum was new to Maine and owned no timberlands, they depended on buying in the open market. Some mills own and operate their own timberlands. Some own, but contract for cutting. Some don't own much land, but have *entrepreneurs de bois* who look after their interests. Some mills with surplus wood sell to other mills. Some mills use spruce but no pine, and so on. But no matter how the wood is grown and acquired, the mill can't operate without it, and the wood buyer is the key man in the whole operation. Brice Booker was the wood buyer for U.S. Gypsum, and in a competitive and far-flung field he was getting all the wood they needed at favorable prices. And one day the vice-president from Chicago came to Brice and said he had inspected everything else and he was now ready to give his attention to the wood-buying department. Brice had heard about the nuisance this fellow had been all through the mill, and he hadn't been looking forward happily to this moment.

"Well, I tell you," said Brice. "Wood buying is kind of an involved matter, and it doesn't have any set location. I keep a desk here in the mill, but sometimes I don't sit at it for a month. I think the best way to handle this is for you to just report that everything is well in hand."

"No," said the vice-president. "I'm obliged to go deeper than that. I want to see how wood is acquired, and I need to know the secrets of an adequate wood supply."

The last thing in the world Brice Booker wanted was to have anybody learn his secrets, because they were exactly what made him the best wood buyer for miles around, but he was stuck with the fellow, so he says, "All right—where are you staying?"

"I'm at the Eagle Hotel in Brunswick."

"Good," says Brice. "Tomorrow morning you be ready at six o'clock, and I'll pick you up and we'll go buy some wood."

The old Eagle Hotel hadn't seen a vice-president that early in the morning, ever, but they had the fellow on the doorstep when Brice drove up. Away they went, and Brice drove without stopping until he came to the town of Guilford, which is pretty-nigh up to Moosehead Lake, in Piscataquis County. He pulled up before a little, shingled office building with a false front, on which a sign said: HORACE MASON, ATTORNEY AT-LAW, REAL ESTATE & INSURANCE, FORESTER & SURVEYOR, NOTARY PUBLIC.

"Here we are," said Brice, and they went in to find a man poking the fire in a potbelly stove. He turned to see who was coming in, and was clearly delighted to see Brice.

After the handshake and "How's the family," Brice said, "Oh, I want you to meet a vice-president of my company."

Then Brice said, "I've been wondering—did you have any luck moving that old theatre building?"

Squire Mason said, "Yes, I did. Fellow from Bangor. Got my money, and he seems happy."

"Good," said Brice. "I've been worried about you on that deal."

"No need to," said the squire. "I made out."

Then there was a little more small talk, and Brice jumped up and said, "Well, we got to be pushing along. Awful good to see you. Shun evil companions!" and he started for the door. And he contrived to let the vice-president go out through the door first, so the vice-president never heard the rest of the conversation, which went like this:

Booker—You going to have some wood for me this season?

Mason—Eyah.

Booker—Good.

Mason—Same amount?

Booker—Eyah.

Mason—Same price?

Booker—Eyah.

Mason—Will do. It's as good as on the cars.

Booker—See ya!

And he shut the door. He got the vice-president in the automobile and drove without stopping back to Brunswick, where he let the vice-president out on the steps of the Eagle Hotel.

"There you are, all safe and sound," said Brice, "and now you've seen how we buy wood."

"Well," said the vice-president. "I've had a pleasant ride, and I've seen a good part of the State of Maine, but I don't see what that trip had to do with buying wood."

"You will," said Brice. "The vouchers will be coming through any day, and you'll see we bought forty-thousand cords at eleven dollars a cord."

PART IV:

FICTION

HARRIET BEECHER STOWE
1811–1896

Harriet Beecher Stowe was born in Litchfield, Conn., one of nine children of Roxana and Lyman Beecher, the famous Calvinist minister. She moved to Cincinnati when her father accepted the presidency of Lane Theological Seminary. Here she taught school, wrote magazine stories, and observed the effects of slavery in neighboring Kentucky; in 1836 she married the widowed Calvin Stowe, a professor at the seminary. The couple moved to Maine in 1850 when Stowe was offered a position at his alma mater of Bowdoin College. Mrs. Stowe cared for her six children, conducted classes in her home, and continued to write. While in Brunswick, she created a serialization that ran for ten months in the *National Era.* Published in book form as *Uncle Tom's Cabin,* the work was a national sensation, sold 300,000 copies within a year, and made Harriet Beecher Stowe an international celebrity. The Stowes left Maine in 1852, but Mrs. Stowe used the area as the setting for one of her later novels, *The Pearl of Orr's Island* (1862). The didactic aspects of *The Pearl* reduce its appeal for the modern reader, but Stowe intended to depict the dignity and nobility of Maine's coastal inhabitants. The plot centers on the love between Mara and Moses, and is resolved by the death of the gentle, saintly girl and the spiritual awakening of the wild youth.

From *The Pearl of Orr's Island*

Naomi

On the road to the Kennebec, below the town of Bath, in the State of Maine, might have been seen, on a certain autumnal afternoon, a one-horse wagon, in which two persons were sitting. One was an old man, with the peculiarly hard but expressive physiognomy which characterizes the seafaring population of the New England shores. A clear blue eye, evidently practiced in habits of keen observation, white hair, bronzed, weather-beaten cheeks, and a face deeply lined with the furrows of shrewd thought and anxious care, were points of the portrait that made themselves felt at a glance.

By his side sat a young woman of two-and-twenty, of a marked and peculiar personal appearance. Her hair was black, and smoothly parted on a broad forehead, to which a pair of penciled dark eyebrows gave a striking and definite outline. Beneath, lay a pair of large black eyes, remarkable for tremulous expression of melancholy and timidity. The cheek was white and bloodless as a snowberry, though with the clear and perfect oval of good health; the mouth was delicately formed, with a certain sad quiet in its lines, which indicated a habitually repressed and sensitive nature.

The dress of this young person, as often happens in New England, was, in refinement and even elegance, a marked contrast to that of her male companion and to the humble vehicle in which she rode. There was not only the most fastidious neatness, but a delicacy in the choice of colors, an indication of elegant tastes in the whole arrangement, and the quietest suggestion in the world of an acquaintance with the usages of fashion, which struck one oddly in those wild and dreary surroundings. On the whole, she impressed one like those fragile wild-flowers which in April cast their fluttering shadows from the mossy crevices of the old New England granite,—an existence in which colorless delicacy is united to a sort of elastic hardihood of life, fit for the rocky soil and harsh winds it is born to encounter.

The scenery of the road along which the two were riding was wild and bare. Only savins and mulleins, with their dark pyramids or white spires of velvet leaves, diversified the sandy wayside; but out at sea was a wide sweep of blue, reaching far to the open ocean, which lay rolling, tossing, and breaking into white caps of foam in the bright sunshine. For two or three days a northeast storm had been raging, and the sea was in all the commotion which such a general upturning creates.

The two travelers reached a point of elevated land, where they paused a moment, and the man drew up the jogging, stiff-jointed old farm-horse, and raised himself upon his feet to look out at the prospect.

There might be seen in the distance the blue Kennebec sweeping out toward the ocean through its picturesque rocky shores, decked with cedars and other dusky evergreens, which were illuminated by the orange and flame-colored trees of Indian summer. Here and there scarlet creepers swung long trailing garlands over the faces of the dark rock, and fringes of goldenrod above swayed with the brisk blowing wind that was driving the blue waters seaward, in face of the up-coming ocean tide,—a conflict which caused them to rise in great foam-crested waves. There are two channels into this river from the open sea, navigable for ships which are coming in to the city of Bath; one is broad and shallow, the other narrow and deep, and these are divided by a steep ledge of rocks.

Where the spectators of this scene were sitting, they could see in the distance a ship borne with tremendous force by the rising tide into the mouth of the river, and encountering a northwest wind which had succeeded the gale, as northwest winds often do on this coast. The ship, from what might be observed in the distance, seemed struggling to make the wider channel, but was constantly driven off by the baffling force of the wind.

"There she is, Naomi," said the old fisherman, eagerly, to his companion, "coming right in." The young woman was one of the sort that never start, and never exclaim, but with all deeper emotions grow still. The color slowly mounted into her cheek, her lips parted, and her eyes dilated with a wide, bright expression; her breathing came in thick gasps, but she said nothing.

The old fisherman stood up in the wagon, his coarse, butternut-colored coat-flaps fluttering and snapping in the breeze, while his interest seemed to be so intense in the efforts of the ship that he made involuntary and eager movements as if to direct her course. A moment passed, and his keen, practiced eye discovered a change in her movements, for he cried out involuntarily,—

"*Don't* take the narrow channel to-day!" and a moment after, "O Lord! O Lord! have mercy,—there they go! Look! look! look!"

And, in fact, the ship rose on a great wave clear out of the water, and the next second seemed to leap with a desperate plunge into the narrow passage; for a moment there was a shivering of the masts and the rigging, and she went down and was gone.

"They're split to pieces!" cried the fisherman. "Oh, my poor girl—my poor girl—they're gone! O Lord, have mercy!"

The woman lifted up no voice, but, as one who has been shot through the heart falls with no cry, she fell back,—a mist rose up over her great mournful eyes,—she had fainted.

The story of this wreck of a home-bound ship just entering the harbor is yet told in many a family on this coast. A few hours after, the unfortunate crew were washed ashore in all the joyous holiday rig in which they had attired themselves that morning to go to their sisters, wives, and mothers.

This is the first scene in our story.

Mara

Down near the end of Orr's Island, facing the open ocean, stands a brown house of the kind that the natives call "lean-to," or "linter,"—one of those large, comfortable structures, barren in the ideal, but rich in the practical, which the workingman of New England can always command. The waters of the ocean came up within a rod of this house, and the sound of its moaning waves was even now filling the clear autumn starlight. Evidently something was going on within, for candles fluttered and winked from window to window, like fireflies in a dark meadow, and sounds as of quick footsteps, and the flutter of brushing garments, might be heard.

Something unusual is certainly going on within the dwelling of Zephaniah Pennel to-night.

Let us enter the dark front-door. We feel our way to the right, where a solitary ray of light comes from the chink of a half-opened door. Here is the front room of the house, set apart as its place of especial social hilarity and sanctity,—the "best room," with its low studded walls, white dimity window-curtains, rag carpet, and polished wood chairs. It is now lit by the dim gleam of a solitary tallow candle, which seems in the gloom to make only a feeble circle of light around itself, leaving all the rest of the apartment in shadow.

In the centre of the room, stretched upon a table, and covered partially by a sea-cloak, lies the body of a man of twenty-five,—lies, too, evidently as one of whom it is written, "He shall return to his house no more, neither shall his place know him any more." A splendid manhood has suddenly been called to forsake that lifeless form, leaving it, like a deserted palace, beautiful in its desolation. The hair, dripping with the salt wave, curled in glossy abundance on the finely-formed head; the flat, broad brow; the closed eye, with its long black lashes; the firm, manly mouth; the strongly-moulded chin,—all, all were sealed with that seal which is never to be broken till the great resurrection day.

He was lying in a full suit of broadcloth, with a white vest and smart blue neck-tie, fastened with a pin, in which was some braided hair under a crystal. All his clothing, as well as his hair, was saturated with sea-water, which trickled from time to time, and struck with a leaden and dropping sound into a sullen pool which lay under the table.

This was the body of James Lincoln, ship-master of the brig Flying Scud, who that morning had dressed himself gayly in his state-room to go on shore and meet his wife,—singing and jesting as he did so.

This is all that you have to learn in the room below; but as we stand there, we hear a trampling of feet in the apartment above,—the quick yet careful opening and shutting of doors,—and voices come and go about the house, and whisper consultations on the stairs. Now comes the roll of wheels, and the Doctor's gig drives up to the door; and, as he goes creaking up with his heavy boots, we will follow and gain admission to the dimly-lighted chamber.

Two gossips are sitting in earnest, whispering conversation over a small bundle done up in an old flannel petticoat. To them the doctor is about to address himself cheerily, but is repelled by sundry signs and sounds which warn him not to speak. Moderating his heavy boots as well as he is able to a pace of quiet, he advances for a moment, and the petticoat is unfolded for him to glance at its contents; while a low, eager, whispered conversation, attended with much head-shaking, warns him that his first duty is with somebody behind the checked curtains of a bed in the farther corner of the room. He steps on tiptoe, and draws the curtain; and there, with closed eye, and cheek as white as wintry snow, lies the same face over which passed the shadow of death when that ill-fated ship went down.

This woman was wife to him who lies below, and within the hour has been made mother to a frail little human existence, which the storm of a great anguish has driven untimely on the shores of life,—a precious pearl cast up from the past eternity upon the wet, wave-ribbed sand of the present. Now, weary with her moanings, and beaten out with the wrench of a double anguish, she lies with closed eyes in that passive apathy which precedes deeper shadows and longer rest.

Over against her, on the other side of the bed, sits an aged woman in an attitude of deep dejection, and the old man we saw with her in the morning is standing with an anxious, awestruck face at the foot of the bed.

The doctor feels the pulse of the woman, or rather lays an inquiring finger where the slightest thread of vital current is scarcely throbbing, and shakes his head mournfully. The touch of his hand rouses her,—her large wild, melancholy eyes fix themselves on him with an inquiring glance, then she shivers and moans,—

"Oh, Doctor, Doctor!—Jamie, Jamie!"

"Come, come!" said the doctor, "cheer up, my girl, you've got a fine little daughter,—the Lord mingles mercies with his afflictions."

Her eyes closed, her head moved with a mournful but decided dissent.

A moment after she spoke in the sad old words of the Hebrew Scripture,-

"Call her not Naomi; call her Mara, for the Almighty hath dealt very bitterly with me."

And as she spoke, there passed over her face the sharp frost of the last winter; but even as it passed there broke out a smile, as if a flower had been thrown down from Paradise, and she said,—

"Not my will, but thy will," and so was gone.

Aunt Roxy and Aunt Ruey were soon left alone in the chamber of death.

"She'll make a beautiful corpse," said Aunt Roxy, surveying the still, white form contemplatively, with her head in an artistic attitude.

"She was a pretty girl," said Aunt Ruey; "dear me, what a Providence! I 'member the wedd'n down in that lower room, and what a handsome couple they were."

"They were lovely and pleasant in their lives, and in their deaths they were not divided," said Aunt Roxy, sententiously.

"What was it she said, did ye hear?" said Aunt Ruey.

"She called the baby 'Mary.'"

"Ah! sure enough, her mother's name afore her. What a still, softly-spoken thing she always was!"

"A pity the poor baby didn't go with her," said Aunt Roxy; "seven-months' children are so hard to raise."

"'T is a pity," said the other.

But babies will live, and all the more when everybody says that it is a pity they should. Life goes on as inexorably in this world as death. It was ordered by THE WILL above that out of these two graves should spring one frail, trembling autumn flower,—the "Mara" whose poor little roots first struck deep in the salt, bitter waters of our mortal life.

SARAH ORNE JEWETT
1849–1909

Sarah Orne Jewett became well acquainted with the area around her home town of South Berwick by accompanying her physician father on his rounds. As a girl Jewett was also moved by Harriet Beecher Stowe's sympathetic treatment of Maine coastal life, and she set for herself the task of recording the commonplace lives of those who dwelt in Maine's quiet towns, dwindling farms, and deserted harbors. At the age of twenty the prestigious *Atlantic Monthly* accepted one of her stories; the series of stories that followed was collected as *Deephaven* in 1877. Jewett published many works in the following decades, and her craftsmanship culminated in *The Country of the Pointed Firs* (1896), which is considered a masterpiece of regional fiction. Through her friend Annie Fields, the wife of a prominent Boston publisher, Jewett enjoyed a cosmopolitan circle of acquaintances. Jewett spent much time in Boston and traveled with Mrs. Fields, but she always returned to the land and people of Maine. With her keen perception Jewett was able to penetrate beneath the surface to reveal the inner natures of the laconic, independent individuals she frequently chose as subjects for her "sketches."

A White Heron

I.

The woods were already filled with shadows one June evening, just before eight o'clock, though a bright sunset still glimmered faintly among the trunks of the trees. A little girl was driving home her cow, a plodding, dilatory, provoking creature in her behavior, but a valued companion for all that. They were going away from the western light, and striking deep into the dark woods, but their feet were familiar with the path, and it was no matter whether their eyes could see it or not.

There was hardly a night the summer through when the old cow could be found waiting at the pasture bars; on the contrary, it was her greatest pleasure to hide herself away among the high huckleberry bushes, and though she wore a loud bell she had made the discovery that if one stood perfectly still it would not ring. So Sylvia had to hunt for her until she found her, and call Co'! Co'! with never an answering Moo, until her childish patience was quite spent. If the creature had not given good milk and plenty of it, the case would have seemed very different to her owners. Besides, Sylvia had all the time there was, and very little use to make of it. Sometimes in pleasant weather it was a consolation to look upon the cow's pranks as an intelligent attempt to play hide and seek, and as the child had no playmates she lent herself to this amusement with a good deal of zest. Though this chase had been so long that the wary animal herself had given an unusual signal of her whereabouts, Sylvia had only laughed when she came upon Mistress Moolly at the swamp-side, and urged her affectionately homeward with a twig of birch leaves. The old cow was not inclined to wander farther, she even turned in the right direction for once as they left the pasture, and stepped along the road at a good pace. She was quite ready to be milked now, and seldom stopped to browse. Sylvia wondered what her grandmother would say because they were so late. It was a great while since she had left home at half past five o'clock, but everybody knew the difficulty of making this errand a short one. Mrs. Tilley had chased the hornéd torment too many summer evenings herself to blame any one else for lingering, and was only thankful as she waited that she had Sylvia, nowadays, to give such valuable assistance. The good woman suspected that Sylvia loitered occasionally on her own account; there never was such a child for straying about out-of-doors since the world was made! Everybody said that it was a good change for a little maid who had tried to grow for eight years in a crowded manufacturing town, but, as for Sylvia herself, it seemed as if she never had been alive at all before she came to live at the farm. She thought often with wistful compassion of a wretched dry geranium that belonged to a town neighbor.

"'Afraid of folks,'" old Mrs. Tilley said to herself, with a smile, after she had made the unlikely choice of Sylvia from her daughter's houseful of children , and was returning to the farm. "'Afraid of folks,' they said! I guess she won't be troubled no great with 'em up to the old place!" When they reached the door of the lonely house and stopped to unlock it, and the cat came to purr loudly, and rub against them, a deserted pussy, indeed, but fat with young robins, Sylvia whispered that this was a beautiful place to live in, and she never should wish to go home.

* * *

The companions followed the shady woodroad, the cow taking slow steps, and the child very fast ones. The cow stopped long at the brook to drink, as if the pasture were not half a swamp, and Sylvia stood still and waited, letting her bare feet cool themselves in the shoal water, while the great twilight moths struck softly against her. She waded on through the brook as the cow moved away, and listened to the thrushes with a heart that beat fast with pleasure.

There was a stirring in the great boughs overhead. They were full of little birds and beasts that seemed to be wide-awake, and going about their world, or else saying good-night to each other in sleepy twitters. Sylvia herself felt sleepy as she walked along. However, it was not much farther to the house, and the air was soft and sweet. She was not often in the woods so late as this, and it made her feel as if she were a part of the gray shadows and the moving leaves. She was just thinking how long it seemed since she first came to the farm a year ago, and wondering if everything went on in the noisy town just the same as when she was there; the thought of the great red-faced boy who used to chase and frighten her made her hurry along the path to escape from the shadow of the trees.

Suddenly this little woods-girl is horror-stricken to hear a clear whistle not very far away. Not a bird's whistle, which would have a sort of friendliness, but a boy's whistle, determined, and somewhat aggressive. Sylvia left the cow to whatever sad fate might await her, and stepped discreetly aside into the bushes, but she was just too late. The enemy had discovered her, and called out in a very cheerful and persuasive tone, "Halloa, little girl, how far is it to the road?" and trembling Sylvia answered almost inaudibly, "A good ways."

She did not dare to look boldly at the tall young man, who carried a gun over his shoulder, but she came out of her bush and again followed the cow, while he walked alongside.

"I have been hunting for some birds," the stranger said kindly, "and I have lost my way, and need a friend very much. Don't be afraid," he added gallantly. "Speak up and tell me what your name is, and whether you think I can spend the night at your house, and go out gunning early in the morning."

Sylvia was more alarmed than before. Would not her grandmother consider her much to blame? But who could have foreseen such an accident as this? It did not appear to be her fault, and she hung her head as if the stem of it were broken, but managed to answer "Sylvy," with much effort when her companion again asked her name.

Mrs. Tilley was standing in the doorway when the trio came into view. The cow gave a loud moo by way of explanation.

"Yes, you'd better speak up for yourself, you old trial! Where'd she tucked herself away this time, Sylvy?" Sylvia kept an awed silence; she knew by instinct that her grandmother did not comprehend the gravity of the situation. She must be mistaking the stranger for one of the farmer-lads of the region.

The young man stood his gun beside the door, and dropped a heavy game-bag beside it; then he bade Mrs. Tilley good-evening, and repeated his wayfarer's story, and asked if he could have a night's lodging.

"Put me anywhere you like," he said. "I must be off early in the morning, before day; but I am very hungry, indeed. You can give me some milk at any rate, that's plain."

"Dear sakes, yes," responded the hostess, whose long slumbering hospitality seemed to be easily awakened. "You might fare better if you went out on the main road a mile or so, but you're welcome to what we've got. I'll milk right off, and you make yourself at home. You can sleep on husks or feathers," she proffered graciously. "I raised them all myself. There's good pasturing for geese just below here towards the ma'sh. Now step round and set a plate for the gentleman, Sylvy!" And Sylvia promptly stepped. She was glad to have something to do, and she was hungry herself.

It was a surprise to find so clean and comfortable a little dwelling in this New England wilderness. The young man had known the horrors of its most primitive housekeeping, and the dreary squalor of that level of society which does not rebel at the companionship of hens. This was the best thrift of an old-fashioned farmstead, though on such a small scale that it seemed like a hermitage. He listened eagerly to the old woman's quaint talk, he watched Sylvia's pale face and shining gray eyes with ever growing enthusiasm, and insisted that this was the best supper he had eaten for a month; then, afterward, the new-made friends sat down in the doorway together while the moon came up.

Soon it would be berry-time, and Sylvia was a great help at picking. The cow was a good milker, though a plaguy thing to keep track of, the hostess gossiped frankly, adding presently that she had buried four children, so that Sylvia's mother, and a son (who might be dead) in California were all the children she had left. "Dan, my boy, was a great hand to go gunning," she explained sadly. "I never wanted for pa'tridges or gray squer'ls while he was to home. He's been a great wand'rer, I expect, and he's no hand to write letters. There, I don't blame him, I'd ha' seen the world myself if it had been so I could.

"Sylvia takes after him," the grandmother continued affectionately, after a minute's pause. "There ain't a foot o' ground she don't know her way over, and the wild creatur's counts her one o' themselves. Squer'ls she 'll tame to come an' feed right out o' her hands, and all sorts o' birds. Last winter she got the jay-birds to bangeing here, and I believe she 'd 'a' scanted herself of her own meals to have plenty to throw out amongst 'em, if I hadn't kep' watch. Anything but crows, I tell her, I'm willin' to help support, — though Dan he went an' tamed one o' them that did seem to have reason same as folks. It was round here a good spell after he went away. Dan an' his father they didn't hitch,— but he never held up his head ag'in after Dan had dared him an' gone off."

The guest did not notice this hint of family sorrows in his eager interest in something else.

"So Sylvy knows all about birds, does she?" he exclaimed, as he looked round at the little girl who sat, very demure but increasingly sleepy, in the moonlight. "I am making a collection of birds myself. I have been at it ever since I was a boy." (Mrs. Tilley smiled.) "There are two or three very rare ones I have been hunting for these five years. I mean to get them on my own ground if they can be found."

"Do you cage 'em up?" asked Mrs. Tilley doubtfully, in response to this enthusiastic announcement.

"Oh, no, they 're stuffed and preserved, dozens and dozens of them," said the ornithologist, "and I have shot or snared every one myself. I caught a glimpse of a white heron three miles from here on Saturday, and I have followed it in this direction. They have never been found in this district at all. The little white heron, it is," and he turned again to look at Sylvia with the hope of discovering that the rare bird was one of her acquaintances.

But Sylvia was watching a hop-toad in the narrow footpath.

"You would know the heron if you saw it," the stranger continued eagerly. "A queer tall white bird with soft feathers and long thin legs. And it would have a nest perhaps in the top of a high tree, made of sticks, something like a hawk's nest."

Sylvia's heart gave a wild beat; she knew that strange white bird, and had once stolen softly near where it stood in some bright green swamp grass, away over at the other side of the woods. There was an open place where the sunshine always seemed strangely yellow and hot, where tall, nodding rushes grew, and her grandmother had warned her that she might sink in the soft black mud underneath and never be heard of more. Not far beyond were the salt marshes and beyond those was the sea, the sea which Sylvia wondered and dreamed about, but never had looked upon, though its great voice could often be heard above the noise of the woods on stormy nights.

"I can't think of anything I should like so much as to find that heron's nest," the handsome stranger was saying. "I would give ten dollars to anybody who could show it to me," he added desperately, "and I mean to spend my whole vacation hunting for it if need be. Perhaps it was only migrating, or had been chased out of its own region by some bird of prey."

Mrs. Tilley gave amazed attention to all this, but Sylvia still watched the toad, not divining, as she might have done at some calmer time, that the creature wished to get to its hole under the doorstep, and was much hindered by the unusual spectators at that hour of the evening. No amount of thought, that night, could decide how many wished-for treasures the ten dollars, so lightly spoken of, would buy.

* * *

The next day the young sportsman hovered about the woods, and Sylvia kept him company, having lost her first fear of the friendly lad, who proved to be most kind and sympathetic. He told her many things about the birds and what they knew and where they lived and what they did with themselves. And he gave her a jack-knife, which she thought as great a treasure as if she were a desert-islander. All day long he did not once make her troubled or afraid except when he brought down some unsuspecting singing creature from its bough. Sylvia would have liked him vastly better without his gun; she could not understand why he killed the very birds he seemed to like so much. But as the day waned, Sylvia still watched the young man with loving admiration. She had never seen anybody so charming and delightful; the woman's heart, asleep in the child, was vaguely thrilled by a dream of love. Some premonition of that great power stirred and swayed these young foresters who traversed the solemn woodlands with soft-footed silent care. They stopped to listen to a bird's song; they pressed forward again eagerly, parting the branches,—speaking to each other rarely and in whispers; the young man going first and Sylvia following, fascinated, a few steps behind, with her gray eyes dark with excitement.

She grieved because the longed-for white heron was elusive, but she did not lead the guest, she only followed, and there was no such thing as speaking first. The sound of her own unquestioned voice would have terrified her,—it was hard enough to answer yes or no when there was need of that. At last evening began to fall, and they drove the cow home together, and Sylvia smiled with pleasure when they came to the place where she heard the whistle and was afraid only the night before.

II.

Half a mile from home, at the farther edge of the woods, where the land was highest, a great pine-tree stood, the last of its generation. Whether it was left for a boundary mark, or for what reason, no one could say; the woodchoppers who had felled its mates were dead and gone long ago, and a whole forest of sturdy trees, pines and oaks and maples, had grown again. But the stately head of this old pine towered above them all and made a landmark for sea and shore miles and miles away. Sylvia knew it well. She had always believed that whoever climbed to the top of it could see the ocean; and the little girl had often laid her hand on the great rough trunk and looked up wistfully at those dark boughs that the wind always stirred, no matter how hot and still the air might be below. Now she thought of the tree with a new excitement, for why, if one climbed it at break of day, could not one see all the world, and easily discover whence the white heron flew, and mark the place, and find the hidden nest?

What a spirit of adventure, what wild ambition! What fancied triumph and delight and glory for the later morning when she could make known the secret! It was almost too real and too great for the childish heart to bear.

All night the door of the little house stood open, and the whippoorwills came and sang upon the very step. The young sportsman and his old hostess were sound asleep, but Sylvia's great design kept her broad awake and watching. She forgot to think of sleep. The short summer night seemed as long as the winter darkness, and at last when the whippoorwills ceased, and she was afraid the morning would after all come too soon, she stole out of the house and followed the pasture path through the woods, hastening toward the open ground beyond, listening with a sense of comfort and companionship to the drowsy twitter of a half-awakened bird, whose perch she had jarred in passing. Alas, if the great wave of human interest which flooded for the first time this dull little life should sweep away the satisfactions of an existence heart to heart with nature and the dumb life of the forest!

There was the huge tree asleep yet in the paling moonlight, and small and hopeful Sylvia began with utmost bravery to mount to the top of it, with tingling, eager blood coursing the channels of her whole frame, with her bare feet and fingers, that pinched and held like bird's claws to the monstrous ladder reaching up, up, almost to the sky itself. First she must mount the white oak tree that grew alongside, where she was almost lost among the dark branches and the green leaves heavy and wet with dew; a bird fluttered off its nest, and a red squirrel ran to and fro and scolded pettishly at the harmless housebreaker. Sylvia felt her way easily. She had often climbed there, and knew that higher still one of the oak's upper branches chafed against the pine trunk, just where its lower boughs were set close together. There, when she made the dangerous pass from one tree to the other, the great enterprise would really begin

She crept out along the swaying oak limb at last, and took the daring step across into the old pine-tree. The way was harder than she thought; she must reach far and hold fast, the sharp dry twigs caught and held her and scratched her like angry talons, the pitch made her thin little fingers clumsy and stiff as she went round and round the tree's great stem, higher and higher upward. The sparrows and robins in the woods below were beginning to wake and twitter to the dawn, yet it seemed much lighter there aloft in the pine-tree, and the child knew that she must hurry if her project were to be of any use.

The tree seemed to lengthen itself out as she went up, and to reach farther and farther upward. It was like a great main-mast to the voyaging earth; it must truly have been amazed that morning through all its ponderous frame as it felt this determined spark of human spirit creeping and climbing from higher branch to branch. Who knows how steadily the least twigs held themselves to advantage this light, weak creature on her way! The old pine must have loved his new dependent. More than all the hawks, and bats, and moths, and even the sweet-voiced thrushes, was the brave, beating heart of the solitary gray-eyed child. And the tree stood still and held away the winds that June morning while the dawn grew bright in the east.

Sylvia's face was like a pale star, if one had seen it from the ground, when the last thorny bough was past, and she stood trembling and tired but wholly triumphant, high in the tree-top. Yes, there was the sea with the dawning sun making a golden dazzle over it, and toward that glorious east flew two hawks with slow-moving pinions. How low they looked in the air from that height when before one had only seen them far up, and dark against the blue sky. Their gray feathers were as soft as moths; they seemed only a little way from the tree, and Sylvia felt as if she too could go flying away among the clouds. Westward, the woodlands and farms reached miles and miles into the distance; here and there were church steeples, and white villages; truly it was a vast and awesome world.

The birds sang louder and louder. At last the sun came up bewilderingly bright. Sylvia could see the white sails of ships out at sea, and the clouds that were purple and rose-colored and yellow at first began to fade away. Where was the white heron's nest in the sea of green branches, and was this wonderful sight and pageant of the world the only reward for having climbed to such a giddy height? Now look down again, Sylvia, where the green marsh is set among the shining birches and dark hemlocks; there where you saw the white heron once you will see him again; look, look! a white spot of him like a single floating feather comes up from the dead hemlock and grows larger, and rises, and comes close at last, and goes by the landmark pine with steady sweep of wing and outstretched slender neck and crested head. And wait! wait! do not move a foot or a finger, little girl, do not send an arrow of light and consciousness from your two eager eyes, for the heron has perched on a pine bough not far beyond yours, and cries back to his mate on the nest, and plumes his feathers for the new day!

The child gives a long sigh a minute later when a company of shouting cat-birds comes also to the tree, and vexed by their fluttering and lawlessness the solemn heron goes away. She knows his secret now, the wild, light, slender bird that floats and wavers, and goes back like an arrow presently to his home in the green world beneath. Then Sylvia, well satisfied, makes her perilous way down again, not daring to look far below the branch she stands on, ready to cry sometimes because her fingers ache and her lamed feet slip. Wondering over and over again what the stranger would say to her, and what he would think when she told him how to find his way straight to the heron's nest.

* * *

"Sylvy, Sylvy!" called the busy old grandmother again and again, but nobody answered, and the small husk bed was empty, and Sylvia had disappeared.

The guest waked from a dream, and remembering his day's pleasure hurried to dress himself that it might sooner begin. He was sure from the way the shy little girl looked once or twice yesterday that she had at least seen the white heron, and now she must really be persuaded to tell. Here she comes now, paler than ever, and her worn old frock is torn and tattered, and smeared with pine pitch. The grandmother and the sportsman stand in the door together and question her, and the splendid moment has come to speak of the dead hemlock-tree by the green marsh.

But Sylvia does not speak after all, though the old grandmother fretfully rebukes her, and the young man's kind appealing eyes are looking straight in her own. He can make them rich with money; he has promised it, and they are poor now. He is so well worth making happy, and he waits to hear the story she can tell.

No, she must keep silence! What is it that suddenly forbids her and makes her dumb? Has she been nine years growing, and now, when the great world for the first time puts out a hand to her, must she thrust it aside for a bird's sake? The murmur of the pine's green branches is in her ears, she remembers how the white heron came flying through the golden air and how they watched the sea and the morning together, and Sylvia cannot speak; she cannot tell the heron's secret and give its life away.

Dear loyalty, that suffered a sharp pang as the guest went away disappointed later in the day, that could have served and followed him and loved him as a dog loves! Many a night Sylvia heard the echo of his whistle haunting the pasture path as she came home with the loitering cow. She forgot even her sorrow at the sharp report of his gun and the piteous sight of thrushes and sparrows dropping silent to the ground, their songs hushed and their pretty feathers stained and wet with blood. Were the birds better friends than their hunter might have been,—who can tell? Whatever treasures were lost to her, woodlands and summer-time, remember! Bring your gifts and graces and tell your secrets to this lonely country child!

GEORGE S. WASSON
1855–1932

Although George (Savary) Wasson was born and raised in Massachusetts, his ancestors had lived on Penobscot Bay for generations. Wasson studied painting for three years in Germany, returned to Boston to pursue a career in marine painting, married in 1885, and moved to Kittery Point in 1888. As economic changes caused a decline in the shipping industry, he turned instead to writing, publishing *Cap'n Simeon's Store* in 1903 and *The Green Shay* in 1905. After the death of his two sons, he moved to Bangor with his daughter-in-law for the remaining sixteen years of his life. His stories are noted for their authentic color and their easy narrative in the vernacular of coastal Maine.

Rusticators at the Cove

One wild January night a furious northeaster drove the fine snow in curling drifts across the narrow road leading to the store. The three great elms in front swayed and creaked in the heavy gusts, between which the dismal moan of the steam fog horn on the Neck was dimly heard mingling with the rote of the sea on that exposed headland. In the Cove the riding-lights of half a dozen coasters at anchor blinked feebly through the driving snow, rising and falling on the long ground swell which worked in from outside, and to a small but select assemblage the red-hot stove and tobacco laden air of the store seemed doubly grateful.

"This 'ere breeze o' wind is pricking on consid'ble tough, you," remarked Cap'n Roundturn, as he unbuckled his overshoes and settled back comfortably in his chair. "Ef the sea keeps on a-makin' same's she has sence noontime, 't wouldn't s'prise me no great ef some of these lumber-loaded fellers out here didn't pile up on the beach afore ever we're through with it."

"Wal, I dunno about that, now," said Simeon dubiously. "I couldn't make out to sight ary vessel outside in that 'ere glinn we had jest afore sundown, and what few there is to anchor in here tonight is all right enough, without this wind should cant to the east'ard furder, and give us a reg'lar-built ole-fashioned combustible. I don't look to see nothin' come ashore, though, myself. Vessels all carries sich tormented heavy ground-taycle now'days to what they used to, we never commence to git the wracks there was thirty year ago.''

''Wouldn't kick a mite to see a little cargo of stove-coal delivered up here on the rocks good and handy about this time o' year, though,'' remarked Sheriff Isaac Windseye, cheerfully. ''My ole coal-bin is gitting to look kind of sick a'ready. Dinged ef these flaws ain't strikin' heftier every minute, you!'' he exclaimed, as a fierce blast drove the snow like sand against the eastern windows.

''You bate they be so,'' assented Simeon. ''It's been breezenin' on stiddy now ever sence noontime. I told my woman last night, s' I, 'We're in for a linging ole east'ly breeze o' wind,' s' I. It's seldom ever I heerd the rote out on them southeast laidges plainer 'n what she was last night, and take it one spell there, and, swan to man! ef 't didn't seem 's though them breakers on the Hue and Cry was right down here back of the saltshed! Wonder what them summer rusticators would say ef they should light down here this weather. S'pose they'd turn to and be rowin' acrost from Skipper's Islant to-night bare-armed and bare-headed same's ever?''

''Godfrey mighty, you!'' cried Job Gaskett, in response to Simeon's ironical inquiry. '''T wouldn't s'prise me one mite to see 'em tryin' of it on. No, sir, 't wouldn't,—not a part'cle! I tell ye them folks doos make out to act so like a parcel of nat'rals when they're down here summer-times, that nothin' they turned to and done wouldn't jar me none now. Why, I seen some on 'em one day here last fall, when 't was raining consid'ble smart, thick o' fog, and a fresh breeze a-goin' from out here to the south'ard and east'ard, damp and cold 's the devil,—there they was, the pore half-fools, rowin' round and round the Cove into one o' them hotel let-bo'ts, nary head-gear onto 'em, and stripped chock to the waist, they was, trying to git theirselves tanned, I cal'late!

''Oh, them 's a ter'ble cur'ous class of folks, them rusticators is, now I'll be jiggered ef they hain't! But lemme tell ye one thing, and that is, you come to take them kind that goes round a-sketchin' and drawrin' out these 'ere portograft views, I cal'late them kind's the biggest cranks o' the whole kerboodle. One time I seen three o' them kind to once setting down drawrin' out a portograft view of that set-fired ramshackle ole wrack of a house Jim Whidden lives into, 'way down on the lower Neck ro'd, there. Why, gracious ever, you, I'll bate high there ain't a flake o' paint left on to the blame' ole trap, nor there hain't been sence my rec'lection, and seems 's though I could 'member chock back to the Concord fight, too!

''Wouldn't wonder myself but what she was built about the time Columbus come ashore up there to Plymouth, but that's jest the very place them rusticators had turned to and gafted onto to sketch out a portograft view on, much as to say, 'This here is the very pootiest-lookin' place we can make out to scare up to the whole o' Killick Cove!' Sich works is a reg'lar dod-blowed slur on the town, and that's allst ever you can make on 'em.

I know blame' well we haint got no gilted palaces, and all them kind o' krawm to make no great brags on, but same time there doos make out to be quite a few real slick and tidy little places here to this Cove, jest as handsome and neat kep' up as ary one ever you'll find up to the west'ard, back o' Baws'n there. Why, I'll un'take to take and name off half a dezen places this minute that's all painted up and blinded off pooty 's ary pictur' ever you see, a set of out-buildin's and everything complete. But set-fire, you! What's them kind amount to, anyways? Them kind hain't no sort of airthly account to them blame' rusticators!

"The way it works, they've allus and forever got to run afoul o' some ole lop-sided wrack of a house, or else a bo't, or a w'arft; dinged little odds I guess, what she is, long's she makes out to be some reg'lar ole has-been, that hain't seen no paint nor fixin' up not sence Adam wa'n't nothin' only a yearling; and then, 'Oh my!' says they right off, 'but hain't that jest lovely, you!' That makes 'em grin right out, same's so many set-fired Chessy cats, that doos. They got to take and heave to then, sure pop, and sketch her all out full bigness, complete, so's to take and lug her off home 'long on 'em.

"Why, Godfrey mighty, you! Ef you'll b'lieve it, ole Sam Grommet there, he told me hisself one o' them same rusticators turned to one time and drawed out a portograft view of him a-standin' there full bigness into his ole dory with a master great jag o' lopster traps stacked up all o' four foot high,—yas, he did so, that's a fact,—and give him an even dollar for his stopping, too! Must made a reg'lar jim-dandy style o' pictur' to take and stick up into a gilted frame, somewheres, now I swanny!

"That plaguey old dory o' his'n come outen the Pilot's Pride, ef I ain't very much mistakened, and it's going on a dezen year sence she was lost, I know, and prob'ly she wa'n't by no means a brand, spangin' noo dory then, neither. Sam he ain't never teched her sence, I guess, in no way, shape, nor manner, without it is to kind o' chinse up her garboards a grain with pieces ripped off'n his shirt-flap; and I'm tellin' of ye she's about as desp'rate-looking an ole packet now as you'll scare up in a month o' Sundays.

"For the matter of that, though, you come to take ole Sam there, and there don't make out to be nothin' so very beautysome about him, neither, specially when he's all ragged out in his ole oil-skins and kag-boots, same's he most allus is, and chock-a-block full o' noo rum at that! And dirty! Wal now, don't say a word! I'll bate he can't remember so fur back as the time he shifted his shirt last, or washed his face and hands, nary one. Seems 's though he allus doos make out to be one of the very lookin'est ole creeturs ever you see, but there, you! Seems 's though he jest suited them rusticator folks right chock up to the handle, and I cal'late myself he's liable to git adopted by some on 'em yit, so's they can allus have him round handy to set and look at to home."

While in general the company present seemed greatly to enjoy this discussion of the rusticators' failings, Sheriff Isaac Windseye, who had recently fitted up his house for their accommodation, took no part in it, but having fashioned a toothpick from a burnt match, sat tilted far back in his chair, using the implement in moody silence.

But Cap'n Simeon Roundturn, who was well known to entertain a supreme contempt for the peculiar class of people in question, now vacated his high perch at the desk, and with spectacles pushed down to the tip of his nose, advanced into the arena.

"The very fust year after them kind of folks struck here to this Cove," began he, "I turned to and laid me in a prime, A No. 1 stock of these 'ere canned goods; not jest merely tomatoes and the like o' them, but real downright fancy lot of canned chicken, canned puddin', blueb'ries, blackb'ries, lopsters and clams, and most every blame' thing else I figgered them style folks would prob'ly be callin' for. Wal, sir, wha' 'd I git for my pains? There them cans set today, the heft on 'em, up there on them top back shelves." And Simeon turned and surveyed his slighted goods with a look of sorrow and indignation.

"I've eat some few scatterin' cans in my own fam'ly," he went on, "and we'll say mebbe I've turned to and give away p'haps half a dezen or so cans all told, but set-fire, you! I hain't never got red of one single, sol'tary can outen the lot to a rusticator yit, nor I don't cal'late ever I shall, now. All the way ever I can figger it, I 've jest went and made me a clean loss on the whole tormented bus'niss. It's only seldom ever one o' the tribe'll so much's set foot inside here at all now'days, and when they do it's jest only to gawk round like, or else take and call for suppin' they know plaguey well I ain't got.

"Now you come to take it here last summer one time; that 'ere little red-headed galoot from Phullydelphy there,—the one that's built them set-fired homely-lookin' barracks down on the ole Spurshoe place, you know,—he come sailin' in here with his short pants, bigger 'n Billy-be damned. Blow my shirt ef he didn't tread up to the counter here same's a chicken doos to a dough-dish, and 'lowed how he wanted some Mocho coffee.

" 'I hain't got her,' s' I. 'Don't never have no call for her, scursely,' s' I.

" 'Got any Jayvy, have ye?' s' he.

" 'No,' s' I. ''Pear to be all cleaned out o' Jayvy jest this minute.'

" 'Wal, what have you got in the way of coffee?' s' he.

" 'Wal, you,' s' I, 'I got some bang-up ole Rio here, good's ever you'll scare up in the State o' Maine, 'twixt here and Quoddy Head.'

"But devil, no, no, that wouldn't never go nohow. That wa'n't nigh costly enough for him, and outdoors he stomped ag'in. Said he was 'fraid his folks wouldn't take to Rio jest rightly; but it's my honest opinion he didn't actilly know nothin' about Rio coffee; like's not never had once give her a good try in his life. When you take and come right down to the fine thing, it's ter'ble little them folks doos appear to know any great sight about, and jest how under the canopy ever they git a livin' at all is suppn' I can't noways fathom.

"P'haps they may be counted dretful big herbs up 'round where they come from, but set-fire! I cal'late honest now, you turn to and plant one on 'em down here somewheres, and it's a chance ef he wa'n't on the town inside o' six months!"

"I kin tell you, sir, jest how't is with them style of folks," put in Cap'n Zenas Roundturn, raising his great forefinger impressively. "The big bulk of these here rusticators couldn't never make out to git their own livin's, noways they could rig it. The thing is, some o' the ole ancient seed-folks was smart enough to acquire consid'ble prop'ty, we'll say, and now all these here creetur's is able to do at this day o' the world is jest only to stand by to heave it away foolish; anyways, most, so's to be red on't clip and clean jest as fast's ever they kin make out. The heft o' these here rusticator folks is more or less lackin' and soft-baked like; anybody that's had truck 'long on 'em kin see that the very fust lick. They'd ought to been turned once more into the oven afore ever they was hauled out; that's my idee of what ails the most on 'em.

"But then there's another class of rusticators that works it on a dif'rent plan like," continued the Cap'n. "You come to take the gin'ral run o' them kind that puts up to these here summer boardin'-houses in room of owning their own places, and I'm knowin' to it for a fact that take it when they're to home, they live same's a cat doos un'neath of a barn!

"Yas, sir, that's eggsac'ly how them kind is apt to live to home. They'll turn to and skin along jammed dretful close to the wind all winter, so's to save up enough money to slide down here for mebbe a month or six weeks summer-times, and try to make our folks think they're sunthin' r'ally quite a little extry-ord'nary, to be sure!"

"Dod-rot 'em! I make out to know 'em root and branch, from stem to starnpost, jest like a blame' book!" cried Cap'n Roundturn, regardless of mixed similitudes in his wrath at the thought of such gross imposition.

"Some on 'em drives hoss-cars and these here electuissic mortars when they're to home, and damned tickled they be to strike the job, too; but soon's ever they come to once git down here with a b'iled shirt and short pants onto 'em, why seems's though nothin' ain't half good enough for 'em!''

After thus relieving his mind, Cap'n Roundturn paused, and glared about menacingly.

''Cal'late to take ary rusticator up there to your place this next summer, do ye, Zenis?'' inquired Simeon, shortly.

''Oh wal, I wouldn't wonder no great,—I wouldn't wonder,'' answered the old man with an air of resignation. ''Every fall reg'lar, soon's ever we once git the house good and clear on 'em, I jest up and vum I won't never have no more truck 'long on sich style folks, noways. It's allus a plaguey nuisance having of 'em and all their dodblowed parafarelly round under foot summer-times; but the thing on't is, our women-folks makes out to git quite a little spendin'-money outen 'em fust and last, and I s'pose likely it'll have to be jest as they say about it ag'in this spring, same 's 't is with ev'rything else.''

KENNETH ROBERTS

1885–1957

Born in Kennebunk, Kenneth Lewis Roberts was descended from a long line of "Down Easters." He graduated from Cornell University and started a career in journalism as a humorous writer for the Boston *Post.* After serving in the army, he worked as a staff correspondent for the *Saturday Evening Post.* In 1928 he began writing full time with the plan of producing a series of historical novels based on New England during the American Revolution. The first to appear was *Arundel* (1930), the story of Benedict Arnold's expedition against Quebec; sequels included *Rabble in Arms* (1933) and *Captain Caution* (1934). Among his other works were *The Lively Lady* (1931); *Northwest Passage* (1937), *Oliver Wiswell* (1940), *Lydia Bailey* (1947), and *Boon Island* (1956). For each book Roberts conducted careful, painstaking research; few critics dispute his accuracy, but they differ widely in appraising him as a novelist. Whether one prefers his facts or his fiction, however, Kenneth Roberts remains among America's most widely read historical novelists.

From ***Arundel***

The lower headland of Swan Island, which is an island five miles long, points down into Merrymeeting Bay like a broad-head arrow with a broken tip; and its nose is embedded in a marsh that extends down river from it like an even larger arrowhead. The front edge of the headland was used as a look-out by the Swan Island Indians, who are Abenakis and very friendly people and a part of the Kennebec tribe, though they live by themselves and have little traffic with the Abenakis who dwell in the town of Norridgewock. So high is the headland that one who stands on it, screened by the trees and bushes, sees spread out beneath him all the winding guzzles in the marsh and the pools through which they pass, as though he gazed down upon a vast map; and he sees at once whatever pools contain swans or geese or brant or mallards or other ducks, no matter how low the tide has fallen below the marsh grass, and can steal out to them in the small flat boats that the Swan Island huntsmen use for the killing of wild fowl.

Behind the front edge of the headland is a deep swale in which there is a good spring; and behind the swale the land rises again to a pleasantly wooded plateau on which the wigwams were placed, some twenty of them. They were strewn irregularly among the oaks and birches, and were made of poles and bark, except for the three houses nearest the swale. These were of logs, one of them being a Long House for meetings, and the other two being smaller: one for the sachem and the other for the *m'téoulin,* or Indian who possesses magic power, which is also known as *m'téoulin.*

Of *m'téoulin* I know nothing whatever. I know that I have difficulty in preserving an air of seriousness when a great *m'téoulin* is mystifying an audience with some such amazing piece of *m'téoulin* as causing a strip of calico to vanish in his hands, for I can do the same thing by drawing it up my sleeve with a piece of string; yet, when I have been badly cut by the razorlike hooves of a deer and burning up with fever I have had a *m'téoulin* sing a *m'téoulin* song over me and burn a wolverine's whiskers and a loon feather in a clam-shell, and I have gone to sleep and awakened without fever, which is a work of *m'téoulin* that I could not do, even though I should be offered a partnership in the Plymouth Company for doing it.

The sachem of the Swan Island Indians was a woman, Rabomis, which is an unusual state of affairs among the Abenakis; for a sachem must be experienced and wise and brave and a successful hunter. It was Rabomis who ran into the water to greet my father, calling him "Steven" as she did so and gazing at him in the same proudly possessive way that a woman gazes at a pleasing jewel on her finger; and I could not understand how she could be a sachem, for she was too young and beautiful, I thought, to be wise or a good hunter.

It seemed to me that our arrival at the island was in the nature of a homecoming, for Rabomis clung to my father's arm, going with him around the point of the headland and into the swale and up the slope to the wigwams; and behind them came the rest of us, squaws carrying our packs and braves carrying our muskets lest a squaw, by handling them, should rob them of strength and cause them to shoot inaccurately, and all laughing and talking together about my father.

I know little concerning these things, because I was young in those days and content with my father, who was both brave and good; and whatever he did was done, I know, for excellent reasons. He went often into the Northern forests while his sour-visaged first wife was yet alive, returning always with a large store of beaver and otter skins; but whether he went always to Swan Island, I know not. He said little to me about it, save in praise of Rabomis, to whom he had taught such tricks of hunting and shooting and governing that she had more skill than any of the braves; but I learned from the talk of the Indians that he had planned the building of the three log houses and supervised the work, and that he had given instruction in the building and maintenance of latrines, and in the value of skins and methods to be followed in trading, and in other matters affecting their health and well-being.

At any rate, it seemed to me that my mother would be as happy if she heard nothing concerning Rabomis, so I afterward remained silent on the subject; and in truth I think all of us would be better off if we spoke and speculated less concerning the private lives of other folk, since we know not the whys and wherefores of their actions, and are ever ready to impose standards of conduct on them that we are unwilling to impose on ourselves. Nor, indeed, would I mention these things now, only that they are bound up with my tale and so cannot be slighted.

I think that my father must have been a great joker with the Indians; for I remember that as we came to the cabin of the *m'téoulin,* the *m'téoulin* stood in the door wearing his swan headdress, the neck curved back so that the head rested on his forehead and the great white wings puffed out around his head and shoulders, and holding an empty kettle toward my father.

"We greet you, Brother," he said, reaching up and taking a rawhide drum from the door post and clapping it over the empty kettle. "If you find our kettles empty you will send word to Glooskap, and Glooskap will hearken to your message and send us many riches. Here, Brother, is a messenger."

With that he snatched the drum from the kettle, and in the kettle was a rabbit which fell clumsily to the ground, scrambled to its feet drunkenly, thumped nervously with its hind leg, and then scuttled off through the trees like a flash of light. At this the Indians behind my father howled with pleasure, and my father gravely extended his hands toward the *m'téoulin.*

"I have sent," said he, "and thus the answer returns." He showed the back of his left hand and the palm of his right: then he showed the palm of his left hand and the back of his right; and both hands were empty. Then he moved them quickly in the air and drew the left hand slowly over the right, and in the palm of the right hand there lay a new clasp knife, very shiny and fine. This, as the Indians slapped their thighs and rocked with laughter, he dropped into the *m'téoulin's* kettle.

Rabomis drew my father on toward her own cabin, but waved the others to the Long House, which lay between the *m'téoulin's* cabin and her own. "We will return at once for a council," she said, and then she opened the door for my father and me to enter.

It was a good cabin, warm, with a stone fireplace, and hung with skins and on the floor a bearskin. She leaned against my father and pointed to a small girl who sat quietly by the fireplace, playing with a doll made from the thigh-bone of a deer. There was something about the girl, for all that her skin was a soft brown, that made me think of my sister Cynthia.

"Jacataqua," said Rabomis.

My father nodded and looked around the cabin. "No change," said he. His glance lingered here and there, and stopped at Rabomis. "No change," he repeated, and smiled at her.

"No change," said Rabomis, and she leaned over suddenly and kissed me, the act being so unsuspected and so without reason, so far as I could see, that I was near to squirming away from her and running from the cabin.

My father went to the fireplace and squatted down by the child Jacataqua, who fondled her doll and regarded him solemnly. Seeing that she viewed him with no alarm, my father picked her up and sat on the bed with her in his arms, and called me to him.

"Stevie," said, he, "I am a great magic-maker. I am *m'téoulin.* I can see that this girl is much like you. She will never get up in the morning unless she must, and it will be many years before she will admit that she likes to be kissed. Therefore I declare that she is your sister and that you are her brother. Say the words, Stevie."

I felt that somehow my father was joking, and yet again I knew that he was not. I said the words of the ritual: "She is my sister and I am her brother."

"At all times and in all places," insisted my father, "until the squirrel again grows greater than the bear."

These words I repeated after him, and then my father pricked my little finger with his knife and placed a drop of my blood on Jacataqua's tongue, and she became my sister.

Rabomis smiled what seemed to me a tremulous smile, and said to my father: "If all the English were like you, Steven, and all the French were like the Frenchman who stopped here yesterday, we would be fighting with you against the French, instead of doing as we are."

My father shot a warning glance at me, and it was fortunate that he did so, else I might have voiced my excitement and hurt our cause by transgressing against Indian custom, which looks askance on a display of emotion.

"So," said my father with an air of indifference, "the French captain is on his way home!"

Rabomis nodded. "Traveling by night," she said, "to escape the forts."

"He was not liked by our brothers to the south," said my father, "because of his high-and-mighty airs. I think it would have been better for this captain—ah—bah, his name slips ever from my tongue—"

"Henri Guerlac," said Rabomis.

"Of course," said my father. "It would have been better, I think, if this Captain Guerlac had taken lessons in common decency before he came into these parts, so that he would not have looked with such contempt on all of us, or made war on unarmed men and little children."

"The little girl seemed happy with him," said Rabomis.

This was more than I could bear, "She was not!" I shouted; "she was not!" and I dragged at my father's arm to get him from the cabin.

My father shook me to keep me quiet. "Here is the truth," he said to Rabomis, "and you never knew me to speak aught else. This Guerlac came among us two nights past. He killed my neighbor and carried away his daughter, who was the dear friend of my son, the brother of Jacataqua. This is apart from the war. This is an evil that he has done to me and to my house. We must come up with him and take the child back and finish him if we can, and avenge ourselves. There can be no end to it until we have done this."

"You will rest here to-night, Steven, and go at dawn?"

"No," said my father, "later we will return; but this evil has been done and we must go. Cook ducks for us and help us on our way."

"What do you want from us, Steven?"

"A canoe and two short bows and two strong braves to paddle," said my father.

Rabomis hesitated, but seeing the tears that were rolling down my cheeks, she kept silent and opened the door of the cabin, leading us to the Long House, where all the braves were assembled. There was a stir and a murmur of welcome when my father entered, but Rabomis faced them silently until they too became silent. "Our brother," said she, "asks for help. Hear him and judge."

My father stood straight and strong before them, as young as any man there, it seemed to me.

"In times past," he said, "I have given you my help and you have called me brother. Now I claim the rights of a brother. Wrong has been done by the Frenchman Guerlac, who has gone to the north, and my son and I are afoot to right that wrong. This is a private matter between the Frenchman and myself, and the war has no part in. If there is fighting between us, my son and I will do it without help. Give us only the means to overtake the Frenchman."

"The Frenchmen are also our brothers," a young brave objected.

"That is idle talk," said the *m'téoulin,* "and unless we are dogs we must do as he asks."

"Give him a canoe and two strong men," said an ancient Abenaki. "He has been wronged and he is our brother. That is talk that we can understand, and if we speak all day we will come no nearer to the heart of the matter."

"You will catch them above Cushnoc," said Rabomis, "and Natawammet knows the river above Cushnoc. Say if you will go, Natawammet, and who you will take."

"Woromquid," replied Natawammet, and stalked from the Long House.

Rabomis gave some directions and we went out, all of us, and down to the beach on the river bank where the marsh is narrowest. The canoes leaned against the high bank, overturned, and the *m'téoulin* pointed to a small, slender one. My father turned it over, picked it up by the thwarts, swung it over his head, and then lowered it gently into the water at the edge of the beach, nodding when the *m'téoulin* observed laconically that it was a very fast canoe.

A brave brought us a moosehide bow case, two quivers, and a bundle of broad-head arrows with grooved shafts. In the case were three short hunting bows, four extra bow strings, and a ball of sinews for fastening arrowheads to shafts. Tied to the case was a bag of arrowheads. Both my father and I had wrapped our arm guards and our finger stalls in our blankets, knowing full well that if we had occasion to borrow bows we would borrow them from folk whose fingers, toughened by constant archery, would know as little of finger stalls as a catfish knows of kittens.

The bows were shorter than any I had ever used, being barely four feet long, made of cedar backed with hickory, and the hickory in turn backed with rawhide. My father tried one of them, borrowing three blunt-head arrows from a child, and the Abenakis watched him closely, for he draws a bow to his jawbone, shooting very accurately at targets, whereas the Abenakis of the Kennebec draw to the breastbone with the bow held diagonally before them, shooting miserably at targets but excellently well at game.

He shot at a block of wood on the edge of the marsh, twenty paces off, and knocked it spinning into the water. Then he shot at a red squirrel sitting on a pine branch, striking the branch below him and causing the squirrel to fly raging into the air with tail and fur a-bristle, at which my father drolly declared that the bow had lost its cast and that the arrow was badly made and that a gust of wind had taken the arrow at the last moment; and the Abenakis, having excused their bad marksmanship with all of these complaints at one time or another, cackled loudly.

He loosed his third arrow at a black duck swimming in a guzzle some sixty paces off; but the duck, hearing or seeing the approaching shaft, sprang into the air as it arrived and struck it somehow with his wing so that he became tangled with it and fell back into the guzzle with a great flopping, and then flew off with a terrific squawking.

When Natawammet and Woromquid had placed our packs and our muskets and two extra paddles in the canoe the men gathered in a circle around the *m'téoulin,* who drew for us a map in the sand.

"The Frenchman left here with two canoes at dusk last night," said he. "Thus he could pass the fort beyond the upper end of the island unseen. The tide was against them, and they could make four miles an hour in the dark, maybe less. Cushnoc is twenty-two miles, though some say eighteen who have never paddled it, and there they must carry, going silently so that the garrison at Fort Western may be unalarmed

"Above Fort Western the water is swift and shallow, and they will make no attempt to travel by night, not knowing the river and fearing to break their canoes. To-day they have gone on, proceeding cautiously and pausing at each bend lest they encounter soldiers moving between Fort Halifax and Fort Western. To-night they lie south of Fort Halifax. To-morrow morning they carry, a long carry, around Fort Halifax and perchance past the Five Mile Ripples, going very carefully and slowly to avoid disaster; for this is the last of the settlements. Once beyond this they are safe and the way is clear to Norridgewock and beyond.

"Now at Ticonic Falls, hard by Fort Halifax, there is a trail through the forest, and this trail is known to Natawammet and Woromquid. It cuts across a great bend in the river and comes out above the Five Mile Ripples. Two leagues from the ripples there is an island, and on one side of the island the water is shoal and quick, but on the other side it is clear, with trees overhead and good shelter on either side. Here is where you can catch the Frenchman, and if you do not catch him here you cannot catch him at all. To do this you must reach Ticonic Falls by dawn. That is an evil journey, and I know of nobody who has made it in any such time."

Natawammet and Woromquid nodded their heads and gazed impassively at my father. He motioned me into the canoe and went around the circle of red men holding each one for a moment by the upper arms. "You are my brothers," said he, "and when we return we will feast together." With that he climbed over me and sat down, and Woromquid stepped into the bow. Natawammet pushed the canoe into the guzzle and guided it through the marsh; and behind us Rabomis waved and called after us: "We shall be happy when you return."

The sun was more than halfway down the sky as we put it at our backs and swung into the broad Kennebec, and the tide still ran strongly upward with the clean smell of salt about it. My father looked around at Natawammet kneeling in the stern. "The Frenchman," said my father, "is a very bad man. If we pass over the trail above Ticonic Falls before the sun is an hour up, I will make fine new muskets for you and Woromquid." Natawammet nodded and rose to a half-standing position, and at each stroke of his paddle the canoe lifted in the water, and the ripples hissed along its side.

Fretted by inaction, my father and I took paddles as well though we helped our speed very little, and only made it possible for Natawammet and Woromquid to work less hard.

Fort Frankfort we passed in an hour's time, shouting our names at the lazy militiaman who came down to watch us pass. As the sun slipped down into the west great flocks of wild fowl passed over our heads, moving south, and heavy-headed moose deer stood and watched us from the shallows. Often we came across black bears fishing at the water's edge, frightening them half out of their wits when we slapped water at them with our paddles and sent them galloping fearfully through the forest, snorting and whistling in an ague of terror.

To hold the beat of our paddles in time, Woromquid sang the ancient Abenaki song of Wuchowsen the Wind Blower, who sits on a great rock at the edge of the sky and causes the winds by flapping his wings.

When the great lord Glooskap came among men, sang Woromquid, he often went in his canoe to shoot sea fowl. At one time the winds blew violently each day, so that he shot with difficulty. Then it grew worse. Then it blew a tempest, so that he could not go out at all. So Glooskap said: "Wuchowsen, the Great Bird, has done this!"

He went, therefore, to find him; and after many days he found him, a large white bird, sitting on a high rock.

Then Glooskap spoke to him saying, "Grandfather, you are too hard upon your children; be easier with your wings, for the wind is too strong."

But the giant bird replied: "I have been here since ancient times, and I moved my wings ere aught else moved or spoke. I will ever move my wings as I will."

Then Glooskap, angered, rose until he touched the clouds, seized the bird-giant Wuchowsen as though he were a pigeon, tied both his wings, and threw him into a cleft between the rocks.

Now the Indians could go out in the canoes all day, for there was no wind. But the waters became stagnant, and they became thick with scum, so that Glooskap could not paddle his canoe.

So, bethinking himself of Wuchowsen, he went again to the cleft in the rock and drew out the great bird, who had suffered no hurt, being immortal.

Untying one of his wings, he put him on his rock again; and since that time the winds have never been as terrible as in the old days.

* * *

Darkness had just fallen when our ears caught the roar of the falls at Cushnoc, at the foot of which lies Fort Western, the best of all the Kennebec forts, not only in the way it is placed, but in the way it is manned. A sentry hailed us at the landing place, and across the river burned a fire, so that the sentry could see, against the path of light in the river, any person who sought to pass the fort. My father gave our names and went up the path with the sentry to see Captain Howard. When the captain heard that we wished to reach Fort Halifax before dawn, he shook his head doubtfully but sped us on our way, giving us news of rapids here and smooth water there, and having food brought to us so that we could eat as we scrambled around the falls.

The traveling above Cushnoc was wretched and laborious. The water was swift and shallow, and hour after hour was a nightmare of low falls and high falls and broken, tumbling water and high banks and roaring rapids and great rocks; of pushing and fending and poling and straining with paddles; of leaping out of the canoe into icy water and scrambling in again; of fighting yard by yard and rod by rod and mile by mile up the river, with the smooth stretches coming so seldom and lasting so short a time that after we had passed them we could scarce believe that they had existed.

The darkness pressed us down, and there were over-many noises of wild animals among the thickets at the water's edge; and our shoulders and stomachs and backs and legs ached from the chill of the water and the pounding of the boulders in the river bed.

How we got through the night I know not; and for my part I think I could never have done so had it not been that I hoped to find Mary on the morrow. I said to myself God knows how many times that nothing on earth could tempt me to do such a thing again, and that the effort was useless and could not be completed; and then I thought, too, how my father was doing this because an evil thing had been done, not to him but to his community, and how Natawammet and Woromquid were doing it for friendship and a new gun; and I knew that there was no way of telling what a man will endure, or why.

At any rate, when the gray light of the false dawn appeared through the trees at our right Natawammet and Woromquid poled the canoe behind a high rock on the west bank of the river, and above the clatter and babble of near-by rapids I heard the distant vibration of falls.

"Ticonic," said Natawammet. We had come two miles an hour for eight hours, and I wanted never to see quick water again.

The Indians drew the canoe onto the high bank and dropped on the ground beside it. In half an hour the real dawn came, and the red men picked up the canoe and moved into the trees, hunting for saplings marked with a small triple slash inclined slightly to the left, which was the mark of the trail.

We clambered through the woods for three hours, burdened by our packs and muskets, whipped by branches and briers, and striving to hold saplings from the canoe and to clear the rocks and vines from under the Abenakis' feet. At the end of the three hours we came to the Kennebec again, and found it running clear, without rapids, and with no sign of other travelers on it.

We drove upstream, peering eagerly around each bend and sick at heart for fear the Frenchman had already passed. The *m'téoulin,* we found, had spoken us fair, for shortly we came to a pleasant island that split the river, and the channel to the right was passable by a canoe; while to the left the water ran over broken rocks, wholly impassable.

The Abenakis put us ashore on the island with our muskets and bows; the canoe, with our packs, they took to the far bank, beyond the shallow channel.

Having seen the lay of the land, we whispered together, my father and I, ever fearful that our labors were in vain and that the enemy had passed.

Being the better shot with arrow and musket, my father decreed that he should lie on the high bank, while I, being quick in the water and an easy swimmer, went and lay by the river bank with a branch thickly grown with leaves. If the canoes came he was to whistle the mournful cry of the yellowleg, and I was to roll into the river with the leafy branch over my face, so that I could see without being seen. When the first canoe reached me, then, I was to upset it with a hand on the gunwale and seize Mary while my father attended to the rest of the matter.

And so, without further words, I cut a goodly branch and went down and lay close to the edge of the water; and above me I could hear my father filling the powder pans and laying out his arrows and arranging himself for action.

* * *

We lay and waited interminably; and I knew then that all the hunting that I had ever done, for geese or turkey or raccoon or bear or moose deer, was as nothing compared to the excitement of the hunting of man.

The sky was overcast, and the morning was still, and the muted call of the chickadees and the scolding of the bluejays and the brawling of the crows and the movements of the wood mice were very loud, and my heart was low in me, for I was sure that Guerlac had pressed on toward Quebec ahead of us.

But when my heart was lowest I heard my father whistle mournfully and low, the four dropping notes of a yellowleg, and I rolled into the river with the branch over my face and my heart pounding as though it would tear my ribs apart.

I worked out toward midstream and could see nothing. I was trembling and shaking under the water as if I would shake myself to pieces.

Then, suddenly, I saw the canoe, with four paddlers rising and dipping and rising and dipping, the paddlers brown and naked, with feathers bound upright to their scalplocks, and green and yellow paint on their faces. My heart stopped pounding and my throat grew dry and rough, and I sank in the water until I could scarce breathe.

The canoe came straight for me, the brown men rising and dipping and rising and dipping.

It loomed high above me, and I looked into the white eye of the bow paddler and saw the deep groove at the corner of his lips. I came up under my branch, reached for the gunwale and missed—reached and caught it and pulled hard.

I heard Guerlac's cold brittle laugh and heard a yell from my father and the twang of a bowstring, and then a blaze of white light engulfed me and blotted out all things. . . .[1]

---

[1]The blaze of white light was the impact of Guerlac's hatchet against Steven's head. Guerlac manages to escape with Mary, and it is several years before Guerlac and Steven encounter each other again. Fortunately, Steven fares much better in the second confrontation.

BEN AMES WILLIAMS
1889–1953

Ben Ames Williams was born in Macon, Miss., raised in the South and Midwest, and educated at Dartmouth. He worked as a reporter for the Boston *American* until 1916, when he resigned to devote full time to writing. In the course of his life Williams would publish over 400 short stories and 35 novels. In 1912 he married Florence Talpey of York, and the couple established a summer home in Searsmont. Known as "Hardscrabble Farm," the property was bequeathed to Williams by A.L. McCorrison, who, as "Chet McAusland," became the chief inspiration for the "Fraternity" stories. In addition to these short stories, Williams wrote several novels set in Maine, including *Evered* (1921), *Honeyflow* (1932), and *Come Spring* (1940). His works contain fine examples of historical fiction and character studies and display what he himself labelled "potency of place."

The Piano

Brad worked with a slow particularity. He was a man with a mechanical turn and such arrangements as this one always interested him. A fox had been stealing his chickens and he was engaged in setting a spring gun to kill the fox.

The first depredation had occurred several days before. The chickens had, during the day, the run of a small wired yard; at night they were accustomed to withdraw within the chicken house. Brad never troubled to lock them in. It was some time since he had been visited by varmints. But one morning he found a sag in the wire; found a few white feathers and the pad mark of a fox in the soft earth of the pen. One of his hens was gone.

That night and thereafter he came out before going to bed and secured the chicken-house door; but there was no sill below the door, and a few days later he discovered that the fox had again entered the yard, dug his way beneath the door and carried off another hen. Brad buried a board in such a way as to form a deep sill below the door. The chicken house had a window, but it did not occur to him to see that this was secure. The window was three or four feet above the ground. It was arranged on hinges, swinging inward at the bottom. Within a few days the marauder returned, pushed in this window, dropped on top of the nest boxes and killed a third hen. By a chance that was fortunate for the fox, the window did not in its fall close tightly; the creature was able to nose it up and escape.

Brad was by nature a mild man, and he guessed the fox was probably hard put to it to feed a litter of kits. Nevertheless he felt it necessary to avenge his hens. There was in the attic an old single-barreled, ten-gauge, muzzle-loading shotgun, unused for years. The muzzle had been blown off when a bit of snow clogged it. Brad unearthed this gun from its long retirement and with a hack saw cut away the jagged metal. He found that the lock was rusted, and he worked at it with screw driver and oil until it functioned smoothly, and he cleaned the nipple where the cap would set; then took the gun, with hammer, saw, nails and a bit of board, into the chicken house and secured it across two roosts opposite the window in such a way that it commanded that avenue of entrance at a distance of about ten feet. He did not yet load the gun. In the miscellaneous junk about his woodshed he found two small metal pulleys, once a part of the mechanism of a big icebox he had made for his wife, now dead. These pulleys he fastened, one behind the butt of the gun, the other under the window. A cod line attached to the trigger passed back through one pulley, across the shed and through the other, and was then secured to the bottom of the window sash.

All this consumed some time, but Brad was in no hurry. A tall, gaunt, slow man, he was never inclined to haste in word or thought or deed. When his simple apparatus was adjusted he tested it by first cocking the gun, then pulling the window inward as it would be thrust by a push from outside. The string tightened, the trigger clicked, the hammer fell.

Thus satisfied, Brad proceeded to load the gun, removing it from its rest for the purpose. He used black powder, and atop the powder put a variegated charge; a few Number Three shot, some BB's and a half a dozen 00 buck. Even at this short range the charge would spread to cover the whole lower half of the window; the buckshot would penetrate the old boards of the wall.

"Anything outside will get peppered some," he decided.

He replaced the gun in its rest and adjusted a cap on the nipple, but did not cock the hammer. Time enough for that after the chickens were roosting. Then there would be no danger of their touching the trigger cord. He would attend to the matter when he locked them in for the night. It was now about half past four in the afternoon.

Brad gathered up his tools and went out through the chicken yard, disturbing the hens, and around to the shed. He put his hammer and saw methodically in their places and began to feed the stock. Two pigs behind the barn, the chickens, four half-grown geese in a box in the dooryard and the horse in his stall. The cows were not yet come in from the pasture when he began; but before he was through they appeared in the lane, and he threw down hay for them, and secured their necks between the upright staves in the tie-up. Now and then, as he worked, he spoke to beasts or fowls in a low, friendly tone.

Brad lived quite alone on his farm on the hillside. He was on a back road and saw few people except in the fall, when woodcock gunners sometimes left their cars in his barnyard while they descended to the alder runs below. Yet the prospect from his farm was worth seeing. The valley was heavily wooded; a silver pond lay a mile away to the left; and directly across, the slopes of the ridge ascended, covered with birch and black growth. The foliage presented through the seasons a bewildering range of lovely colors. When the sun was low above the hills behind the house, these eastward slopes assumed a purple hue so rich that to look upon it was a delight almost physical.

Brad's kitchen was as neat as it had been when his wife—dead last spring—was alive. The red-painted cream separator, bolted to the floor, stood beside the sink; the bright pails were stacked there ready for his hand. He drew water from the pump in the shed and went out into the tie-up and methodically milked his cows, washing their teats with the water, pressing his brow against their flanks while the milk hissed into the foaming pails. His kine were not heavy milk producers. Of fairly good stock, their only feed was pasturage, hay, or the beets and squash and turnips Brad raised in the garden behind the barn. Yet they yielded milk enough so that he had a surplusage of cream for butter, which he sold at the store. He drove to the store every evening, if only to get his paper from the post office there. The routine of his life was little changed by his wife's death; there was only a little more work for him to do.

Some of the younger folk in Fraternity derided Brad for staying on at the farm, for it was known that he had come into money a few months before. His uncle, a man with a reputation for wealth well hoarded, had died in town; Brad and two brothers shared the estate. In the gossip of the countryside the amount varied widely. Some loose talkers set Brad's share as high as fifty thousand dollars. It had been, as a matter of fact, a little over thirty-five hundred. Even this might have tempted some men into an adventurous journey to Boston; but Brad's life was settled. He stayed at home and worked as he had always done. The money was in the bank, in town.

His only outward evidence of prosperity was the purchase of a piano. This instrument was of yellow varnished oak. It stood upright against the west wall of the parlor of the little farmhouse, with an old sampler hung above it, a carpet-covered spring rocker beside it and a haircloth sofa across the room. The other furniture was conspicuously old, but rather mellowed by age than rendered shabby.

Even the sofa had a certain beauty about it. The windows of the room were small and admitted little light, so that the piano stood always in a sort of reverential dusk. Atop it there was set a framed photograph of a woman, Brad's wife. She had been, at the time of the photograph, middle-aged and very weary. Her hair, unnaturally pompadoured for the occasion, made her seem uncomfortable and ill at ease; she had somewhat the aspect of one who balances a bowl upon her head. Only her head and shoulders appeared, but you were quite sure that her hands must be gnarled and scarred with many labors. Beside this photograph stood a little white china vase containing a bouquet of artificial flowers of the variety called everlasting. The top of the piano was free from dust; the paneled front of it was snugly shut; the lid that covered the keys was closed and locked.

Before beginning to prepare his supper this day Brad went into the parlor and in the failing light of late afternoon surveyed the piano for a moment without moving. His bearing was that of a reverent man in a holy place. Then he crossed the room to where the instrument stood, and with a soft cloth he had brought from the kitchen began to wipe its gleaming surfaces. This was a ceremonial task performed twice a day. He stroked its sides and front; he passed his cloth across its top. In the process he lifted for a moment the framed photograph, and there was an awkward tenderness in his movements, somehow pitiful. When he set the picture down again there was, or seemed to be, drama in the simple gesture. With a key from his pocket he unlocked the cover and wiped the ivory keys, evoking now and then a throb of sound from the wires within. At such moments he seemed to listen for something he could not quite hear. When at last he left the room, closing the door behind him, the closing of the door was like the falling of the curtain at the play.

Brad's was one of those tragedies which are so common, so poignant and so little understood; the tragedy of a man who was inarticulate. Most of us suffer under this cross. We find it easy to upbraid or blame, but very hard to praise. We are afraid of seeming sentimental. Yet how a little affection, frankly expressed from friend to friend, can temper the winds of life!

What harm can it do to say to your son, "You're a fine boy and I like you"? To your friend, "You're a mighty decent sort of fellow and I'm very fond of you"? To your wife, "I love you dearly"?

Yet ancient reticences hold our tongues; we do not speak; till some day we perceive, abruptly, that there is no longer an ear to hear what we may have wished to say.

Marriages have before now been wrecked upon this rock; many which escaped shipwreck have nevertheless been lifelong tragedy. Such was Brad Miller's. New Englanders are a silent breed, hard of shell and not easily warmed. Their feelings are apt to be buried deep.

Brad was born, no doubt, a normal boy; hungry for affection, eager for caresses; friendly as a dog. But—he was born on a New England farm, and his father and mother disciplined themselves for the good of their son; and from the time he was a baby no one ever kissed him except with the kiss of ceremonious greeting or farewell. When he loved May Stoneman it was in a dumb and silent fashion; and she, being of the same breed, expected nothing more. No doubt they had at first their moments of warm passion, of frank and affectionate communion when each opened his heart to the other. But as the years of their marriage passed these moments came more seldom. Each surrendered to the ancient inhibitions; the time came when a kiss passed between them would have tortured either Brad or his wife with acute embarrassment.

There is no testimony that Brad was ever unkind to his wife; but life upon a barren farm may be sufficiently unkind. There was work to be done; work for both of them. Each did the tasks assigned; each, upon occasion, prompted the other to some forgotten duty.

"Brad, you ain't mended the leak by the chimney!"

"May, I told you to keep that hen shut up; she wants to set."

"Brad, I need more wood in the box."

"Where's the milk buckets, May?"

They had no children, they were much alone; and there were days when they exchanged no word except in connection with the stark duties of life. They rose about six in the morning in winter, earlier in summer. May got the meals, Brad did the outside work. When dusk gave them respite from toil they shared the evening paper which Brad fetched from the store, and then went stolidly to bed. The fact that they shared the same bed had no significance whatever; they were in many ways as remote, one from the other, as though they had lived a thousand miles apart.

May, as a girl, had liked to play on her mother's piano; and sometimes she tried to get Brad to buy one. But habits of frugality were bred in him; he always put her poor pleadings aside with the brutal folly of expediency as his justification. He told her the money was needed for taxes; that they ought to buy a new cow; that the hay crop was so short he would need to be buying hay in the coming winter. May submitted humbly enough to these rebuffs. She had at times a vague feeling that if she could play a piano now and then she would not mind having one or two fewer cows to tend. But she was inarticulate as he, and could not put these feelings into effective words. Besides, Brad always meant to get her a piano sometime. The thing was simply postponed; postponed from year to year, to weary years—till May died.

There was no outward reason to suppose that Brad's love for her was more than long habit. Their daily contacts had been rude enough, and empty of all tendernesses. Through the hideous ceremonies of the interment he preserved an impassive demeanor. But when a little later on, his uncle's death made the purchase possible, he bought the piano and had it brought out to his lonely farm. This was his memorial to her. He himself knew nothing of its mechanism; but his rough fingers liked to touch the keys and evoke soft vibrations from the wires within. The merchant who had sold him the instrument had played for him.

Brad's only comment was, "It sounds pretty. I'll take it, then."

To those who wondered at his purchase he had but one explanation to give.

"May always wanted one," he would say. "She was always wanting a piano."

Back in the kitchen, this day, he prepared his supper, scrambled eggs, boiled potatoes, doughnuts and milk. Having eaten, he went to the chicken house and, since it was now dark and the fowls were settled for the night, he cocked the old gun; then shut and secured the door. His day's work was now done; there remained to him the only social pleasure which his life held. He hitched his horse to the buggy and drove slowly over the hill and down into Fraternity village, to Will Bissell's store.

A number of men were there before him, and he found them grouped around the cold stove or leaning against the long counter. Young Evered, from over beyond the Swamp, was telling Jim Saladine of a string of trout he had that day taken from the brook below the meadow. Will Belter and Zeke Pitkin, reprehensible men, huddled side by side on the bench by the stove and talked in low tones. Lee Motley and Will Bissell, men of substance, were also drawn apart; and when Brad came in they asked his opinion of the proposal to increase taxes and rebuild the Liberty road. He recognized this as a tribute to his new importance in the town—he was a moneyed man now—and the subtle flattery pleased him. While they spoke together, a man came in through the front door, whom none of them knew, and bought half a dozen cheap cigars from Andy Wattles and sat down beside Will Belter. His coming put a damper on the general conversation. The men in the store watched him with silent attention, waiting for him to speak.

This man had the bearing of the city; yet his clothes were worn and his countenance was not prepossessing. Jim Saladine, given to reflection, wondered more acutely than the others; observed the fact that though the man seemed physically vigorous, he wore a certain pallor, as though he had been for long indoors.

Brad made some purchases of small amount. He wanted a sack of feed, but Will's supply had run short and his truck had failed to return from town, so Brad had to cross the bridge to the other store.

"I'll come back and git the mail," he told Bissell as he departed.

When he was gone they spoke of him. The fact of his inheritance was common knowledge; the amount was fit subject for conjectures.

"I heard in town yest'day that the corner block his uncle owned brought over thirty thousand by itself," Zeke Pitkin announced.

Gay Hunt, just come in, asked "Who?"

"Brad Miller."

"I'll bet he come in to a hundred thousand if it was a cent," Gay asserted. He was always a fanciful man. Joe Race added to that.

"The lawyer told me, himself, it was more than that," he swore, being by nature a liar for the sake of the sensation his lies might create.

But the stranger beside Belter did not know Joe Race or Gay Hunt. His head was bowed forward; smoke from his cigar clouded his eyes. Even Jim Saladine could not read his expression.

"And Brad had some himself," Will Belter declared. "If you'd hunt up the first dollar he ever made you'd find it right up against the last one."

"Never spent a cent in his life till he got him that piano," Gay agreed.

Jim Saladine ventured a word: "You know, you never noticed any of this about Brad until this summer."

"I always knowed he was close as his shirt," Gay insisted.

"You never told me," Jim replied, faint mockery in his smile; and Gay was silenced. But no one could silence Will Belter, the bearer of tales.

"He don't keep it in no bank, neither," Will announced. "He—"

But the talk ended there, for Brad returned. When he entered through the front door, bringing with him that guilty silence which is apt to prevail on such occasions, the stranger remarked the silence, raised his eyes, saw Brad and dropped his head again. Thereafter his eyes followed Brad covertly, till a few minutes later he rose and spoke to Andy Wattles at the cigar counter; asked if there was a chance for day labor thereabouts. They discussed the question in low tones.

Then the stranger went out, and Saladine asked Andy, "Who's he?"

"Just tramping, I guess," said Andy. "He wanted to know about work, but he didn't act hungry for it. And he asked me the road to town."

"He's been somewheres in jail," Saladine commented.

"Well, they got a jail in town," Andy replied dryly, "if that's what he hankers after."

"Walking, ain't he?"

"There's a good moon," Andy assented. "He figured he'd go on in tonight."

They saw Brad preparing to depart, and Saladine called, "Good night, Brad!"

Brad responded, went out through the side door to where his horse was fastened. Across the bridge he stopped at the other store to load aboard his bag of feed, then turned his horse's head homeward and allowed the beast to amble at its own pace. The night was warm and still; the moon, half full, illumined all the road. Brad relaxed in his seat, his thoughts drifting; the amiable thoughts of a mild and gentle man.

Such men may upon occasion become just and terrible.

Arrived at home, Brad unharnessed and turned the horse into the stall. He drew the door of the barn half shut, came into the house through the shed and lighted the lamp in the kitchen. The fire in the stove was quite burned out; and he got kindling and wood ready for the morning, and filled the teakettle and the water reservoir in the end of the stove itself. Then he carried the lamp into the dining room and sat down there to read the paper he had brought from the store.

Two or three cats—there were a dozen or more of all ages about the place—bestirred themselves at his coming, and reminded him by their low complaints that they had not been fed. He responded at once, apologized to them.

"Poor kits. Well, I forgot you, didn't I? Old Brad forgot the kits. Well now! There, there!

The aimless, kindly mutterings of a man much alone. He put milk in their basin by the stove and they lapped contentedly. Then he returned to his paper and read it slowly, word by word, from front to back, with a conscientious care.

When the paper was done there remained nothing more to do. The lamp in his hand, he went once more into the front room and stood in the doorway, looking fondly at the piano in its glory there; then retraced his steps. His own room was off the dining room. He undressed with slow movements that were nevertheless effective, and at length blew out the lamp and got into bed. The moonlight came in through his window. From the woodland down the hill he heard the occasional whistle of a coon. Far away a dog barked. The night was full of little noises. They lulled him, and presently he slept. In sleep he was either a comic or a tragic figure, according to your mood. Flat on his back, his mouth open, his thin neck bare, he slept noisily, ridiculously; yet he was so utterly alone.

Something, by and by, recalled him from slumber. He choked, strangled, opened his eyes and returned to normal, quiet breathing. The house seemed still; yet he felt vaguely that he had heard a noise.

His own snores had more than once awakened him. He thought this might be the present explanation, but was not wholly satisfied. Then he remembered the fox, and wondered if the gun had been discharged; but his hens were quiet. In the end he got out of bed, absurdly tall, absurdly thin, his nightshirt flapping about his shins, and stepped slowly into the dining room without troubling to light a lamp.

He was immediately conscious of a tumult of color; soundless color which filled his universe. No pain attached to the spectacle; but after a moment the colors passed and he knew nothing more until he woke from not unpleasant dreams to a throbbing headache and to the discovery that his bodily freedom was restricted by bonds. When his senses had somewhat cleared he perceived that he was tied down to an iron cot which had long served as a couch in the corner of the dining room. Save for the moonlight, the room was dark. Analyzing his situation, he found that his ankles were tied separately, tied fast to the foot of the cot; that his wrists were drawn down and attached to the iron frame; and that there was a rope around his neck which made it painful to move his head.

The experience was utterly incredible. He was filled with conjectures. Someone, he now understood, had struck him on the head as he came out of his room; the same person, no doubt, had tied him here with bits of his own closthesline, from the yard. Someone, therefore, had broken into the house. This in itself was inconceivable to Brad; it had never happened to him before. He had read in the paper of burglaries, but they were always remote. A burglar in his own house, now. . . . He wondered how the marauder had entered, and why. And where was he now?

His ears answered that question presently; he heard footfalls overhead. Someone was up there in the unfinished attic tumbling things about. Brad was more bewildered than ever at this realization. There was nothing of value in the attic; nothing of value in the house anywhere, except a few bills in his worn leather pocketbook. The sounds overheard became more boisterous. He heard a succession of blows as of metal on stone, digging at the bricks of the chimney.

Brad was not gifted with imagination. He set himself to a sober effort to escape from his bonds; but their very simplicity made them effective. The ropes cut his wrists and crushed them; they yielded no play at all. The line about his neck, he discovered, was a noose; and he was near strangling after an effort to pull his head to one side. This vaguely angered him. He wished he might get free so as to overpower this marauder. He would load his gun. But at this he remembered that his double-barreled gun had been loaned a day or two before for the destruction of a hawk, and the only other weapon in the house was that which he had set to kill the fox.

At about this period in his thoughts he heard steps descending the stairs in the kitchen wall, and a moment later the light of a lamp shone in his eyes.

Then a man's voice said harshly, "Come to, have you?"

Brad's eyes, becoming accustomed to the light, saw this man as a bulky figure with a cap pulled low. Before he could adjust his vision to details, the man withdrew into the kitchen, and again reappeared a moment later with a red handkerchief tied about his mouth and nose, his eyes mere slits below the cap's visor.

Brad, wriggling, asked impatiently, "What in time do you want, anyhow?"

The man set the lamp on the table and inspected Brad's bonds. Then he leaned back against the table edge and spoke in a voice utterly dispassionate.

"I'm looking for whatever there is in the house," he replied. "They tell me you've come into a pile of dough and that you keep it here. You got a nice farm here to support you. I guess I need the money worse than you do. Where is it at?"

Brad said irritably, "You darned fool, I don't keep money in the house!"

"They tell me you do."

"Who?"

The stranger lighted a cheap cigar.

"Folks," he replied airily. He leaned forward more intently. "Now listen!" he warned. "I'm not kidding a damned bit, and you can't fool me a damned bit. And we're going to argue this out between us, just you and me. Ain't anybody going to happen in. Now, you'll save trouble if you'll come across, old man."

Brad said furiously, "I'll bust you all to pieces!"

The other shook his head.

"No you won't," he answered. "You ain't going to get a chance. That's why I clouted you with the stove wood. As long as you kep' on snoring I let you alone; but you had to go and wake up, and so there wasn't anything else for me to do. Now you'll save me a lot of hunting around by just spilling the whole dope. Let it all come up in mamma's hand, mister. Where is it?"

Brad lay still for a moment, considering. He was, after all, a sensible man. And there was nothing in the house worth taking; nothing worth fighting for. His thoughts found words.

"There ain't twenty dollars in the house," he said.

"Git out!"

"There ain't."

The man flicked ashes on the floor.

"Well, where's that?"

"In my pants pocket," said Brad. "In there."

The man went into Brad's bedroom and returned with the garment in question; found the old leather fold and extracted half a dozen bills.

"Fourteen dollars," he commented, "Well, it ain't enough, old man."

"What do you think I'd keep money here for?" Brad demanded petulantly.

"Where is it, then?"

"In the bank, in town."

The man considered this.

"Then you must have a bank book around."

Brad hesitated; decided there could be no harm in this much yielding.

"It's in the drawer of the table over there," he replied.

The other crossed the room without comment, opened the drawer, rummaged among a litter of papers and found the book. He flipped the pages, stared at Brad truculently.

"Thirty-three hundred and fifty-two," he commented. "That's all there is here."

"That's enough, ain't it?"

"Where's the rest of it?"

"There ain't any more."

The man laughed.

"Say, mister," he replied, "that ain't a bit of use. I've got all the dope on you. I know you've got a pile stowed away somewhere here. I can dig it out if I take the time; but I'm lazy. I don't want to take a house all apart when you can save me the trouble."

Brad shook his head and the rope about his neck irked him.

"They've been lying to you," he replied. "They've all got the notion that I got a lot of money. I let 'em think it. It ain't any of their business. But that's all there was—about thirty-six hundred. I spent some on a piano. That's all—"

"What did you want with a piano, anyhow? You don't look musical."

"My wife always wanted one," said Brad simply; and the man laughed, so that a deeper anger began to stir in Brad.

But a moment later the other said curtly, "You think I'm kidding you."

And he bent and pressed the cigar's lighted end against Brad's leg, thrusting it home till the fire was stifled, the cigar crumpled into dust. Brad, save for a low exclamation, made no sound. The man stepped back and lighted another cigar, and Brad stared at him, more amazed than hurt, with wide eyes.

"I mean what I say," the man explained mildly. "You'll tell me where the stuff is hid or you'll get hurt."

"There ain't any more money in the house," Brad muttered stubbornly, and at the words the man's self-control fled.

He leaped forward with a ferocity that was terrifying; and he groped and caught the rope beneath Brad's head, and jerked at it till the noose tautened stranglingly; jerked and jerked again, till the bound man's convulsive struggles began to weaken; only then relaxed the pressure and stepped back while Brad choked to full consciousness again.

Before he was able to speak once more Brad heard a rooster crow. The sound made him remember again his plan to kill the fox. His wits were working more swiftly now; and he lay with closed eyes, gasping and choking, and thought what he might do.

The thought was horrible to him; he was unable to contemplate it without a shudder; and the man, watching him fight back to life, marked this shudder and chuckled to himself.

"You'll see what I mean," he said coldly.

Brad abruptly perceived that the game was in his own hands; the discovery gave him a sense of superiority. He had an overwhelming weapon—if he chose to use it. Though he did not choose to use the weapon, yet the mere fact that he possessed it gave him an assurance and a certainty which was reflected in his tones when a moment later he spoke; spoke with a negative movement of his head, with eyes still closed.

"You ain't going to kill me," he remarked mildly. "It wouldn't do you a mite of good. I'm kind of sorry for you too. If I had some money here, enough to help you out, you could have it and welcome. I guess you need it bad enough. But there ain't any more here than what you've got, no matter what you do."

The man stood erect, looking down, his face twitching beneath the handkerchief.

"Honest," he said, "I hate to hurt you. You're a game old coot." His tones hardened. "But you got to come across or go across, old man. I'm not kidding you. I ain't going to hurt you any more; but I'll give you just about five minutes. If you don't come through then I'll fix you. That's the straight goods. Now what do you say?"

"There ain't a cent of money in the house," Brad replied.

"Then you're out of luck," the man said equably. "Because if there ain't you're due to leave these parts."

Brad lay still, with closed eyes. The man sat down beside the table; then rose and went into the kitchen and got the alarm clock ticking there. He set it on the table and sat down again.

"It's ten minutes past two," he said. "I'll give you till quarter past."

"You won't kill me," Brad told him calmly. "I ain't a mite afeard."

"You got five minutes."

"If I go to sleep," said Brad, "you wake me up, will you?" And he moved a little as though relaxing for slumber.

The other leaned forward.

"Is it hid in the attic?" he asked. "In the cellar? I'm going down and look." Brad did not move. "In the house somewhere?"

His eyes roamed around the room. He rose. A sewing machine —Brad's wife had used it—stood by the window. He lifted the cover and replaced it; rummaged in the table drawers; pulled out the round plate that stopped the flue, where in winter a stove stood to heat the house, and looked into the black hole, thrusting in his fumbling hand; went restlessly into the kitchen and tumbled pans and pots about; groped along the shelves. A sudden fury of greed seized him; he stormed to and fro with destructive hands; went into the woodshed and returned with the ax to split away the wainscoting about the room. Through the tumult Brad lay still, sure of his own ultimate victory. The man would in the end give up the search; he would go away. Brad had no fears.

"It's quarter past," the man announced.

"You woke me up," said Brad; and the man struck him in the face, pounded him with furious blows. Brad, calm and unmoved, heard the other's gasping breath, sensed the madness that possessed him.

"Now will you come across?" the man asked at last, looking down at Brad's bloody countenance.

"You've got all there is," said Brad.

The man became abruptly still. He stepped back, and there was such an ominous threat in this silent withdrawal that Brad opened his eyes and spoke without his own volition: "What?"

"Why, sure! That's it!"

"What's what?"

"It's in the piano," the man cried. "That's what you got the piano for. It's in there." He snatched the lamp and started toward the other room. And Brad, passively confident till now, abruptly wrenched at his bonds.

The man saw the movement; he cried exultantly. "I knew it!" And was gone; back in a moment. "Where's the key?" he asked hotly.

"You let that piano alone!" Brad cried.

The man struck him.

"Damn it, where's that key?"

"There ain't a thing in there."

"You old fool—"

"I got that piano 'cause my wife always wanted one. Don't you go monkeying with it!"

"I'll monkey with it! I'll monkey with you!" He saw the ax

against the wall and caught it up. "I'll bust the thing wide open!"

"Please, don't you—"

The man laughed and leaped through the door. After an instant Brad heard the crash of an ax; and he groaned aloud and surged against his bonds so that they tore the skin of wrists and ankles. But they did not yield. He shouted something, got no reply save the repeated blows of the ax; and abruptly he relaxed, lay still, eyes closed. Tears flowed from between his closed lids; the blows were as though they fell upon his heart.

By and by the man came back, more furious than ever.

"You old hound, it wasn't there!" he cried.

"I told you to leave it alone," Brad answered implacably.

The man looked around him, enraged by his own futility; caught up the lamp from the table, and knelt and held it below where Brad's hand was fast to the side of the cot.

"Where is it?" he cried. "Damn it, where's that money?"

"I'll tell! I'll tell!" Brad exclaimed. "Oh, Lord, take it away!"

The man withdrew the lamp. He laughed.

"That got you! Well, spill it quick!"

"In the henhouse."

"Where?"

"Go through the shed and out. You'll see a window."

"Quick, damn it!"

"Push the window open and reach down inside. There's a nest there. Lift it off. It's in a tin box underneath."

The man drew back.

"If it ain't you'll wish you was dead."

Brad said slowly, "It's there!"

The man departed swiftly. Brad, left alone, wondered whether the piano were utterly destroyed.

"I can get another," he reminded himself. "She always wanted one." Considered his own situation. "Someone'll drop in tomorrow morning," he decided.

Then he heard the roar of a big-gauge gun, heavily loaded.

There was no other sound; not even a cry.

ARTHUR R. MACDOUGALL, JR.
1896–

Born in Enfield, Arthur Raymond Macdougall, Jr., is a longtime resident of Bingham and was for many years pastor of the Bingham Congregational Church. A fly-rod expert himself, Macdougall has written many stories centered on Dud Dean, an old Maine guide with a dry sense of humor who knows the ways of fish and sportsmen. Macdougall's works capture the flavor of the upper Kennebec region of Maine.

And the Sun Stood Still

It was past sundown and a moment before twilight. The clear, flute-like call of a deep-woods thrush played up and down the sweetest scale of music in the world. A spell of lazy light moved over the lake, while a distilling tint of yellow was passing in the west.

The sense of well-being that follows the satisfaction of hunger sat lightly on my heart. If the calm in Dud's lean and kindly face was assurance, the same sense of tranquillity dwelt with him. And as for our guest, Dick Lord, he had been unrestrained the livelong day in declaring his continual delight. The cup—the fisherman's cup—was full to the brim.

"Over in the west cove," began Dud, carefully filling his pipe as he spoke, "thar's a big hatch of caddis flies goin' on, I bet. An' accordin' to the time-honored custom, the big trout are goin' luny. D'know's I blame them. A caddis hatch is a kind of miracle. A poor fumblin' critter comes up from the bottom, an' produces a pair of wings. If we hadn't got used to it, we'd be jist as surprised as though we'd seen a horse climb up on a fence an' fly away, or as if we, ourselves, had suddenly sprouted tails. An' speakin' of tails, why does this business that eddicated men call 'evolution' always go ahead, in the main? Why don't it turn an' go back'ards?"

At that soliloquy Dud lapsed into silence and fired his pipe.

I stood up to light a lamp. Its yellow light softly invaded the camp. Outside, the ancient quiet of the night possessed the world again.

Dick Lord slid down a bit in the chair he occupied, and wiggled his toes inside the sock on his right foot.

"I suppose," he said, "that each of us has some eventful fishing trip that stands out in his memory—a day when, we might say, that the sun stood still. Mr. Dean, I wish that you would tell us about the day's fishing that comes back, most often, in your memory."

"Well," Dud responded, "I can run back'ards in my mind to days when trout was unbelievably plentiful. I can't say that I remember the fust of my fishin' so clearly as I remember some I've had of late years. Ye see, we uster hoss 'em out on the end of a stiff pole. The idea was to git as many as ye c'ud. Now all in all, I'd say that the memory of the fishin' trip that comes most readily to my mind ain't more'n ten years old. An' it took place no more'n eight miles above our town on the old Kennebec. I know that I never did see more trout in one place, er bigger ones."

"But I had not realized that trout were really abundant on the Kennebec, in late years," said Dick.

"So they ain't. Jist so-so, as a rule, although it's always good fishin', at that, if ye know where they lay. This time, that I'm thinkin' of, was jist afore an' durin' a thunder storm."

Perhaps I turned quickly to look into Dud's face, for he chuckled.

"Mak, here," he said to Dick, "is beginnin' to recollect. Sh'udn't be a mite surprised if he kinda review's that fishin', hisself, now an' then."

"Do you mean just above the old Gutt, below the Berry Place?" I asked.

Dud nodded.

"An' I mean that I never saw anythin' to beat that show in all my life. When I got home that night, I felt a little like Sherm Clark. Sherm was an innocent kind of a feller. Ye liked him becuz his mind always smelt clean. One time Sherm went down to Bangor, er somewheres, an' while he was thar, some of the boys got him inter one of them shows that hain't exactly approved of in polite society. Before Sherm got home, almost, somebudy had tipped off the boys, here, an' they was layin' fer Sherm. Fust off, they tried questionin' him. 'Don't ask me nothin',' says Sherm. 'I can't remember any details, thar was so many of them.'

"That's erbout how I felt concernin' that fishin'. An' by crotch, if Mak an' me sh'ud live to be a hundred, we'd likely never see anythin' like it ag'in."

"How many fish did you get?" asked Dick.

"They was *trout,*" replied Dud, "I can't remember how many we got."

"Five," I said, for the whole event was coming back to me.

"Did we?" asked Dud, indifferently, "I c'udn't have told to

save my winter's pay, but I do know that it all happened quick, an' that lightnin' struck twice—once up on Pleasant Ridge, an' ag'in over in back of us. Say, Mak, whatever did become of that feller, what's his name?''

''But there's something I don't get,'' interrupted Dick. ''I have always understood that trout will not rise during a thunder storm.''

Dud chuckled. ''Young feller, a trout feeds when he's hungry, if thar's anythin' to eat. An' if ye sh'ud happen to be fishin', when Gabriel blows his horn, my advice w'ud be to keep right on fishin'. Like e-nough he won't be lookin' for you, anyway. Anyhow, right that min-it, the trout might begin to rise.

''Thunder an' lightnin' does seem to bother the fishin' as a rule. I've seen the time when they'd be comin' good, an' a little bluff of a storm w'ud blow up an' spoil the fun fer the rest of the day. Then ag'in, it don't. If I knew all erbout fishin' fer trout, I'd give it up, an' tackle sunthin' more int'restin'.

''Say, why don't ye git Mak to tell ye the story erbout that special fishin'. He oughter remember it, becuz that was the time he busted off short the best rod he ever owned.''

''Big trout?''

''No. He stepped on it, hisself. Say Mak, the more I think erbout it, the more I feel like spinnin' the yarn myself. Crotch! How the years come an' go, like a nigger dodger's head. B'fore ye can hit 'em square in the middle they're in Kingdom Come. So the motto is, go fishin' now. . . . What was that feller's name, Mak?''

''McComick.''

''Aya, that was his name. Seein' he was a friend of yours, he was prob'ly Scotch.''

''He was not.''

''No? Crotch, this yarn ain't gittin' nowhere, as Doc Brownin' uster say, when he'd be tellin' erbout the time he got lost in a ten-acre lot. Well, this feller, McComick, come up to visit Mak. It was in August becuz I remember that I warned them that at that season it warn't much use to fish anywhere, much less in the river. However, I finally agreed to go. But, by crotch, when I see that feller's wife, I felt like backin' out. Anybudy c'ud see that she didn't favor fishin', much.

''They had a brand new car that was as long as a string of hoss sheds, an' she was seated in the front. 'How d'ye do,' she says to me, when we was interduced. 'Fair to middlin',' I says, but of course I know that she didn't care a durn. Her face showed she was one of them kind that don't take no int'rest in anythin' but their own comforts.

''When Mak started to git in the backseat, she took one look at his old boots an' britches, an' says, 'Spread out that robe on the cushions.'

"Mak says, 'Oh thank ye, but we won't need it this weather.'

"'Spread it out on the *seat,'* she says. 'It's one we keep fer the dog.'

"Mak jist begun to look all around fer the dog. But I spread the blanket on the seat. An' after we'd told McComick where to go, we started out. In them days, the old road ran close to the Kennebec in places. It was narrow an' crooked. Now, it's under erbout fifty feet of water. The old dugway, as we called it, give Mrs. McComick the jitters. But I think that she'd have kicked erbout the road to glory—an' have turned back, most likely.

"Her husband was built like an elephant. His neck was wide an' short. Thar was three upholstered rolls on it, an' they kept gittin' redder an' redder, as his wife talked. After a while, he said a few words, that was as red as his neck, but the lady never wavered. If thar's anythin' in all the world more uncomfortable than listenin' to somebody else's family row, I'm glad that I've missed it.

"Bine-by, we drew up opposite the Gutt. Thar was a little field between it an' the road, where they sometimes landed logs. This Gutt was a split off the main river. It ran shallow an' fast by a point of interval land, an' then turned an' come inter the river ag'in. We uster git some nice trout in the Gutt. An' I can remember gittin' some nice messes on the other side of the little island. But off the upper p'int, in the main river, was a favorite spot. Off an' on, I've seen some nice trout thar.

"When we got out of McComick's car, we agreed that him an' Mak w'ud maybe try the Gutt, an' then go over on the p'int, while I went up to the Berry Place, a quarter of a mile above, an' fished down to them. McComick suggested that his wife w'ud drive me up, but I said not to bother. An' she didn't. As 'twas, it seemed to me passin' lucky that she was content to set in the car, an' warn't int'rested in fishin'. When I was leavin', she said that it was surely goin' to rain, an' although Mak said sunthin' optimistic, I agreed with her, on that.

"But the water in the river was jist right. Thar had ben a 'head' earlier in the day, but the river was back to normal pitch. I started 'ith wet flies, of course, but somehow they didn't start nothin' that afternoon. Thar was the funniest run of wild flies on the water I ever see. They was erbout number 16 size, an' all over a reddish brown. The queer part of it was that they all seemed to be dead. I rec'lect that I never see one in the air. They was oily an' floated high an' dry. I was puzzled becuz I c'udn't figger where they come from unless it was from up the river quite a ways. But so far as I c'ud see, on my way down, thar warn't a fish that paid any attention to the things. In fact, thar didn't seem to be any fish.

"So I warn't long in gittin' down to the p'int of land. Fer erbout a hundred an' fifty feet erlong that p'int, thar was some good sized oaks. I was busy fishin', an' didn't pay any attention to Mak an' his company, beyond noticin' that they was out thar. At the head of the p'int, at erbout the fust oak tree, the water ran fast, over some big rocks, an' on inter a couple of turn-in-and-out pools. An' right thar, I see that them brownish flies was uncommon plentiful. They was comin' down at a fast clip. An' thar was where I noticed the fust signs of trout; an' hooked two little fellers, 'bout ten inches long.

"Thinks I to myself, 'Might's well keep 'em, becuz it looks like dry fishin',' as Doc Brownin' said, the time a feller offered him a bunch of skunk skins fer services rendered. It was when I bent over to unhook the second trout that one of them wide-open blasts of thunder let go, like a crack of doom. I warn't exactly surprised, becuz it had been grumblin' up on Pleasant Ridge fer ten min-its, er more. But I *was* taken back, when that woman of McComick's opened up. The river makes a lot of noise in a place like that, but the yell she let out of her, carried like a 10-gauge gun beside of a pop gun.

"'Har-ry! Har-ry!' she screams.

"Crotch, ye w'ud have thought that she had been hit, until it come to ye, that she c'udn't have yelled like that, if she had been struck. I looked down the river, an' see McComick drop his duffle, an' dust out of thar as fast as a man wearin' boots c'ud run. Of course, I reeled-up, an' went down where Mak was castin', as though thar hadn't been any thunder, er commotion.

"'Guess the lady was scared, wasn't she?' I says.

"Mak looked up, an' it was the fust notice he had taken of me bein' thar. 'Dud,' he says, this river if full of trout, old codgers!' An' then he went to castin' ag'in, like mad.

"That was the fust attention I paid to the river, down thar, becuz I had decided that we'd have to git out before Mrs. McComick got as wet as an old hen in a rain barrel. When I come to look at the river erlong where Mak was castin', I see that it was literally full of feedin' trout. Maybe thar warn't a million, but I bet thar was a hundred big fellows. They was lyin' right thar in two an' three feet of water— takin' them brown flies as they come down. It really looked like all the trout in the Kennebec had congregated in that place. Fust, ye'd see a big, flat sided cuss roll up. Then Mak 'ud begin to cast inter the boil. Then, maybe twenty feet farther out in the river, up w'ud come another, an' Mak 'ud switch to him.

"By jumpin' hornpouts, it was some perfermance! An' I was jist as long as it took me to wade out gittin' inter it myself. I fergot all erbout the McComicks, an' of course Mak had never remembered them. But it didn't do me no good to join the party. A man might jist as well have been castin' in a haymow. Them trout simply w'udn't look at a wet fly. Jist the same, we kept right at it, castin' at the rises.

"Purty soon, a trout that was past five pounds sprung clean out of the water, an' says, 'Hello, hayseeds!' An' I reckon that was too much fer Mak, becuz he reeled in his line, an' stumbled a-shore, lookin' like a man that had been knocked down an' trumped on. Out of the corner of my eye, I see him goin' through that old ducks-back huntin' coat of his'n that holds a half ton of stuff. After he'd pulled out a fist full of last year's shells, a tin cup, an' an old felt hat—in fact, erbout everythin' but a prayer book, which was what we needed, by crotch—he hauled out a little box erbout four inches square.

"'Dud!' he yells, like I was clean across the river, 'come in here!'

"When I got thar, he says, 'Now pick out a dry fly that looks like them nat'rals.'

"All the time we was gittin' fixed up 'ith lighter leaders, an' them new flies, the thunder was gittin' louder, an' the sky was gittin' blacker. When we started out inter the river ag'in, the rain come. It come at us in a straight wall, like ye've seen it, sometimes. An' it come so evenly that ye'd have thought the devil hisself was drivin' a water cart at us. At a hundred feet away, the river was a-pelt with big drops, an' not a sprinkle touchin' us. Then it hit us. At sech times, a man knows that all this talk erbout controllin' nature is danged foolish.

"I had made jist one cast, a-fore that rain hit us. When it got thar, it sunk that fly like a stick of pulpwood in white water, an' then I felt a bigger an' wider trout than I ever see take that fly from underneath. I don't use number seven shot fer ducks, an' I don't use number sixteen flies fer *big* trout, when I'm choosin'. But jist that moment thar warn't nothin' as per *my* specifications. When I set the hook, that trout jist rolled over, as mad as a skunk at a tea party. So I let him run, until he'd taken practically all my line out inter the river, an' then I tried to turn him, while he was pullin' cross-ways of the current. Well, thar's sunthings we jist can't do, although it's up to a man to try.

"Erbout that time. I got the rain water out of my eyes, an' made-out that Mak was fast to a nice trout. The line sliced the water like a knife drawn through sour-milk cheese. Up an' down it went, an' all over the lot, until finally Mak got him backed in shore, where I c'ud git the landin' net under him. He was—the trout I mean—mighty beautiful in that wild, weird light. A trout is purty in any light. I've always said that thar ain't no fish like a nice trout. An' they're firm an' pink-meated inside, givin' the lie to that old saw that beauty is only skin-deep.

"Wel-el, what a spell of weather we had! When the wind an' the rain had passed over us, it looked like it might clear up; so we waded out ag'in. But that was jist a lull before the decks was cleared fer action, an' in a min-it, the heavens turned loose a broadside that rumbled an' roared, an' exploded like all hell was on a drunk. Once thar was a crack of white-hot light, as wide as a door, that run from the top of the universe to the bottom. An' either I had some wet matches in my pocket, er I actually smelled brimstone. An' three or four times, it looked like a hand that we c'udn't see had cut a slit a hundred miles long in the black sky. Them slits let through the most uncomfortable yeller light that a man ever see. Then streaks of lightnin' w'ud go dodgin' across the sky like a three-legged rabbit in front of a bow-legged hound."

Dick, who had been trying to get in a word, interrupted Dud at this point. "Do you mean to say that those trout were risin' in all that inferno?"

Dud chuckled and poked at the fire.

"No, no. I don't say that. I really don't know what them trout was doin'. Fer the fust time in my whole life I had lost all int'rest in fishin'. Mak an' me was lyin' down flat. Ye see, the storm was a little too much fer a man to stand up under. The wind w'ud blow like a cyclone, an' then the rain 'ud come by spells. An' the thunder never missed a cue. Crotch.

"Wel-el, that sort of passed. So we raised up, an' begun to wonder erbout them trout. We fixed on some more flies. But 'bout then McComick appeared. He was as wet as we was.

"'My wife insists on goin' home,' he says.

"'Well, I don't blame her a bit,' says Mak, as he waded out in the river ag'in.

"Then, by crotch a-mighty, it came!—a flash of light as white as a frog's belly. I can remember jist how Mak looked, out thar in the river up to his knees. I can remember jist how everythin' looked, an' I thought I was lookin' at it fer the last time. That crash beat anythin' that ever happened, I guess. It hit a big pine up on the hill, on our side of the river.

"Now a quarter of a mile is a quarter of a mile, but when it's that near to a charge of lightnin' like that 'un, it's only a hair. McComick had jist picked up his own rod an' basket, preparatory to goin', but they jist fell out of his hands, like sunthin' he'd never need again. An' his face looked like his soul had left him, an' was already six miles down the road. But almost always in a time like that, sunthin' earthly happens to bring a man around. An' it did then.

"'Har-ry!'

"'That's my wife,' says McComick, lickin' his lips.

"Funny how different we react to this an' that. Mak had his arm comin' up to make a cast, when that crack came. It scared him so that it paralyzed him right in the act. When it was over, an' his senses come back, nothin' c'ud be more natural than that he sh'ud finish the cast."

Dud broke off, turning to me. "You tell this feller what happened after that cast. He'll never, never believe me."

"A trout hit it," I said.

"A trout," reitereated Dud, with his heavy eyebrows drawn together, and his grey eyes daring Dick to question the statement.

Dick did not indicate belief or disbelief, and Dud went on with his story.

"Now I had been all set to go home, like a gentleman. But thar was Mak, fast to another trout. An' at that second another boiled within ten feet of the shore. McComick see it, too, but he jist moaned, 'My wife insists—'

"What c'ud I do? C'ud I leave Mak, an' him fast to a trout? 'By crotch,' thinks I, 'it's your wife, not mine.' An' I waded out with the landin' net. We got that fish. An' thar was signs of some more. I dropped erbout forty feet of line up the river, an' watched my fly. Blub! she goes. An' the fun was on. It run clean to the end of my line, but it warn't more'n two min-its before I was pullin' slack line—so much that it got out of my left hand, an' trailed down the river. That trout took it inter his head that he had more places to visit than a pie-eyed crane c'ud keep track of. Ye understand that all this was goin' on in fairly quick water, an' at the end of a guess-and-by-gosh leader. Wel-el, thar's an end of all important things—one end or another—an' I finally got that trout so's he'd float belly-up, er on his side, an' didn't care which it was. Mak got the net under him, an' two-thirds of that fish was on the outside, I mean that the small half was inside. So we started fer shore, an' got erlong nice, until Mak slipped. He didn't go down, but pitched forward, and kept goin'. That's how he come to walk all over his nice rod, which he had put down when he got ready to net my fish.

"But we got that old-timer where he c'ud only flop a little. An' right then was when the sun tried to come out. Ye might say, Dick, that it had been standin' still. But it c'udn't seem to make a go of shinin' through them clouds. Everythin' looked like a circus ground the day after the circus had gone.

"And then is when Mak remembered the McComicks. 'Dud,' he says, 'how are we ever goin' to face that woman?'

"Crotch, it did look like we was up ag'inst sunthin' worse than the thunder storm. But it had to be faced. So we waded round the p'int and across the little brook that run out of the interval, an' then climbed up the bank to the car. Only . . . thar warn't no car!

"But thar sot McComick on a rock. 'She's gone,' he says to us, 'with the car.'

"'Man, man,' says Mak, 'we're sorry erbout this! Why didn't ye go with her?'

"An' then McComick begun to laugh. 'She must of left,' says he, 'jist after that last crack.'

"Well, we all felt purty mean, but jist then I see a car comin' down from Caratunk, an' waved my arms in a sign of dire distress. It was Albert Clark, an' he took us in."

"You haven't finished the story," I said. "Why not tell Dick what you *did* with the big trout?"

"I weighed him. That's what I done, b'crotch. Nine pounds an' two ounces!"

"And then—" I prodded.

"An' then, like a danged fool, I sent him to that Mrs. McComick, erlong 'ith my apologies fer the thunder storm, an' all thunder storms, past an' future. Sunthin' had to be done, didn't it? I never did blame her a mite, except . . . well, crotch . . . she. Well! thar was them trout a-jumpin'."

Dick burst out laughing, as though he could stand it no longer. "Did she, ha, ha, did she ever forgive you?"

"Aya. She had sense enough, after all . . . to see that I was in bad company. Sent me a nice little note, writ on paper that smelled like the lotus islands, which Nancy says is a wicked place."

ERSKINE CALDWELL
1902–

Born in Coweta County, Georgia, Erskine Caldwell is known primarily as a southern writer and is noted for his short stories and for such graphically naturalistic novels as *Tobacco Road* (1932) and *God's Little Acre* (1933). After attending Erskine College, the University of Pennsylvania, and the University of Virginia, Caldwell moved to Maine with his wife (the first of four), and lived in the state from 1925–32. He held a series of odd jobs and struggled as a writer until he caught the attention of Maxwell Perkins, who offered encouragement and accepted some stories for *Scribner's Magazine.* Caldwell left Maine to work as a script writer in Hollywood and as a foreign correspondent in Prague, Moscow, Mexico, Spain, Russia, and China. In 1939 he married the photographer Margaret Bourke-White, with whom he collaborated on several documentaries, among them *You Have Seen Their Faces* (1937). A prolific writer, Caldwell has sold hundreds of editions and many millions of copies of his works throughout his career. Books which are set in Maine include *A Lamp for Nightfall* (1952) and *American Earth* (1931), a collection of short stories.

The Lonely Day

For a week the wet mid-summer mists had been creeping over Maine from the south, from the coast; sheets of low-hanging gray vapor spread over the country like dirty steam and levelled the foot-hills into smooth fields, while the mountains had been wrapped in wet gray clouds and put away from sight towards the north, towards Canada. Yesterday the mists had lifted over the housetop, almost over the tops of the elm trees; but to-day, Sunday, the lower air was so wet that the meshes of the window-screens were filled with panes of opaque water.

Katherine hurried across the wet grass from the garden and went into the house. She opened the kitchen-door quietly and closed it slowly as she stood back against it.

The old woman struck at her with the heavy end of the crutch and cursed her.

The girl jumped away and ran to the other side of the kitchen.

The room was wet with the mid-summer mists. There were little balls of water in the dusty spider-web over the stove and a thin stream of water trickled at intervals down the table-legs to the floor.

"Go pick me some berries," the old woman cried at her. "GO PICK ME SOME BERRIES!" she shouted. "Do you hear me? You damned little sneak! Bring me a pail of berries before I take this crutch and kill you!"

"All right," Katherine whimpered. "I'm going."

"Well, why don't you run? I'll break your head if you don't get out of here after those berries!"

Katherine took the berry-pail from the kitchen-table and ran outside before the old woman could strike her again. The wet mists clung to her hair as she ran towards the pasture, and tears fell on her dampened cheeks. The berry-field was on the other side of the stream, beyond the sheep pasture. Bordering the field was the State road, running north and south.

She gathered the wet berries as quickly as she could. She knew the old woman was even then waiting at the kitchen-door to strike her with the crutch because she had not returned sooner. She tried as hard as she could, but she could not pick them any faster.

Several hundred yards away automobiles passed in both directions, going up into the Provinces, coming back into Maine. All around her was the forest, the deep dark forest where men worked in winter, in the white frozen snow, cutting pulp wood. The men who worked there were French from Canada and she could not understand what they said. Now there was nobody near. The closest settlement was forty miles to the south and the only people who came through the woods were tourists, passing but never stopping. She had never gone so far as the road, but when she picked berries she could hear the roar of the speeding automobiles and occasionally the laughter of men and women. The old woman would not let her go near the road.

While she was gathering the wet berries she thought she heard one of the automobiles stop. As she listened, there came shouts and laughter from the direction of the road, but she was too far away to hear what the people said. She bent over the berry-bushes and tried to fill the pail as quickly as she could.

It was noon before the pail was full. She ran towards the house where the old woman sat waiting for the berries.

While she ran down the hillside toward the stream in the sheep pasture she heard again the shouts and laughter of several persons. When she reached the footbridge she could see them in dim outline through the mists. There were five or six men and girls farther down the stream toward the lower lake.

Katherine crossed the footbridge and went down the stream where the men and girls were. At first she thought they were fishing, but almost before she knew it, she was within a hundred yards of them; and then she saw that they were swimming and diving into the stream. The low-hanging cloud had cleared along the banks of the stream for a few moments and she saw them plainly only a short distance away.

She stared wild-eyed as she saw one of the men and a girl wade out of the water and stand on the bank a moment before diving in again. Then others came out to dive and she saw that none of them was wearing a bathing-suit.

She was so confused by what she saw that she could neither cry out nor run away. Her heart was beating madly and her body trembled with excitement.

While she stood in amazement before the scene, one of the girls climbed to the bank of the stream and ran out across the pasture. The girl turned and called to one of the men.

"You can't catch me, Jimmy!"

Laughing, the naked girl ran off and disappeared in the heavy mists.

"I'll catch you if I don't catch a cow first!" the man shouted after her.

The other men and girls were laughing and splashing water in the stream.

Suddenly the girl who had disappeared in the misty pasture cried out:

"Oh, Jimmy, come quick and find me! I've caught a sheep!"

"I can't, Helen!" the man called to her. "I'm all tangled up in a wire fence!"

The other men and girls climbed to the bank of the stream, shouting ridiculous suggestions telling how to hold a sheep and how to get out of a wire fence. They all fell down on the grass hysterical with laughter.

Katherine stood beside the stream, above them. She had never seen anything such as this happen before in her life, and she could barely believe that men and girls could have such a good time together. It was too incredible to be true, but she could hear everything they said and see everything they did. And still the scene was unreal to her. She had never been with men and girls of her own age, and she was bewildered with the strangeness of their behavior.

Her heart was racing so excitedly that she could stand still no longer. She wanted to run as fast as she could and fall in the midst of those men and girls and laugh with them. Then suddenly she felt the weight of the berry-pail in her hand, and she turned and ran as quickly as she could to the house where the old woman waited.

The old woman snatched the pail of berries from her hands and began eating the fruit. Katherine went to her room and closed the door. She stood beside her bed trembling with excitement, remembering what she had seen and heard down at the stream in the sheep pasture. She ran from window to window trying to see through the wet mists. If only there had been no mists, she knew she could have seen the men and girls in the pasture. But she could see no further than the windows. The mists covered everything outside.

While the old woman sat in the kitchen eating the berries, Katherine slipped quietly from the front of the house and ran towards the stream. As she ran down the hillside she tried to hear the things the men and girls were saying. She wanted to run, just as they were, into their midst and throw herself on the grass beside them. She wanted to laugh and dive into the stream and splash water over everybody.

Running wildly towards the stream, she suddenly saw that the men and girls were not there. They had taken their clothes and gone back to the automobile to dress, and by now they were probably several miles away. Now there was nothing she could do. She did not want to stay at the stream alone. She wanted to be with someone, with men and girls who laughed and splashed water, and to have them see her. Alone, she stood crying by the stream. Once she looked at herself, but she was alone. She wanted men to see her, and girls, and she wanted to see them.

The wet mists chilled her body and she began to shiver. The warm tears fell cold and hard on her arms and hands.

Slowly she turned and walked up the hillside toward the house. She repeated over and over the words she thought she had heard as she was running so happily to the stream a few minutes before.

The old woman had not missed her. She still sat in the kitchen eating from the pail the berries Katherine had picked that morning.

Katherine sat on the bed in her room crying. She fell backward and crushed a pillow over her face so the old woman could not hear her.

Later in the afternoon she got up and undressed. She walked around the room, stopping at a window and trying to penetrate the gray mists that hung over the earth. But taking off her clothes, putting them on, taking them off again was not enough. There was no one to see her, there were no men and girls she could see. It was not what had happened in the sheep pasture that morning, when the gray mists were filled with laughter and the stream with splashing water. It was not the same thing. And she could not laugh aloud.

After supper, when the old woman had gone to bed, Katherine stole out of the house and ran through the wet dark night towards the pasture. When she reached the stream she could see nothing, not even the grass at her feet. All about her she felt the clinging wet clouds of vapor. The black mists covered everything. Over the hill she thought she heard an automobile speed along the road towards the Provinces. Her nightgown had fallen at her feet on the wet grass, but she could not keep from feeling that she had not taken off as much as the men and girls had that afternoon. She pulled at her arms and waist as if she expected to find something else to throw off from her. She tried again, but she could not laugh aloud in the wet mists.

She ran across the berry-field until she reached the road where the automobiles passed. When she got there she stood in the road and waited. It was then after midnight. She waited but no car came from either direction.

While she stood in the centre of the road she distinctly heard in the distance the same laughter that had made her so excited that afternoon. Clearly she heard a girl's voice. Someone was calling, "You can't catch me, Jimmy!" Almost immediately the voice of a man could be heard out in the far darkness somewhere, "I'll catch you if I don't catch a cow first!" And then, all around her, men and girls were shouting and laughing, just as she had heard them that afternoon in the pasture. From the music of their voices she knew they were splashing water in a stream and lying naked on the grassy banks beside the water. But they were so far away she knew she could never find them while everything was so black and misty.

She waited and listened for an automobile to come up or down the road. But there was none. It was after midnight. She wanted to stand in the centre of the road and have the men and women see her.

The first light of day broke through the mists and found her lying in the road, her body made lifeless by an automobile that had shot through the darkness an hour before. She was without motion, but she was naked, and a smile that was the beginning of laughter made her the most beautiful woman whom tourists speeding to the Provinces had ever seen.

EDWARD M. HOLMES
1910–

Born in Montclair, N.J., Edward M(orris). Holmes received his A.B. from Dartmouth College, M.Ed. from the University of Maine, and M.A. and Ph.D. from Brown University. In addition to teaching, Holmes has worked as a clerk, salesman, stage carpenter, business manager for a health cooperative, news reporter, and organizer of fishermen's cooperatives and credit unions. Affiliated with the University of Maine at Orono since 1956, he was named professor emeritus in 1977. Holmes has contributed stories and articles to numerous journals, is the author of a critical work on Faulkner, and has produced three collections of short stories: *Driftwood* (1972), *A Part of the Main* (1973), and *Mostly Maine* (1977). Holmes won the Emily Clark Balch Prize in 1971 for "Drums Again" and was represented in *The Best American Short Stories of 1972.*

Lost and Found

After they lost the *Ellen Jay* on Outer Litchfield Ledge off Fishhawk Point, Ev Miller and Hank Torey did the best they could not to speak to Hal Gustavsen, or—what amounted to the same thing—come face-to-face with him anywhere here in Rockhaven. And they had to work at it: neither one of them, of course, could come down to my wharf just after daybreak when most of the men was going aboard their crafts, or if it was one of them halfway bad days when a man didn't know whether it was fit to go out and haul or not, standing around the bait shed talking about going out, and needling each other the way they do. Nor, sometimes, did the two of them even dare go to the post office at mail time nor to the movies nights. Hank Torey see Hal coming toward him one day on the road that passes the fish factory, but before Hal got anywhere near him, Hank slipped off between two buildings somewhere and went right out of sight. I know because Hal told me about it himself.

I got to admit there was no reason at first Ev or Hank either should be down to my wharf any time, since neither one of them had a boat to go fishing in any more, and both of them knew enough to think twice before coming to me for credit to buy one. Still, it must have been trying for them in a place this size to keep from meeting a man.

They had been setting trawls in the *Ellen Jay* two three months before they lost her. Hal Gustavsen had gone out of his way to get them to fish in her on shares. I don't know what the deal was exactly, but I dare-say it was twenty-five percent for the boat, twenty-five percent to the owner, and twenty-five percent to each man—something like that. Anyway, Ev and Hank had nothing to lose out of it except their labor, if you've a mind to count that.

None of us ever asked why Hal Gustavsen didn't fish in the *Ellen Jay* himself any more because the reason was obvious. He had fished in her for years—even before his wife died—and then in June in the year I am speaking of he went out to make a set and took some visitor from away—name of Redford—and his son Ben (Hal's son, I mean) with him. Ben was about twenty, a fisherman in his own right—hauled summer and winter in a twenty-eight foot lobster boat and was pressing the high-liners. He went with Hal and Redford that day only for the fun of it, kind of a start-the-summer celebration. Trouble with Ben was he had a bad heart, or so Dr. Norwood tells me, and along with that, high spirits and plenty of energy. Way Hal and Redford told it later, they was three miles off shore, and Ben was standing on the after deck, one hand on the mast that supports the *Ellen Jay*'s riding sail. Everything was going fine—some swells, but no rough seas nor high winds nor nothing—until Hal glances aft for a second and sees that the stern deck is empty. Well sir, he pulled back on the *Ellen Jay*'s throttle, swung her around as fast as he could, and retraced her wake a short time to what he thought was the right place—though how he could guess one spot was more right than another I don't pretend to know. Then he puts the *Ellen Jay* in neutral, kicks off his boots and dives overside, dives deep, like he thought he could make it to the bottom even in all them fathoms, or get a-holt of Ben before he was clean out of sight—which of course he couldn't.

Not only that: he had the devil's own time getting back to the surface without drowning himself, and even staying on the surface long enough for Redford to pull up alongside and drag him aboard. Lucky for him that Redford knew enough to handle the *Ellen Jay* even a little bit.

Reason he was in such hard plight was he was wearing quite heavy trousers, and a wool sweater, and jacket, and though he had kicked off his boots—something hard for any man to forget to do if he knows he is going overside and has any chance—still, with his whole heart and soul suddenly right up there in his mouth, he never thought to take off anything else.

Worst of it was, he blamed himself for Ben's death, claiming if he (Hal) had stayed cool for a minute, him and Redford might have sighted Ben when he surfaced. Hal couldn't believe Ben hadn't surfaced at least once. But the way it was, Redford put all his attention on saving the man he could see, and it took him five or six minutes to do that. So Hal blamed himself, took the whole load on himself. Set right here in my office, in that chair you're setting in, shaking his head and telling me, then putting his head down in his hands, and the tears rolling off his face in a freshet.

It wasn't just me he told; it was everyone, anyone who would listen and I guess there wasn't no one but felt he had to listen so long as Hal wanted to talk. This thing had left him all alone in the world, so to speak, and we felt mighty bad for him, deep-down bad where there wasn't really no way to say it. But there wasn't one of us, not a single one, nor any of us together, could get him to see that it wasn't his fault, that he shouldn't go around day and night thinking, "I drowned my son. If I hadn't done what I did, diving overside we could have saved him." We tried, and tried, and tried, with no results. So it was no wonder to us he did not want to step foot aboard the *Ellen Jay*. We all understood that.

So what he did was dig up Ev Miller and Hank Torey to take the *Ellen Jay* on shares and go trawling. They weren't the best men for the work, as he knew quite well, or any of us could have told him. They was not too responsible, nor ambitious, nor energetic, and perhaps not too smart neither. But the best men for such work was already busy on their own. Hal didn't really have much choice. Meanwhile, Hal went lobsterfishing, using his son's boat. It didn't bother him any to do that; maybe it even made him feel better, just a mite. And afternoons when the *Ellen Jay* was due in from a trip he would be down here to the fishwharf to watch the count and then divide with Ev and Hank whatever it was the trip had stocked.

And that was how things went until that September Ev and Hank rowed in here in a skiff in the dark and told us the *Ellen Jay* was lost. They never reported to Hal, never dared to. I picked up the phone here myself and called him, but at first he was out or the party line was busy or something, and by the time I could reach him, Ev and Hank had talked it all over with them that was here on the wharf, and by the time Hal got here, Ev and Hank had gone off into the darkness, and home I guess. Hal could have followed them up, of course. I asked why he didn't.

He was silent for a minute, and his eyes had that kind of distant look. Then he said: "What difference would it make?"

The way Ev and Hank told it, and the way I and no doubt several others told it to Hal, was about like this: toward dark, just as they was coming in, the *Ellen Jay*'s engine conked out. Neither one of them ever seemed too certain what was wrong with it. First Ev said it was the condenser, and Hank said no, it was the coil; then Ev thought perhaps it was the timer, and Hank said well, it could have been worn points or a corroded battery terminal. Other times they talked about the gas filter, the fuel pump, and the air-intake. In other words, they didn't know what it was, and when the engine failed, with the ebb tide setting toward Litchfield Ledge not too far to port like a black sea beast groaning as the waves flushed over it, they was so jeezily scared they didn't know where to turn. They didn't try anchoring nor kedging, and whether either one could have saved the *Ellen Jay* we'll never know.

First off, Ev jumps into the big skiff they was towing and has Hank pass him the *Ellen Jay*'s bow line; then rowing against tide and swells both, he tried to tow her clear of the ledge. Time he got her bow swung around, he was about wore out; so then he comes back alongside, Hank gets into the skiff with him, and with two pair of oars they give it another try. They get her started away from the ledges all right, but it isn't enough. When the tide picks up, most they can do while they have their strength is hold their own, and soon as they begin to wear down, the current takes them. Last of it, they have to cast off the *Ellen Jay* or go on the rocks with her, and with the end of their breath, they row away, hearing the splintering crash of the *Ellen Jay*'s transom against the ledge. She was a complete loss all right; here and there some of us picked up a few bits and pieces.

Four, maybe five weeks after that, Hal Gustavsen come down to see me on the wharf in one of them slack times when nobody else was around. Not that I hadn't been seeing him two three times a week anyway when he come up to the wharf to buy gas or bait, or perhaps more or less as a favor or because he needed cash, to sell me a catch instead of carring it. But this time he comes on foot.

"Carl," he says finally, "how long do I have to put up with it?"

"With what?" I said.

"Them fellows dodging away from me."

"Oh. Well—"

"Like I was cursed or something."

"I wouldn't go so far as to say that," I told him. "You know why they're dodging away from you."

"Yeah." He sounded tired.

"Because they blame themselves," I said, "the same as—"

"All right, all right, Yeah, I know. But I don't like it. I don't know that I can go on standing it."

"Go see them. Go to their house one at a time," I said. "They'll listen. They got to listen."

Hal leaned back against the counter and scratched his head. "I don't want it to be like that. I want them and me to be together sometime when neither one of us can help it."

"Well, stick around here," I said.

"Why? They ain't been down here."

"Not til yesterday," I said. "But they'll be back."

"What for?"

"They got hold of a boat," I said, "Hank's father's boat. It ain't much."

"So?"

"But it still floats. It goes, even."

"Yeah?"

"And they figure to go lobsterfishing in it, that is if they can get credit for gear."

"And you're going to extend it to them?"

"Not by a damned site I ain't. I been stung on that kind of fisherman before this."

Hal nodded. "I see. Not even if I was to co-sign their note?"

"Well, that might make a difference."

"When do you think they'll be here?" he said.

"Not today," I told him. "It's late now, and more boats will be in before you know it. Tomorrow maybe, middle of the morning, after they figure everyone's gone out, you included."

"Thanks," said Hal. "What am I supposed to do? Hide my boat somewhere so they won't see it to the mooring."

"I don't believe you have got to go quite so far as that," I said.

And he didn't. But he was down here, perhaps an hour after the last of the boats had gone out, not here in my office, you understand, where I was, but out there where the counter is and the coils of potwarp and the paint and hardware and whatnot, just hanging around. And about ten-thirty Ev and Hank wanders in, and there they was right in front of Hal, and no way to back out without seeming silly. So they looks at each other, and there is a little shuffling of feet, and then Hal says, "Hi, fellows," and they said, "Hi," and "How is everything?" back.

"Not too good," said Hal.

"No?" Ev says.

"How's that?" says Hank.

"Some of my friends ain't speaking," said Hal. "They don't even want to meet me on the street."

"Yeah, that's us, Hal," Ev said. "And you know why, don't you?"

"Do I?" said Hal.

"Because we lost you a boat. We lost you the *Ellen Jay* and you know we can't make it up to you, not if we work the rest of our goddamned life."

"That's right," Ev said.

I heard Hal take a step or two, like he was coming toward them, but instead of lifting his voice, it was like he whispered: "You think I care about that? You think I care about a goddamned boat?"

"Thousands of dollars," one of them said. "Thousands . . . We know that."

"Yeah. And I'd give it up, that and three times over, ten times over if I had it—for something." For a few seconds there was silence. Then again I heard him: "Don't you fellows know that I know what can happen when something terrible comes to you on the water, when a man is afraid and can't hardly draw a breath, or see, or think straight, and loses his head? For Christ's sake, you think I don't know about *that?*"

There was more shuffling of feet. I heard a board squeak, and some breathing, and someone open a cooler lid. Then Hank says, "Which is it you'd rather have, Hal, a root-beer or a Seven-Up?"

Hal said something, and Ev said something, and there was a little laughter, and I heard the coins ring on the counter top.

Ordinarily I would have left my desk and gone into the store part at that, but I didn't. I stared out the window at Hal's boat at the mooring, and felt my muscles relax. When, finally, I did go out, there was the change, with a few cents over, on the counter top, and through the window I could see all three of them sauntering up the road, drinks in one hand, and talking together like they was right in the middle of summer, or something like that.

PART V:
POETRY

HENRY WADSWORTH LONGFELLOW
1807–1882

Born and raised in Portland, Henry Wadsworth Longfellow graduated from Bowdoin at the age of eighteen with the intention of becoming a writer. His alma mater offered him a position as professor of modern languages and literature that allowed him to spend nearly four years traveling and studying in France, Italy, Germany, and Spain. He remained at Bowdoin for six years, spent more time abroad, and then moved to Harvard, where he taught until 1854. Longfellow's first collection of verse, *Voices of the Night,* was published in 1839; his output over the next decade made him the most popular poet in the country and one of the well known poets of the world. After the tragic death of his second wife, Longfellow devoted himself to a translation of Dante's *Divine Comedy* (1865–67) and to *Christus: A Mystery* (1872), which was intended to symbolize three great periods in history; these efforts were followed by several additional volumes of verse until his death. While Longfellow at times displays excessive sentimentality, he can be highly praised for the technical skill displayed in his sonnets and reflective verse, his experiments in adapting foreign forms and metres, and his compelling narratives that came to be regarded as national epics.

A Psalm of Life
What the Heart of the Young Man Said to the Psalmist

Tell me not, in mournful numbers,
  Life is but an empty dream!—
For the soul is dead that slumbers,
  And things are not what they seem.

Life is real! Life is earnest!
  And the grave is not its goal;
Dust thou art, to dust returnest,
  Was not spoken of the soul.

Not enjoyment, and not sorrow,
  Is our destined end or way;
But to act, that each to-morrow
  Find us farther than to-day.

Art is long, and Time is fleeting,
  And our hearts, though stout and brave,
Still, like muffled drums, are beating
  Funeral marches to the grave.

In the world's broad field of battle,
  In the bivouac of Life,
Be not like dumb, driven cattle!
  Be a hero in the strife!

Trust no Future, howe'er pleasant!
  Let the dead Past bury its dead!
Act,—act in the living Present!
  Heart within, and God o'erhead!

Lives of great men all remind us
  We can make our lives sublime,
And, departing, leave behind us
  Footprints on the sands of time;

Footprints, that perhaps another,
  Sailing o'er life's solemn main,
A forlorn and shipwrecked brother,
  Seeing, shall take heart again.

Let us, then, be up and doing,
  With a heart for any fate;
Still achieving, still pursuing,
  Learn to labor and to wait.

Mezzo Cammin

Half of my life is gone, and I have let
  The years slip from me and have not fulfilled
  The aspiration of my youth, to build
  Some tower of song with lofty parapet.
Not indolence, nor pleasure, nor the fret
  Of restless passions that would not be stilled,
  But sorrow, and a care that almost killed,
  Kept me from what I may accomplish yet:
Though, half-way up the hill, I see the Past
  Lying beneath me with its sounds and sights,—
  A city in the twilight dim and vast,
With smoking roofs, soft bells, and gleaming lights.—
  And hear above me on the autumnal blast
  The cataract of Death far thundering from the heights.

The Evening Star

Lo! in the painted oriel of the West,
Whose panes the sunken sun incarnadines,
Like a fair lady at her casement, shines
The evening star, the star of love and rest!
And then anon she doth herself divest
Of all her radiant garments, and reclines
Behind the sombre screen of yonder pines,
With slumber and soft dreams of love oppressed.
O my belovèd, my sweet Hesperus!
My morning and my evening star of love!
My best and gentlest lady! even thus,
As that fair planet in the sky above,
Dost thou retire unto thy rest at night,
And from thy darkened window fades the light.

My Lost Youth

Often I think of the beautiful town
That is seated by the sea;
Often in thought go up and down
The pleasant streets of that dear old town,
And my youth comes back to me.
And a verse of a Lapland song
Is haunting my memory still:
"A boy's will is the wind's will,
And the thoughts of youth are long, long thoughts."

I can see the shadowy lines of its trees,
And catch, in sudden gleams,
The sheen of the far-surrounding seas.
And islands that were the Hesperides
Of all my boyish dreams.
And the burden of that old song
It murmurs and whispers still:
"A boy's will is the wind's will,
And the thoughts of youth are long, long thoughts."

I remember the black wharves and the slips,
And the sea-tides tossing free;
And Spanish sailors with bearded lips,
And the beauty and mystery of the ships,
And the magic of the sea.
And the voice of that wayward song
Is singing and saying still:

  "A boy's will is the wind's will,
And the thoughts of youth are long, long thoughts."

I remember the bulwarks by the shore,
  And the fort upon the hill;
The sunrise gun, with its hollow roar,
The drumbeat repeated o'er and o'er,
  And the bugle wild and shrill.
    And the music of that old song
    Throbs in my memory still:
  "A boy's will is the wind's will,
And the thoughts of youth are long, long thoughts."

I remember the sea-fight far away,
  How it thundered o'er the tide!
And the dead captains, as they lay
In their graves, o'erlooking the tranquil bay
  Where they in battle died.
    And the sound of that mournful song
    Goes through me with a thrill:
  "A boy's will is the wind's will,
And the thoughts of youth are long, long thoughts."

I can see the breezy dome of groves,
  The shadows of Deering's Woods;
And the friendships old and the early loves
Come back with a Sabbath sound, as of doves
  In quiet neighborhoods.
    And the verse of that sweet old song,
    It flutters and murmurs still:
  "A boy's will is the wind's will,
And the thoughts of youth are long, long thoughts."

I remember the gleams and glooms that dart
  Across the school-boy's brain;
The song and the silence in the heart,
That in part are prophecies, and in part
  Are longings wild and vain.
    And the voice of that fitful song
    Sings on, and is never still:
  "A boy's will is the wind's will,
And the thoughts of youth are long, long thoughts."

There are things of which I may not speak;
  There are dreams that cannot die;
There are thoughts that make the strong heart weak,

And bring a pallor into the cheek,
  And a mist before the eye.
    And the words of that fatal song
    Come over me like a chill:
  "A boy's will is the wind's will,
And the thoughts of youth are long, long thoughts."

Strange to me now are the forms I meet
  When I visit the dear old town;
But the native air is pure and sweet,
And the trees that o'ershadow each well-known street,
  As they balance up and down,
    Are singing the beautiful song,
    Are sighing and whispering still
  "A boy's will is the wind's will,
And the thoughts of youth are long, long thoughts."

And Deering's Woods are fresh and fair,
  And with joy that is almost pain
My heart goes back to wander there,
And among the dreams of the days that were,
  I find my lost youth again.
    And the strange and beautiful song,
    The groves are repeating it still:
  "A boy's will is the wind's will,
And the thoughts of youth are long, long thoughts."

My Cathedral

Like two cathedral towers these stately pines
  Uplift their fretted summits tipped with cones;
  The arch beneath them is not built with stones,
  Not Art but Nature traced these lovely lines,
And carved this graceful arabesque of vines;
  No organ but the wind here sighs and moans,
  No sepulchre conceals a martyr's bones,
  No marble bishop on his tomb reclines.
Enter! the pavement, carpeted with leaves,
  Gives back a softened echo to thy tread!
  Listen! the choir is singing; all the birds,
In leafy galleries beneath the eaves,
  Are singing! listen, ere the sound be fled,
  And learn there may be worship without words.

EDWIN ARLINGTON ROBINSON
1869–1935

Born in Head Tide, Edwin Arlington Robinson and his family soon moved inland to Gardiner, the "Tilbury Town" of his poems. The years following Robinson's graduation from high school were marked by family illnesses and economic instability; he entered Harvard at the age of twenty-two but withdrew after only two years. After privately printing *The Torrent and the Night Before* in 1896, Robinson decided to go to New York to make his living by writing. Over the next decade Robinson faced further financial insecurity, bouts of depression, and dependence upon alcohol. Theodore Roosevelt secured him a sinecure as a customs clerk that lasted from 1905 to 1910, and in 1911 Robinson spent the first of many summer residences at the MacDowell Colony, an artists' retreat in New Hampshire. Robinson now concentrated upon writing longer works, among them the Arthurian poems: *Merlin* (1917), *Lancelot* (1920), and *Tristram* (1927). His first edition of collected poems (1921) won a Pulitzer Prize, as did *The Man Who Died Twice* (1924) and *Tristram*. *Tristram* was also a national best seller, so for the remaining years of his life Robinson was finally free of financial worries.

Robinson is noted for his ability to delve into the paradoxes of human character in a few lines. His vision is somewhat somber, for he recognized and described limitations of existence. He presented a universe of impenetrable mysteries, but, at the same time, he conveyed the necessity of enduring adversity and of continuing to search for the answers. To achieve his purposes, Robinson preferred to utilize the traditional sonnet, dramatic monologue, and narrative; whatever the form, though, his consciousness of his craft and his meticulous attention to detail earned him his reputation as one of America's great poets.

Eros Turannos

She fears him, and will always ask
  What fated her to choose him;
She meets in his engaging mask
  All reasons to refuse him;
But what she meets and what she fears
Are less than are the downward years,
Drawn slowly to the foamless weirs
  Of age, were she to lose him.

Between a blurred sagacity
  That once had power to sound him,
And Love, that will not let him be
  The Judas that she found him,
Her pride assuages her almost,
As if it were alone the cost.—
He sees that he will not be lost,
  And waits and looks around him.

A sense of ocean and old trees
  Envelops and allures him;
Tradition, touching all he sees,
  Beguiles and reassures him;
And all her doubts of what he says
Are dimmed with what she knows of days—
Till even prejudice delays
  And fades, and she secures him.

The falling leaf inaugurates
  The reign of her confusion;
The pounding wave reverberates
  The dirge of her illusion;
And home, where passion lived and died,
Becomes a place where she can hide,
While all the town and harbor side
  Vibrate with her seclusion.

We tell you, tapping on our brows,
  The story as it should be,—
As if the story of a house
  Were told, or ever could be;
We'll have no kindly veil between
Her visions and those we have seen,—
As if we guessed what hers have been,
  Or what they are or would be.

Meanwhile we do no harm; for they
  That with a god have striven,
Not hearing much of what we say,
  Take what the god has given;
Though like waves breaking it may be,
Or like a changed familiar tree,
Or like a stairway to the sea
  Where down the blind are driven.

Luke Havergal

Go to the western gate, Luke Havergal,
There where the vines cling crimson on the wall,
And in the twilight wait for what will come.
The leaves will whisper there of her, and some,
Like flying words, will strike you as they fall;
But go, and if you listen she will call.
Go to the western gate, Luke Havergal—
Luke Havergal.

No, there is not a dawn in eastern skies
To rift the fiery night that's in your eyes;
But there, where western glooms are gathering,
The dark will end the dark, if anything:
God slays Himself with every leaf that flies,
And hell is more than half of paradise.
No, there is not a dawn in eastern skies—
In eastern skies.

Out of a grave I come to tell you this,
Out of a grave I come to quench the kiss
That flames upon your forehead with a glow
That blinds you to the way that you must go.
Yes, there is yet one way to where she is,
Bitter, but one that faith may never miss.
Out of a grave I come to tell you this—
To tell you this.

There is the western gate, Luke Havergal,
There are the crimson leaves upon the wall.
Go, for the winds are tearing them away,—
Nor think to riddle the dead words they say,
Nor any more to feel them as they fall;
But go, and if you trust her she will call.
There is the western gate, Luke Havergal—
Luke Havergal.

The Clerks

I did not think that I should find them there
When I came back again; but there they stood,
As in the days they dreamed of when young blood
Was in their cheeks and women called them fair.
Be sure, they met me with an ancient air,—
And yes, there was a shop-worn brotherhood

About them; but the men were just as good,
And just as human as they ever were.

And you that ache so much to be sublime,
And you that feed yourselves with your descent,
What comes of all your visions and your fears?
Poets and kings are but the clerks of Time,
Tiering the same dull webs of discontent,
Clipping the same sad alnage of the years.

For a Dead Lady

No more with overflowing light
Shall fill the eyes that now are faded,
Nor shall another's fringe with night
Their woman-hidden world as they did.
No more shall quiver down the days
The flowing wonder of her ways,
Whereof no language may requite
The shifting and the many-shaded.

The grace, divine, definitive,
Clings only as a faint forestalling;
The laugh that love could not forgive
Is hushed, and answers to no calling;
The forehead and the little ears
Have gone where Saturn keeps the years;
The breast where roses could not live
Has done with rising and with falling.

The beauty, shattered by the laws
That have creation in their keeping,
No longer trembles at applause,
Or over children that are sleeping;
And we who delve in beauty's lore
Know all that we have known before
Of what inexorable cause
Makes Time so vicious in his reaping.

The Dark Hills

Dark hills at evening in the west,
Where sunset hovers like a sound
Of golden horns that sang to rest
Old bones of warriors under ground,
Far now from all the bannered ways

Where flash the legions of the sun,
You fade—as if the last of days
Were fading, and all wars were done.

Mr. Flood's Party

Old Eben Flood, climbing alone one night
Over the hill between the town below
And the forsaken upland hermitage
That held as much as he should ever know
On earth again of home, paused warily.
The road was his with not a native near;
And Eben, having leisure, said aloud,
For no man else in Tilbury Town to hear:

"Well, Mr. Flood, we have the harvest moon
Again, and we may not have many more;
The bird is on the wing, the poet says,
And you and I have said it here before.
Drink to the bird." He raised up to the light
The jug that he had gone so far to fill,
And answered huskily: "Well, Mr. Flood,
Since you propose it, I believe I will."

Alone, as if enduring to the end
A valiant armor of scarred hopes outworn,
He stood there in the middle of the road
Like Roland's ghost winding a silent horn.
Below him, in the town among the trees,
Where friends of other days had honored him,
A phantom salutation of the dead
Rang thinly till old Eben's eyes were dim.

Then, as a mother lays her sleeping child
Down tenderly, fearing it may awake,
He set the jug down slowly at his feet
With trembling care, knowing that most things break;
And only when assured that on firm earth
It stood, as the uncertain lives of men
Assuredly did not, he paced away,
And with his hand extended paused again:

"Well, Mr. Flood, we have not met like this
In a long time; and many a change has come
To both of us, I fear, since last it was
We had a drop together. Welcome home!"

Convivially returning with himself,
Again he raised the jug up to the light;
And with an acquiescent quaver said:
"Well, Mr. Flood, if you insist, I might.

"Only a very little, Mr. Flood—
For auld lang syne. No more, sir; that will do."
So, for the time, apparently it did,
And Eben evidently thought so too;
For soon amid the silver loneliness
Of night he lifted up his voice and sang,
Secure, with only two moons listening,
Until the whole harmonious landscape rang—

"For auld lang syne." The weary throat gave out,
The last word wavered, and the song was done.
He raised again the jug regretfully
And shook his head, and was again alone.
There was not much that was ahead of him,
And there was nothing in the town below—
Where strangers would have shut the many doors
That many friends had opened long ago.

Lost Anchors

Like a dry fish flung inland far from shore,
There lived a sailor, warped and ocean-browned,
Who told of an old vessel, harbor-drowned
And out of mind a century before,
Where divers, on descending to explore
A legend that had lived its way around
The world of ships, in the dark hulk had found
Anchors, which had been seized and seen no more.

Improving a dry leisure to invest
Their misadventure with a manifest
Analogy that he may read who runs,
The sailor made it old as ocean grass—
Telling of much that once had come to pass
With him, whose mother should have had no sons.

Many Are Called

The Lord Apollo, who has never died,
Still holds alone his immemorial reign,
Supreme in an impregnable domain

That with his magic he has fortified;
And though melodious multitudes have tried
In ecstasy, in anguish, and in vain,
With invocation sacred and profane
To lure him, even the loudest are outside.

Only at unconjectured intervals,
By will of him on whom no man may gaze,
By word of him whose law no man has read,
A questing light may rift the sullen walls,
To cling where mostly its infrequent rays
Fall golden on the patience of the dead.

The Sheaves

Where long the shadows of the wind had rolled,
Green wheat was yielding to the change assigned;
And as by some vast magic undivined
The world was turning slowly into gold.
Like nothing that was ever bought or sold
It waited there, the body and the mind;
And with a mighty meaning of a kind
That tells the more the more it is not told.

So in a land where all days are not fair,
Fair days went on till on another day
A thousand golden sheaves were lying there,
Shining and still, but not for long to stay—
As if a thousand girls with golden hair
Might rise from where they slept and go away.

MARSDEN HARTLEY
1877–1943

Although his fame rests on his painting, Marsden Hartley also produced noteworthy poetry. Hartley was born in Lewiston and spent his boyhood in Maine. At the age of fifteen he moved to Cleveland, where he began his studies in art. He received further training in Paris and Berlin, and lived in such diverse areas as New Mexico, Nova Scotia, and Bermuda. In the last years of his life he divided his time between New York City and the coast of Maine. At his death he left three privately printed slender volumes of poetry (*Twenty-five Poems*, 1922; *Androscoggin,* 1940; and *Sea Burial,* 1941) and over five hundred poems in manuscript; *Selected Poems of Marsden Hartley* (1945) was drawn from all of these sources. His verse is technically sophisticated and deals with many of the same subjects that appear in his paintings—powerful landscapes of his native state, the sea, contemporary and historical individuals, and aesthetic and metaphysical concerns.

Islands in Penobscot Bay

Here they sit
in the manner of black notes
upon a metal sheet of music—
sol-fa-mi-re-do—
timed, tempered, toned,
submerged with indigenous sharps.

How often have we seen
such islands—even in
the faces of men and women we know—
as dark winged ducks at evening
who, for no reason at all, become
restless at the edges of their
evening,
as if the downfall of the sun
being perfect
impelled another area for sleep.

Plain birds racing from almost
loquacious skies,
among those smileless branches
of the pine, the fir, the spruce,
the hemlock,
emitting some casual diatonic array,
some casual melody on a theme
that evening comprehends—
tapering off time to silences
empirical.

People crawl into these bird
sanctuaries in the early beaming
of summer,
like beavers into their dams, thinking
themselves immune from secular invasion.
They say that every now and then a
moose appears from the main,
crossing the waters of the bay,
a bay that is just more distant waters.
Perhaps they like the sting of the salt
upon the shins and nostrils—
for even animals covet—as we—
interstitial release—
as we—from all but sinister
functioning.

Islands say, when they are alone
(do they take their speech from us?)
"we are too much like ourselves,
rivers of vision flow by our cliffs and marshes,
now and then a wing dropping a feather,
the loon loving the teardrop of a lake
seen upon cosmic lids.
North birds go to sleep among the
swirling lilies,
then swing out at flush of sudden morning,
and we are left alone,
so like—ourselves."

"An island is something to be discouraged"—
said an aged one—
"it wants itself and hates to give it up"—
sol-fa-mi-re-do
besieged with indigenous sharps.

Kennebec

Austere to the prospect
and the mighty millimeters
of entoned existence
enervating the listless afternoon.

The bevy of fluffed ornithoptera
enveloping the silk of the milkweed
that flutters like a rended veil at
the wedding of some postponed interrogation;
one silken epitome mounting up the hill at
go-down of sun as if impaled upon a lance
of sudden-gusted air,
the spirit entombed therefore
among curves of encumbered silence.

A sail would have relieved the drifting
of the wave
but there was no sail or nothing
coming over from Phippsburg
but a diagonally uncalled for wind;
the houses parting company on this
shore—separating with the idea, patricianly:
"we have had enough of it ourselves
now you take it and see what you can do
with it"; laughing in their very faces
through the twelve bronze gates of the calendar,
the wind, the planets exchanging ochreous sneers
clandestinely.

Fisherman's Last Supper

For wine, they drank the ocean—
for bread, they ate their own despairs;
counsel from the moon was theirs
For the foolish contention.

Murder is not a pretty thing
yet seas do raucous everything
to make it pretty—
for the foolish or the brave,
a way seas have.

He Too Wore a Butterfly

He wore a butterfly upon his flanks,
upsetting the woman and the ship in their angles,

and down his midrib the image of Christ, the feet
and the nails, touching his navel.
He wore a butterfly upon his shoulder blade and
one above his knee, as if—like the Indian in the
race, whose thighs are brushed with eagle feathers to
give him speed in the run.
He wore a butterfly upon his flanks as though he
felt the fear of being musclebound,
or, saying to himself—"I must have the breath of
spring upon my beam"—that smiling morning of a man;
and as if the sea had crowded all its waves
within his eyes, making him think of numberless
casual afternoons, the lashes curling up to let the
floods of evening in,
staving off for later years the pale textures of
immitigable distance.

Perusing Mallarmé in Maine

Mallarmé,
with this equestrian cliff clutching
at sky-reins hyper-fervently
protecting ponderously the fragrant
width of words,
wind pounding sea-froth into frozen
curds
against the curves of sleek, world-without-
end wandering birds,
words fragile, if you will, but as most
fragile things, profound,
yet following in grooves the still
insensate ground,
thought leaping after fleet anxieties
of subtle sense,
pursuing soft compensatory ways
though they but seem as driftwood,
heart-stunned hordes.

"Yielding the initiative to the words."
Sound recompense with breath of poetry
for clue,
desperate the sheen of truth craving
to be true
climbs precipice of pride but then,
like shattered plunder among men,
to fall and downwardly disperse

and take a seawashed, throat-filled vow
between a then, and now.

How true a poet is,
contrives a sheaf of centuries;
a branch will break, a stone will roll
away,
and then the poet builds his day.

WILBERT SNOW
1884–1977

The son of a member of the Coast Guard, (Charles) Wilbert Snow was born on White Head Island, St. George, Maine. The large family lived on the island until Snow was seven and then moved to Spruce Head Village. Snow received his A.B. from Bowdoin and his A.M. from Columbia; he taught at numerous colleges and universities throughout the country, including one year at Bowdoin. In 1921 Snow joined the faculty of Wesleyan University and remained there for over thirty years. Active in politics, he served as Connecticut's lieutenant-governor and governor from 1945–47. As the titles of his works indicate, Snow's poetry centers on Maine's coastal region: *Maine Coast* (1923), *The Inner Harbor* (1926), *Down East* (1932), *Selected Poems* (1936), *Before the Wind* (1938), *Maine Tides* (1940), *Sonnets to Steve, and Other Poems* (1957), *Spruce Head* (1958), and *The Collected Poems of Wilbert Snow* (1963 and 1973). Many of his poems deal with homely themes, and he captures the simplicity and integrity of coastal life with force in both his long stories in verse and his brief lyrics.

The Paving Quarry

Our pathway led through birches shoulder-high;
'Twas autumn, and the little yellow leaves,
So slender were their stems, seemed poised in air,
And gaily did they flutter in the wind.
The huckleberry leaves shone brilliant red,
And bayberry scattered incense on our way,
As now we walked through plots of velvet moss,
And now on granite ledges gray and hard.
Abruptly came our journey to a stop,
And there in ragged grayness lay the quarry.

"This pavin' motion," my companion said,
"Was goin' to make me rich, and made me poor.
'Twas in the *'eighties* I began work here,
When all great cities paved their streets with blocks.
A nickel apiece they were, and I could reel

Two hundred blocks or more each blessed day.
The reelin' wa'n't much like the reelin' now:
'Most anything would do. Along this hump
Were fifty motions clickin' every day.
Beside that barrel there filled up with chips
I reeled, the happiest hours of my life,
I wouldn't say how many thousand blocks,
While Fred, my butty, plug-drilled and broke stone.
I somehow liked the music of the sound,
The click-clack-clickin' of a hundred drills
From all these motions in among the trees.
How different now, when all you ever hear
Is chickadees, or crickets, or the frogs!
I sometimes think they liked the noises, too,
Of hammers clickin', and the rattlin' wheels
Of wagons, or the creakin' of the hames
In horses' collars on these rocky roads.
For we were prosp'rous then; at half-past four
'Most any night but Friday you could smell
Beefsteak a-fryin' anywhere in town,
And hear the snap and sizzle in the spider.
(We can't afford to eat beefsteak today.)
'Twas fun at night to see the youngsters bolt
To meet their daddies, grab the dinner pail,
And find a cookie or a piece of cake
Left there like toll-bait to be sure they came.
'Twas fun just after supper to drop 'round
To Em'ry's store, and hear the boys run on.
They'd smoke, and fight John L.'s big mills again,
With Paddy Ryan, Mitchell, Jake Kilrain—
They never loved another like John L.
And sometimes, when the bottle went around,
The boys would sing. I wish you could'a'heard
Mike Flemin' sing 'The Wind that Blew Across
The Wild Moor'; somethin' in his Irish voice
Would make you think o' lonely winds at night,
And cryin' children strayin' on the moor.
And then on Saturdays we'd have a dance,
And start it with a breakdown in the store.
I always liked the breakdown best; the boys
Were keyed just right, the jew's-harp twanged and twanged,
The harmonica began with 'Home Sweet Home,'
And Cowin', wounded at Bull Run, would clog,
And dance the 'buck and wing' in perfect time.
Then all would leave to join the 'march and circle'
Except the old men who would set and smoke.

Ah, them were jolly days; I never thought
They'd leave us as they did; the price went down,
And cities paved with asphalt room o'blocks;
The young folks moved away, but we were old,
Too old to think of other towns as home—
And there we were without a place to farm,
Who might'a'had ten acres turned to field.
Perhaps it's just as well. A hundred hens,
A little garden truck, a chance to fish,
And time to talk of pranks we did as boys—
One way of life's as good's another, I guess,
If we just take it right—that's all that counts."

He gazed along the west; the golden sun
Was streaming through a clump of tall spruce trees.
The dead, low limbs, transfigured in the light,
Had brought the sunset near; the background stood
In lemon-colored glory; back we turned
Without a word, and down a birch-fringed path
We found the road that led our footsteps home.

Harbor

Apart from pull and haul of modern aims,
Beyond all other spots on earth I know,
This harbor in the early morning glow
Of July sunlight presses me with claims
No city street can match: the boats that bask
At anchor in the bight, the lobster car
Bleached out upon the sand, the smell of tar
The sun tries out of herring nets, the flask
As toggle on a lobster pot not far
From ledges where the quiet wash of waves
Incessantly beats out its varying tone;
And out across the mussel-studded bar
The sound of sea gulls reaching umber caves
Mingles its music with the ocean's own.

Thelma Maloney

She closed the tale of *Dora Thorne* to dream
Of balls where counts and dukes in velvet capes
And glittering swords swept broad-brimmed hats across
Their breasts for tribute to her comeliness,
Fencing with one another to secure
Her smile in one brief waltz across a hall
Made beautiful by ladies long since dead.

With *Ishmael* she rode to hounds and viewed
The charm of English country lanes; her own
Peculiar charm impelling men to stay
Behind and flatter her in courtly speech
Till envious dames acknowledged her as queen.

The rubber boots of Edgar clomping in
Made thunder for these lightning words, "My God,
Ain't you begun to get my dinner yet?"

She saw white yachts go up the bay in June
With brassworks luminous as minted gold,
Beneath whose awnings stylish ladies sat,
And on whose deck a pilot stood alert
In navy blue and white, binoculars
Each moment at his eyes—the bay as calm
As any mill pond resting in the hills,
With fragrance far more pungent, and a light
More dazzling than the glow of inland waters,
Both light and fragrance tempting one to dream
As she dreamed every sunny morning through,
Till ragged unwiped Johnny tugged her skirt
Whining, "I want a piece of b'e'd and butta."

When forty winters had depressed her lips,
Turning their blood-red warmth to parching white,
She built her dreams around the man who wore
The seamless robe and dared to speak of lilies.
The robe, clean teeth, and tones of him who came
To be their minister had set her mind
On loftier things; she loved to feel him near,
Drink from his youth the waters of a stream
That welled within herself and overflowed
Into a bank-erasing summer flood.
She told him all the troubles of her soul,
And strove to make his village church a place
Of warmth and cleanliness, acquiring zeal
To press religious duties on her mate,
At which he badgered her, swearing, "I'll see
Myself in hell before I humor you,
Or go to hear that pindlin' Christer preach."

Her last long illness came on suddenly,
And in its train delirium seized her mind
And held it to the end; she lived again
Her girlhood dreams, with music, castle walls,

White pleasure yachts against the forenoon's blue,
And glad church bells on Easter Sunday morning;
She felt the patient soul of Nazareth
Come close beside her bed and hold her hand,
With pressure like the preacher's soft white palm,
Guiding her through the low-tide caves of death;
And at the last she rallied for an hour
And heard two daughters snarling on the stairs,
Like midnight cats, disputing which should wear
The gown put by to serve her in the grave.

Visitor

What I beheld last night how can you know
Who move about among material things?
The ghostly presence of a favoring soul,
Perhaps some gracious lady who abode
Inside these old colonial walls returned.
The white lace on the collar and the sleeves
Of her black gown of watered silk that made
No rustle when she walked; the dignified
Patrician outline of her face against
White paneling where maple boughs and elms
Cast shadows in the moonlight, made her seem
As much at home among us as the trees.
Under the pressure of her gaze I woke,
Whereat she turned away and stood awhile
Beside my first-born's crib, and gently smiled
When he laughed out at something in his dreams.
Then farther off she glided till she came
To baby's cot, and stood there still and long;
Her left hand stretched as if in benediction
Over his soft white limbs and rosy face.
The memory of my mother moving round
At night to see if her large brood were safe,
Moving around in darkness quietly—
Relieved what might have been a midnight fear
And led me into fellowship with her
Who peered through deep recesses of the night.

A Maine Winter's Night

The earth, in frozen drapery of snow,
On which the great stars delicately light,
Is quiet as the Milky Way whose bright
Uneven pennons match Orion's glow;
The brooklets trickling on their wintry flow

In muted monotone, hurry their flight
Close by the ocean whose patrols at night
Boom deep with dark December's undertow.

O winter night on cold Penobscot Bay,
Your crystal stars through crystal air appear
Transfigured like the tall brown cliffs that stand
By waiting groves of spruce to watch the play
Of shadows on dark waters hovering near,
Bringing full nets of beauty to the land.

There Is an Hour at Evening

There is an hour at evening on the sea
When the white yacht of day is not yet gone,
And the black barge of night is coming on,
That never fails to leave its wake in me:
The mingled blacks and grays that cannot free
Their strands to one clear pattern; the weird chill
Of nightfall with its shuddering breeze; the spill
Of shadows on the bay's periphery—
These awe me standing on a seaside bank;
But on a sloop at anchor as she rides
Silently in the harbor, a thin plank
The only sheath between me and the tides,
I feel Eternity has snubbed the barque
Of Time caught hurrying onward toward the dark.

After a Storm

After a storm brown ledges glow
Like northern stars on Arctic snow;
The waves pound in with fuller thump
Although the calm has smoothed each lump
On the grape-green surface, leaving beneath
Strong undertow with shattering teeth.
The trees in moss more pensive stand,
As if they wondered what gaunt hand
Had thrust itself through last night's air,
Uprooting their brothers, and seeking to tear
From their own firm trunks each parrying limb,
Now clean as an athlete's after a swim.
The clouds are gone that trailed buff wings
Down close to the boughs where the damp still clings
And the goblet of sky holds many a white
Ebullient cloud shot through with light.
The chickadees gather in groves of fir

To carol their joy that the rage and stir
Of the night before have given place
To the turquoise sky and mirrored face
Of cove and harbor where tossed-up shells,
Brown kelp, and eelgrass' lusty smells
Conspire to make complete amends
In a moving peace as the great storm ends.

EDNA ST. VINCENT MILLAY
1892–1950

Born in Rockland and raised in Camden, Vincent (as she was called by her family) made her literary debut in 1912 by reading her poem "Renascence" at a hotel party. Millay left Camden to attend Vassar and after her graduation settled in Greenwich Village, where she pursued a bohemian lifestyle and acted with the Provincetown Players. She published several books of verse in rapid succession: *Renascence* (1917), *A Few Figs from Thistles* (1920), *Second April* (1921), and *Ballad of the Harp-Weaver* (1923), which won the Pulitzer Prize. She married a businessman in 1923; the pair lived on a farmstead in the Berkshires of New York and often spent summer vacations on their other property, Ragged Island in Casco bay. During the thirties her works touched more frequently on social and economic problems, and her poetry was less well received. Her critics also felt that she was too bound by the traditions of the Elizabethans, Metaphysicals, and Romantics. At her best, however, Millay displays great lyrical talent and technical ability in dealing with the recurring themes of love, youth, and death.

Renascence

All I could see from where I stood
Was three long mountains and a wood;
I turned and looked another way,
And saw three islands in a bay.
So with my eyes I traced the line
Of the horizon, thin and fine,
Straight around till I was come
Back to where I'd started from;
And all I saw from where I stood
Was three long mountains and a wood.

Over these things I could not see:
These were the things that bounded me.
And I could touch them with my hand,
Almost, I thought, from where I stand!
And all at once things seemed so small
My breath came short, and scarce at all.

But, sure, the sky is big, I said:
Miles and miles above my head.
So here upon my back I'll lie
And look my fill into the sky.
And so I looked, and after all,
The sky was not so very tall.
The sky, I said, must somewhere stop . . .
And—sure enough!—I see the top!
The sky, I thought, is not so grand;
I 'most could touch it with my hand!
And reaching up my hand to try,
I screamed, to feel it touch the sky.

I screamed, and—lo!—Infinity
Came down and settled over me;
Forced back my scream into my chest;
Bent back my arm upon my breast;
And, pressing of the Undefined
The definition on my mind,
Held up before my eyes a glass
Through which my shrinking sight did pass
Until it seemed I must behold
Immensity made manifold;
Whispered to me a word whose sound
Deafened the air for worlds around,
And brought unmuffled to my ears
The gossiping of friendly spheres,
The creaking of the tented sky,
The ticking of Eternity.

I saw and heard, and knew at last
The How and Why of all things, past,
And present, and forevermore.
The Universe, cleft to the core,
Lay open to my probing sense,
That, sickening, I would fain pluck thence
But could not,—nay! but needs must suck
At the great wound, and could not pluck
My lips away till I had drawn
All venom out.—Ah, fearful pawn:
For my omniscience paid I toll
In infinite remorse of soul.

All sin was of my sinning, all
Atoning mine, and mine the gall
Of all regret. Mine was the weight

Of every brooded wrong, the hate
That stood behind each envious thrust,
Mine every greed, mine every lust.

And all the while, for every grief,
Each suffering, I craved relief
With individual desire;
Craved all in vain! And felt fierce fire
About a thousand people crawl;
Perished with each,—then mourned for all!

A man was starving in Capri;
He moved his eyes and looked at me;
I felt his gaze, I heard his moan,
And knew his hunger as my own.
I saw at sea a great fog bank
Between two ships that struck and sank;
A thousand screams the heavens smote;
And every scream tore through my throat.

No hurt I did not feel, no death
That was not mine; mine each last breath
That, crying, met an answering cry
From the compassion that was I.
All suffering mine, and mine its rod;
Mine, pity like the pity of God.

Ah, awful weight! Infinity
Pressed down upon the finite Me!
My anguished spirit, like a bird,
Beating against my lips I heard;
Yet lay the weight so close about
There was no room for it without.
And so beneath the weight lay I
And suffered death, but could not die.

Long had I lain thus, craving death,
When quietly the earth beneath
Gave way, and inch by inch, so great
At last had grown the crushing weight,
Into the earth I sank till I
Full six feet under ground did lie,
And sank no more,—there is no weight
Can follow here, however great.
From off my breast I felt it roll,
And as it went my tortured soul

Burst forth and fled in such a gust
That all about me swirled the dust.

Deep in the earth I rested now.
Cool is its hand upon the brow
And soft its breast beneath the head
Of one who is so gladly dead.
And all at once, and over all
The pitying rain began to fall;
I lay and heard each pattering hoof
Upon my lowly, thatchèd roof,
And seemed to love the sound far more
Than ever I had done before.
For rain it hath a friendly sound
To one who's six feet under ground;
And scarce the friendly voice or face,
A grave is such a quiet place.

The rain, I said, is kind to come
And speak to me in my new home.
I would I were alive again
To kiss the fingers of the rain,
To drink into my eyes the shine
Of every slanting silver line,
To catch the freshened, fragrant breeze
From drenched and dripping apple-trees.
For soon the shower will be done,
And then the broad face of the sun
Will laugh above the rain-soaked earth
Until the world with answering mirth
Shakes joyously, and each round drop
Rolls, twinkling, from its grass-blade top.

How can I bear it, buried here,
While overhead the sky grows clear
And blue again after the storm?
O, multi-coloured, multi-form,
Belovèd beauty over me,
That I shall never, never see
Again! Spring-silver, autumn-gold,
That I shall never more behold!—
Sleeping your myriad magics through,
Close-sepulchred away from you!
O God, I cried, give me new birth,
And put me back upon the earth!
Upset each cloud's gigantic gourd

And let the heavy rain, down-poured
In one big torrent, set me free,
Washing my grave away from me!

I ceased; and through the breathless hush
That answered me, the far-off rush
Of herald wings came whispering
Like music down the vibrant string
Of my ascending prayer, and—crash!
Before the wild wind's whistling lash
The startled storm-clouds reared on high
And plunged in terror down the sky!
And the big rain in one black wave
Fell from the sky and struck my grave.

I know not how such things can be;
I only know there came to me
A fragrance such as never clings
To aught save happy living things;
A sound as of some joyous elf
Singing sweet songs to please himself,
And, through and over everything,
A sense of glad awakening.
The grass, a-tiptoe at my ear,
Whispering to me I could hear;
I felt the rain's cool finger-tips,
Brushed tenderly across my lips,
Laid gently on my sealèd sight,
And all at once the heavy night
Fell from my eyes and I could see!—
A drenched and dripping apple-tree,
A last long line of silver rain,
A sky grown clear and blue again.
And as I looked a quickening gust
Of wind blew up to me and thrust
Into my face a miracle
Of orchard-breath, and with the smell,—
I know not how such things can be!—
I breathed my soul back into me.

Ah! Up then from the ground sprang I
And hailed the earth with such a cry
As is not heard save from a man
Who has been dead, and lives again.
About the trees my arms I wound;
Like one gone mad I hugged the ground;

I raised my quivering arms on high;
I laughed and laughed into the sky;
Till at my throat a strangling sob
Caught fiercely, and a great heart-throb
Sent instant tears into my eyes:
O God, I cried, no dark disguise
Can e'er hereafter hide from me
Thy radiant identity!
Thou canst not move across the grass
But my quick eyes will see Thee pass,
Nor speak, however silently,
But my hushed voice will answer Thee.
I know the path that tells Thy way
Through the cool eve of every day;
God, I can push the grass apart
And lay my finger on Thy heart!

The world stands out on either side
No wider than the heart is wide;
Above the world is stretched the sky,—
No higher than the soul is high.
The heart can push the sea and land
Farther away on either hand;
The soul can split the sky in two,
And let the face of God shine through.
But East and West will pinch the heart
That can not keep them pushed apart;
And he whose soul is flat—the sky
Will cave in on him by and by.

Passer Mortuus Est

Death devours all lovely things:
  Lesbia with her sparrow
Shares the darkness,—presently
  Every bed is narrow.

Unremembered as old rain
  Dries the sheer libation;
And the little petulant hand
  Is an annotation.

After all, my erstwhile dear,
  My no longer cherished,
Need we say it was not love,
  Just because it perished?

["And you as well must die, belovèd dust . . ."]

And you as well must die, belovèd dust,
And all your beauty stand you in no stead;
This flawless, vital hand, this perfect head,
This body of flame and steel, before the gust
Of Death, or under his autumnal frost,
Shall be as any leaf, be no less dead
Than the first leaf that fell,—this wonder fled,
Altered, estranged, disintegrated, lost.
Nor shall my love avail you in your hour.
In spite of all my love, you will arise
Upon that day and wander down the air
Obscurely as the unattended flower,
It mattering not how beautiful you were,
Or how belovèd above all else that dies.

["Pity me not because the light of day . . ."]

Pity me not because the light of day
At close of day no longer walks the sky;
Pity me not for beauties passed away
From field and thicket as the year goes by;
Pity me not the waning of the moon,
Nor that the ebbing tide goes out to sea,
Nor that a man's desire is hushed so soon,
And you no longer look with love on me.
This have I known always: Love is no more
Than the wide blossom which the wind assails,
Than the great tide that treads the shifting shore,
Strewing fresh wreckage gathered in the gales:
Pity me that the heart is slow to learn
What the swift mind beholds at every turn.

ROBERT P. TRISTRAM COFFIN
1892–1955

Robert P(eter). Tristram Coffin was born in Brunswick and raised on a saltwater farm. After graduating from Bowdoin, Coffin received an M.A. from Princeton and was a Rhodes Scholar at Oxford. Coffin taught at Wells College for thirteen years and then returned to Bowdoin to become Pierce Professor of English. A prolific writer, Coffin's output included verse, essays, novels, biographies, lectures, histories, and texts. His sixth book of verse, *Strange Holiness* (1935), received the Pulitzer Prize, and he built up interest in his poems with a heavy schedule of lecture-readings throughout the country. Coffin presents detailed observations of nature and local scenes in his works, and he celebrates the lives of the people who inhabit Maine's coastal farms. His enthusiasm can result in exaggeration and overstatement, but his love for his native state is always apparent.

Winter-Piece

Firelight on stemmed glasses,
  Firelight on the walls,
Words tossed lightly back and forth
  Like thin, crystal balls.

Sucking pigs are kneeling
  With lemons in the mouth,
Emerald grapes and amber
  Plumped with the South.

In comes the king of ganders,
  Lord of all gray geese,
The fork is in his wishbone,
  He lies at utter peace.

The windows are a garden
  Full of jewelled ferns,
A hundred years of sunlight
  Where the red oak burns.

The marrowbones are broken,
  The hounds sleep nose on tail,
The world's as wide's a candle shines,
  The panes are drummed with hail.

Age's as good as youth is,
  And both sit knee to knee,
Minds turned dust from opened books
  Tell us what to see.

Snow upon the sashes,
  Snow on the tablespread,
Nuts and the bronze Baldwins,
  And a thousand miles to bed!

The Woodland Orchard

These apple trees were lost for good
When the little house which stood
Nearby to keep them safe and sound
Sank moldering into the ground
And the children went away.
The waiting forest won the day,
And came and took the orphaned trees
Upon its dark and kindly knees.

The sun comes down more golden here
Than it comes ever in the clear;
The grass is greener for the wall
Of the forest round it all,
There are no feet to tramp it down,
Except the little ones in brown
Beneath a deer that comes to stand
And wonder at this tame, sweet land.

You might say this was a spot
Where tame and wild for once forgot
Their old hate; the partridge feeds
On fruit sprung of men's tended seeds
And pecks the apples touched by frost.
But these are trees that have been lost;
Here one draws a careful breath,
This loveliness is so like death.

A Mess of Clams

The fields are high with all the Winter's snows,
But somewhere there is cawing and glad crows,
And ice upon bare birches feels the sun
And twinkles and is starting in to run.
An old, old man, with no tooth in his head,
Is walking fast, and Spring is in his tread
As he wades the snowdrifts of his farm,
His clam-hoe and clam-basket on his arm.
Down below him, all his bay is white,
But out towards sea the dark place overnight
Has widened, and blue waves are twinkling clear
Above the first and best clams of the year.

The March sun burns upon the man's bent bones,
His wife is lying where the slanting stones
Are hidden by the Winter. All his sons
Are begotten and have begot new ones.
He is alone, but he can go and bring
His mess of clams home in his eightieth Spring
As he could in his twentieth one, and he
Can pick his dinner up out of the sea
Just as well as any man alive
And think of things like young men fit to wive,
His head is high, and handsome as a ram's,
And life is good and tastes of sweet young clams.

ELIZABETH JANE COATSWORTH
1893–

Born in Buffalo, N.Y., and educated at Vassar and Columbia, Elizabeth Jane Coatsworth spent much of her early life traveling throughout the world. She married the author Henry Beston, and the couple ultimately chose "Chimney Farm" in Nobleboro, Maine, as their residence. Coatsworth's productive writing career includes numerous children's books, essays, novels (*Here I Stand,* 1938), and poems (*Fox Footprints,* 1923; *Compass Rose,* 1929; *Country Poems,* 1942; *Poems,* 1957; *Down Half the World,* 1968). Her quiet voice lends itself well to the sensitive recording of Maine coastal and farming scenes.

The Ledge in the Forest

Hollow and haunting comes the wood-wind call
Of thrushes from the darkness of the woods,
Thrush answering thrush across the interval
Of silence slow and grave.
The sun beats down
Upon the great rock mirroring its heat
In granite fierceness, rising from the wave
Of the green forest. Here the mica shines,
Here pass the butterflies. Here the wind dies
Lost in the fragrant caverns of the pines.
Hither some Indian woman may have brought
Berries in baskets of birchbark to dry
Between the heat of rock and burning sky,
And sat, as now I sit, herself in shade
And listened to the thrushes, and perhaps thought
Quietly without sorrow, "As the smoke
Rises from wigwams, and is gone again
Upon the wind, so pass the lives of men,
A something and then nothing."
She may have sat as now I sit,
And leaned against a tree,
While somewhere thrushes called in dark tranquillity.

November Farmyard

Now by the farmhouse door the first snow falls
Upon the last chrysanthemum, the phlox
Stands white above its whitening leaves, the cat
Walks with a hesitant step, and the tall cocks
Stand angry-eyed, then like brass trumpets, sound
Across the silent snow, that turns the trees
To branching coral growing in a world
More soft and pale and secret than the seas.
The farmer's steps from shed-door to barn-door
Seem patterns laid on a pearl-powdered floor.

The Swan

Hawks stir the blood like fiercely ringing bells
or far-off bugles;
even on their perches
they are all latent fury and sheathed power;
and peacocks trail the glory of the world.
But calm, white calm, was born into a swan
to float forever upon moon-smoothed waters
cool placid breast against cool mirrored breast,
and wings curved like great petals
and long throat
bent dreamingly
to listen to the ripple
that widens slowly in a tranquil arrow
reaching the shores, and lisping on the sands.

LOUISE BOGAN
1897–1970

The grand-daughter of a Portland sea-captain, Louise Bogan was born in Livermore Falls and attended Mount St. Mary's Academy, Boston Girls' Latin School, and Boston University. She married in 1916 and was left a widow with a daughter four years later; her second marriage to the poet Raymond Holden ended in divorce. Starting in 1931 she served as poetry editor for the *New Yorker* and also contributed literary criticism to *Nation, Poetry,* and *Atlantic Monthly.* In the course of her career Bogan received critical acclaim and numerous prizes for her poetry, which includes *Body of This Death* (1923), *Dark Summer* (1929), *The Sleeping Fury* (1937), *Poems and New Poems* (1941), *Collected Poems, 1923–1953* (1954), and *The Blue Estuaries: Poems, 1923–1968* (1968). Working in the metaphysical tradition, Bogan produced lyrical poetry that is both intensely personal and highly controlled. Her language is compressed, her lines uncluttered, and her images precise. The New England landscape held both delight and terror for her, and many of her poems contain elements of this tension.

Medusa

I had come to the house, in a cave of trees,
Facing a sheer sky.
Everything moved,—a bell hung ready to strike,
Sun and reflection wheeled by.

When the bare eyes were before me
And the hissing hair,
Held up at a window, seen through a door.
The stiff bald eyes, the serpents on the forehead
Formed in the air.

This is a dead scene forever now.
Nothing will ever stir.
The end will never brighten it more than this,
Nor the rain blur.

The water will always fall, and will not fall,
And the tipped bell make no sound.
The grass will always be growing for hay
Deep on the ground.

And I shall stand here like a shadow
Under the great balanced day,
My eyes on the yellow dust, that was lifting in the wind,
And does not drift away.

Statue and Birds

Here, in the withered arbor, like the arrested wind,
Straight sides, carven knees,
Stands the statue, with hands flung out in alarm
Or remonstrances.

Over the lintel sway the woven bracts of the vine
In a pattern of angles.
The quill of the fountain falters, woods rake on the sky
Their brusque tangles.

The birds walk by slowly, circling the marble girl,
The golden quails,
The pheasants, closed up in their arrowy wings,
Dragging their sharp tails.

The inquietudes of the sap and of the blood are spent.
What is forsaken will rest.
But her heel is lifted,—she would flee,—the whistle of the birds
Fails on her breast.

Winter Swan

It is a hollow garden, under the cloud;
Beneath the heel a hollow earth is turned;
Within the mind the live blood shouts aloud;
Under the breast the willing blood is burned,
Shut with the fire passed and the fire returned.
But speak, you proud!
Where lies the leaf-caught world once thought abiding,
Now but a dry disarray and artifice?
Here, to the ripple cut by the cold, drifts this
Bird, the long throat bent back, and the eyes in hiding.

Division

Long days and changing weather
Put the shadow upon the door:
Up from the ground, the duplicate
Tree reflected in shadow;
Out from the whole, the single
Mirrored against the single.
The tree and the hour and the shadow
No longer mingle,
Fly free, that burned together.

Replica, turned to yourself
Upon thinnest color and air—
Woven in changeless leaves
The burden of the seen
Is clasped against the eye,
Though assailed and undone is the green
Upon the wall and the sky:
Time and the tree stand there.

The Cupola

A mirror hangs on the wall of the draughty cupola.
Within the depths of glass mix the oak and the beech leaf,
Once held to the boughs' shape, but now to the shape of the
  wind.

Someone has hung the mirror here for no reason,
In the shuttered room, an eye for the drifted leaves,
For the oak leaf, the beech, a handsbreadth of darkest reflection.

Someone has thought alike of the bough and the wind
And struck their shape to the wall. Each in its season
Spills negligent death throughout the abandoned chamber.

The Mark

Where should he seek, to go away
That shadow will not point him down?
The spear of dark in the strong day
Beyond the upright body thrown,
Marking no epoch but its own.

Loosed only when, at noon and night,
The body is the shadow's prison.

The pivot swings into the light;
The center left, the shadow risen
To range out into time's long treason.

Stand pinned to sight, while now, unbidden,
The apple loosens, not at call,
Falls to the field, and lies there hidden,—
Another and another fall
And lie there hidden, in spite of all

The diagram of whirling shade,
The visible, that thinks to spin
Forever webs that time has made
Though momently time wears them thin
And all at length are gathered in.

Old Countryside

Beyond the hour we counted rain that fell
On the slant shutter, all has come to proof.
The summer thunder, like a wooden bell,
Rang in the storm above the mansard roof,

And mirrors cast the cloudy day along
The attic floor; wind made the clapboards creak.
You braced against the wall to make it strong,
A shell against your cheek.

Long since, we pulled brown oak-leaves to the ground
In a winter of dry trees; we heard the cock
Shout its unplaceable cry, the axe's sound
Delay a moment after the axe's stroke.

Far back, we saw, in the stillest of the year,
The scrawled vine shudder, and the rose-branch show
Red to the thorns, and, sharp as sight can bear,
The thin hound's body arched against the snow.

To Be Sung on the Water

Beautiful, my delight,
Pass, as we pass the wave.
Pass, as the mottled night
Leaves what it cannot save,
Scattering dark and bright.

Beautiful, pass and be
Less than the guiltless shade
To which our vows were said;
Less than the sound of the oar
To which our vows were made,—
Less than the sound of its blade
Dipping the stream once more.

RICHARD EBERHART
1904–

Richard (Ghormley) Eberhart was born in Austin, Minn., and educated at Dartmouth, Cambridge, and Harvard. He was a tutor to the son of King Prajadhipok of Siam for a year and taught at St. Mark's school from 1933–41. During World War II he served as a naval aircraft gunnery instructor. After the war he began spending part of his summers in Maine on Cape Rosier, where he maintained a house named Undercliff and pursued his hobby of kite-flying. For six years he was an assistant manager for a business firm in Boston; he then returned to teaching at leading institutions throughout the country. Eberhart's first volume of poetry, *A Bravery of Earth,* appeared in 1930 and was followed by over twenty more, including *Collected Poems 1930–1960* (1960) and several plays. This prolific output has resulted in a certain unevenness, but the high quality of his best works has brought him such honors as the Bollingen Prize, the Pulitzer Prize, and membership in the National Institute of Arts and Letters. Considered a major lyric poet, Eberhart is especially known for his anti-war verse. Many of his poems deal with the mystery of death and are infused with intense religious and moral convictions.

For a Lamb

I saw on the slant hill a putrid lamb,
Propped with daisies. The sleep looked deep,
The face nudged in the green pillow
But the guts were out for crows to eat.

Where's the lamb? whose tender plaint
Said all for the mute breezes.
Say he's in the wind somewhere,
Say, there's a lamb in the daisies.

The Groundhog

In June, amid the golden fields,
I saw a groundhog lying dead.

Dead lay he; my senses shook,
And mind outshot our naked frailty.
There lowly in the vigorous summer
His form began its senseless change,
And made my senses waver dim
Seeing nature ferocious in him.
Inspecting close his maggots' might
And seething cauldron of his being,
Half with loathing, half with a strange love,
I poked him with an angry stick.
The fever arose, became a flame
And Vigour circumscribed the skies,
Immense energy in the sun,
And through my frame a sunless trembling.
My stick had done nor good nor harm.
Then stood I silent in the day
Watching the object, as before;
And kept my reverence for knowledge
Trying for control, to be still,
To quell the passion of the blood;
Until I had bent down on my knees
Praying for joy in the sight of decay.
And so I left; and I returned
In Autumn strict of eye, to see
The sap gone out of the groundhog,
But the bony sodden hulk remained.
But the year had lost its meaning,
And in intellectual chains
I lost both love and loathing,
Mured up in the wall of wisdom.
Another summer took the fields again
Massive and burning, full of life,
But when I chanced upon the spot
There was only a little hair left,
And bones bleaching in the sunlight
Beautiful as architecture;
I watched them like a geometer,
And cut a walking stick from a birch.
It has been three years, now.
There is no sign of the groundhog.
I stood there in the whirling summer,
My hand capped a withered heart,
And thought of China and of Greece,
Of Alexander in his tent;
Of Montaigne in his tower,
Of Saint Theresa in her wild lament.

Rumination

When I can hold a stone within my hand
And feel time make it sand and soil, and see
The roots of living things grow in this land,
Pushing between my fingers flower and tree,
Then I shall be as wise as death,
For death has done this and he will
Do this to me, and blow his breath
To fire my clay, when I am still.

At Night

In the dust are my father's beautiful hands,
In the dust are my mother's eyes.
Here by the shore of the ocean standing,
Watching: still I do not understand.

Love flows over me, around me,
Here at night by the sea, by the sovereign sea.

Gone is that bone-hoard of strength;
Gone her gentle motion laughing, walking.

Is it not strange that disease and death
Should rest, by the undulant sea?

And I stare, rich with gifts, alone,

Feeling from the sea those terrene presences,
My father's hands, my mother's eyes.

The Horse Chestnut Tree

Boys in sporadic but tenacious droves
Come with sticks, as certainly as Autumn,
To assault the great horse chestnut tree.

There is a law governs their lawlessness.
Desire is in them for a shining amulet
And the best are those that are highest up.

They will not pick them easily from the ground.
With shrill arms they fling to the higher branches,
To hurry the work of nature for their pleasure.

I have seen them trooping down the street
Their pockets stuffed with chestnuts shucked, unshucked.
It is only evening keeps them from their wish.

Sometimes I run out in a kind of rage
To chase the boys away: I catch an arm,
Maybe, and laugh to think of being the lawgiver.

I was once such a young sprout myself
And fingered in my pocket the prize and trophy.
But still I moralize upon the day

And see that we, outlaws on God's property,
Fling out imagination beyond the skies,
Wishing a tangible good from the unknown.

And likewise death will drive us from the scene
With the great flowering world unbroken yet,
Which we held in idea, a little handful.

Seals, Terns, Time

The seals at play off Western Isle
In the loose flowing of the summer tide
And burden of our strange estate—

Resting on the oar and lolling on the sea,
I saw their curious images,
Hypnotic, sympathetic eyes

As the deep elapses of the soul.
O ancient blood, O blurred kind forms
That rise and peer from elemental water:

I loll upon the oar, I think upon the day,
Drawn by strong, by the animal soft bonds
Back to a dim pre-history;

While off the point of Jagged Light
In hundreds, gracefully, the fork-tailed terns
Draw swift esprits across the sky.

Their aspirations dip in mine,
The quick order of their changing spirit,
More freedom than the eye can see.

Resting lightly on the oarlocks,
Pondering, and balanced on the sea,
A gauze and spindrift of the world,

I am in compulsion hid and thwarted,
Pulled back in the mammal water,
Enticed to the release of the sky.

Sea Burial from the Cruiser *Reve*

She is now water and air,
Who was earth and fire.

Reve we throttled down
Between Blake's Point and Weestern Isle,

Then, oh, then, at the last hour,
The first hour of her new inheritance,

We strewed her ashes over the waters,
We gave her the bright sinking

Of unimaginable aftermaths,
We followed her dispersed spirit

As children with a careless flick of wrist
Cast on the surface of the sea

New-cut flowers. Deeper down,
In the heavy blue of the water,

Slowly the white mass of her reduced bones
Waved, as a flag, from the enclosing depths.

She is now water and air,
Who was earth and fire.

A Wedding on Cape Rosier

Today there is another marriage
Of the very young by the side of the sea.
The caterer is so pleasant he seems one of the guests.
The parents are divorced but the yachting young
Take communion along with their vows
In a forest chapel looking out over the ocean.
A small boy strews rose petals one by one,
So delicate and beautiful an operation

As to defy the desires of poetry,
While a dog comes into the service
With rude life to remind us
Of the charm and stability of the animal kingdom,
Which we deny in singing
The praises of life everlasting,
That deepest wisdom of centuries of Christendom
Which speaks for the vanishing of everything present
Although the young couple in their youth's beauty
Could not be more evident, capable, or potential.

Father Emerson puts out the candles.
His father knew Emily Dickinson.

It takes so short a time to get married,
We noticed no change in the tide.

Old Tree by the Penobscot

There is an old pine tree facing Penobscot Bay,
On the bank above the tide,
Like a predecessor. Its fate
Will be that of its forebear.
I watched the former tree ten years
While it faced the surge of the sea.

Whelmings of the tide, line storms
Buffeted the root system of the pine
Twenty feet above the tide.
I watched the changes of the seasons,
Each year returning assessed
Somber change, a kind of stalwart declination.

As children grew up the pine tree grew down,
Threw down its length in defiant slowness,
Until one summer it was almost horizontal.
Even then, with jags of dead branches, it clung
To life, until further summers dipped it down
Until it lay a dry myth along the shore.

There is something ominous in the new tree
Erect on the high bank, at the very edge,
The sea's hands pulling out earth from the roots,
Slowly displacing a system of boulders,
As I watch through soft afternoons.
The tides have slowly taken the children away.

Then this new tree, about to begin to fall
Through subtle gradations of the strength of years,
Took on the force of a grisly apparition,
My memory was forced down to defeat,
My riches gone, my corpse on the beach,
Dry bones, dry branches, I too a myth of time.

GEORGE OPPEN
1908–

George Oppen was born in New Rochelle, N.Y., and educated in public schools in California. Oppen has worked as a tool and die maker, cabinet maker, experimental mechanic, production manager, and building contractor. In 1929 Oppen went to France and operated the Objectivist Press with Louis Zukofsky. He joined the Communist Party in the mid-thirties to help alleviate mass hunger and was politically active during the following decades. Although he had served as a combat infantryman during World War II, Oppen was harassed by the McCarthy Committee. He fled to Mexico with his wife and child in 1950 and returned to this country in 1958 after McCarthy's death. With his world view, Oppen can write about the city or the rural landscape of Maine viewed during summer vacations at Deer Isle. Among his works are *Discrete Series* (1934); *The Materials* (1962); *This in Which* (1965); *Of Being Numerous* (1968), which was awarded the Pulitzer Prize in 1969; *Alpine: Poems* (1969); *Collected Poems* (1973); and *Seascape: Needle's Eye* (1973). Oppen is noted for the precision and spareness of his language in examining such characteristic themes as history, knowledge, love, and death.

Chartres

The bulk of it
In air

Is what they wanted. Compassion
Above the doors, the doorways

Mary the woman and the others
The lesser

Are dreams on the structure. But that a stone
Supports another

That the stones
Stand where the masons locked them

Above the farmland
Above the will

Because a hundred generations
Back of them and to another people

The world cried out above the mountain

Penobscot

Children of the early
Countryside

Talk on the back stoops
Of that locked room
Of their birth

Which they cannot remember

In these small stony worlds
In the ocean

Like a core
Of an antiquity

Non classic, anti-classic, not the ocean
But the flat
Water of the harbor
Touching the stone

They stood on—

I think we will not breach the world
These small worlds least
Of all with secret names

Or unexpected phrases—

Penobscot

Half deserted, has an air
Of northern age, the rocks and pines

And the inlets of the sea
Shining among the islands

And these innocent
People
In their carpentered

Homes, nailed
Against the weather—It is more primitive

Than I know
To live like this, to tinker
And to sleep

Near the birches
That shine in the moonlight

Distant
From the classic world—the north

Looks out from its rock
Bulging into the fields, wild flowers
Growing at its edges! It is a place its women

Love, which is the country's
Distinction—

The canoes in the forest
And the small prows of the fish boats
Off the coast in the dead of winter

That burns like a Tyger
In the night sky. One sees their homes and lawns,
The pale wood houses

And the pale green
Terraced lawns.
'It brightens up into the branches

And against the buildings'
Early. That was earlier

The Occurrences

Limited air   drafts
In the treasure house moving and the movements of the living
Things fall   something balanced   Move
With all one's force
Into the commonplace that pierces or erodes

The mind's structure but nothing
Incredible happens
It will have happened to that other
The survivor   The survivor
To him it happened

Rooted in basalt
Night hums like the telephone dial tone blue gauze
Of the forge flames the pulse
Of infant
Sorrows at the crux

Of the timbers
When the middle Kingdom
Warred with beasts Middle Things the elves the

Magic people in their world
Among the plant roots   hopes
Which are the hopes
Of small self interest called

Superstition chitinous
Toys of the children wings
Of the wasp

LOUIS OSBORNE COXE
1918–

Louis Coxe was born in Manchester, N.H., and received his B.A. from Princeton University. After serving in the Navy, he taught at Princeton, Harvard, and the University of Minnesota; he has been at Bowdoin College since 1955. His poetry includes *The Sea Faring and Other Poems* (1947), *The Second Man and Other Poems* (1955), *The Wilderness and Other Poems* (1958), *The Middle Passage* (1960), *The Last Hero and Other Poems* (1965), *Nikal Seyn, Decoration Day: A Poem and a Play* (1966), and *Passage: Selected Poems, 1943–1978* (1979), as well as contributions to numerous periodicals. He is also the author of plays and two critical works on Edwin Arlington Robinson. Displaying a sense of history as a cyclic process, Coxe searches for the answers to fundamental questions in his poetry.

From the Window Down

I follow from my window down
The paths my children's feet have mown
Running to the rim of bank
Where I stood once. Yarrow is rank,
Saint Johnswort straggles at the verge,
The paths like past and future merge
In a single child, myself or mine,
Poised there a season out of time,
And blown like the burrowing swallow he
Shall next in time drop down to sea
Dropping below my sight to find
Salt desolation: I am blind:
Another watched me so. I gaze
And see myself, a child, and raise
The head that I held so before
The bank undid me to the shore.

Union Soldier

South and west from the tiding of Calais Maine
In the tousled commons squared off by elms

He grows in local stone grey on the green
Like a hull a bight becalms
And stock-still on the granite plinth can see
Under the kepi through the blind stone eyes
His land slipping from him between
Towns leveling to prairie and the terrible skies
Of rotting Hollywood and Los Angeles.

Whoever botched him into statue knew
Skill out of place for this, grace out of order.
The grounded gun no more familiar grew
Or shapelier to him, murder
Less than his rebel blood running him aghast
From Bull Run and the squealing enemy behind.
And died in the shallows, tramped askew
Under the hot passage of the southern wind
To rot for richer texture in that ground.

Now he is stone. Topsfield, Litchfield, towns
Moving to bloody Kansas tore their quarries
To tier him up, blind anonym, for clowns
Touring the summer boroughs
And for the sliding vista of his land
Dropping beyond to newer monuments.
The eyes surpass three cairns
Of cannonballs, two fifteen-pounder guns,
The fieldpieces he learned and lived by once.

Quivering like the tune the tree toad yells
Here by last summer light, your heart
Can never hark back feeling the lumped hills
As he did burst apart
With shaken host of enemy horse and man
Crying on faith in what they killed for, lust
To hold on, violent cells
Calm at the center of their holy trust.
His land was north and winter to the touch.

And died in that country, part of the one land
Sloping from Saint Croix, died against his will,
Misled, the fool of folly, killed to stand
Today inland from ocean swell.
Erect, unreconciled, he moves against
The fumbling dark of trees, lighter than air,
Than your vision wiser. His hand

Along his left thigh empty as his stare
Waits for a sign, the ultimate cease-fire.

Mocker of all who will against heart's truth,
Soldier stand up, stone gunbutt at your heel:
The special man kills with the skill of youth,
Feels what two metals feel
Joined in the senseless torsion of a lathe
That holds him still against a working part
Bright to the eye. In death
He turns to slag. You in your blacked-out park
Bend the night back around you in an arc.

Squaring the Circle

A bear cub chained and tethered to a stake
Prowled in a Humble service station yard
In a rubble of popcorn, apple cores, dumped cars
And tourists giving him 7-Up to drink.
He swept a centrifuge arc over arc
Like a windshield wiper, and his chain and collar clanked:
Four paces left—does freedom die that hard?—
Four paces right, till the center wound him back.
Beyond the dump, meadow and swamp meet trees
Grown dark as they crawl the Appalachian chain;
Ahead, the freeway flumes the traffic east,
Scatters sunlight and dips to the Gulf of Maine
Where the lobsterman prowls the hundred-fathom curve
And the yacht swings on her mooring like a slave.

DANIEL HOFFMAN

1923–

A frequent visitor to the coast of Maine, Daniel (Gerard) Hoffman was born in New York and received his A.B., M.A., and Ph.D. from Columbia University. After serving in the Air Force during World War II, he began teaching in leading institutions throughout the country; he has been on the faculty of the University of Pennsylvania since 1966. The recipient of numerous awards, grants and fellowships, Hoffman was a poetry consultant for the Library of Congress (1973–74) and has been chancellor of the Academy of American Poets since 1972. Hoffman is known for his skillful use of sounds and rhythms, and he utilizes his poetry to explore aspects of myth, history, and immediate personal experiences. His poetry includes *An Armada of Thirty Whales* (1954), *A Little Geste and Other Poems* (1960), *The City of Satisfactions* (1963), *Striking the Stones* (1968), *Broken Laws* (1970), *The Center of Attention* (1974), and *Able Was I Ere I Saw Elba: Selected Poems 1954–74* (1977). Hoffman has also written scholarly works about myth and folklore in literature, as well as studies of Stephen Crane and Poe.

The Seals in Penobscot Bay

hadn't heard of the atom bomb,
so I shouted a warning to them.

Our destroyer (on trial run) slid by
the rocks where they gamboled and played;

they must have misunderstood,
or perhaps not one of them heard

me over the engines and tides.
As I watched them over our wake

I saw their sleek skins in the sun
ripple, light-flecked, on the rock,

plunge, bubbling, into the brine,
and couple & laugh in the troughs

between the waves' whitecaps and froth.
Then the males clambered clumsily up

and lustily crowed like seacocks,
sure that their prowess held thrall

all the sharks, other seals, and seagulls,
And daintily flipped the females,

seawenches with musical tails;
each looked at the Atlantic as

though it were her looking-glass.
If my warning had ever been heard

it was sound none would now ever heed.
And I, while I watched those far seals,

tasted honey that buzzed in my ears
and saw, out to windward, the sails

of an obsolete ship with banked oars
that swept like two combs through the spray

And I wished for a vacuum of wax
to ward away all those strange sounds,

yet I envied the sweet agony
of him who was tied to the mast,

when the boom, when the boom, when the boom
of guns punched dark holes in the sky.

The Hermit of Cape Rosier

The hermit of Cape Rosier has three houses:
One's atop the cragged bluff that leaps
splashing spruce out of the water, hackled pines
sawing a jagged hole in heaven. There
the hermit's house is: no door, windows like wounds,
a ribcage in a hat whose brim is eaves.
You have to know the path up there to find it;
even if you know the old back trail
you have to know the cut-off to the hermit's,
and when you get there, through the thorned blackberries
with the arched gulls shrill in the steep wind

you see   Keep Out   No Trespassing   assigned
on trees and staves. Perhaps you are not welcome.
'Hello! Hello!' The winds snatch 'Lo!' and dash it
cragward, crumpled, down. A seahawk's nest
in winter, filled with lichen and picked fishbones
would be as hospitable as is this homestead.
Why would anyone not born to feathers
seek such isolation in the sun?
All that the senses touch up here is cleanly,
scoured by solitude in the harsh height.
Yet grant a hermit reasonable cause
to abjure our fendered comforts, still one might
search his self for the natural parts of man
in scenes more clement. Not the bleak of air
but ripeness of the earth, in summertime:
sometimes, beneath the blackberries, he searches there.

The second house the hermit lives in
some people wouldn't call a house, unless
sleeping in a cave's compatible
with the human lot. No one at Harborside
knows what got into Jethro
crouching like a woodchuck in his tunnel
while a scourge of moles rips furrows his father turned.
He's got good lands back there he never touches
except a potato plot and a row of beans;
nobody knows why Jethro won't be seen
at Meeting, store, or trade; nobody knows
just how he lives there, holed up like a marmot
while rains fall, and hay rises, and teams
move from field to field in hot July.
In woods, in the dead of summer, there's the smell
of green gone sour, of flesh the owl has killed;
delicate leafmould works its webbed decay,
a footstep stirs the leaves, and simmering death
bursts from earth behind a canopy
of green hands, giddy in the wind, that grasp the sun.
The cool of cave-mouth in the hill is dank,
the spindling spider hangs numb from his wheel,
the hemlock-guarded air is cold and still.

The other house the hermit lives in
was once a boathouse, but he has no boat.
You pass clam baskets, broken, pyramided,
and mattocks worn down at the shiny tines,
split oars, stacked driftwood, a pile or two of shells.

Peering through the fogstained saltpocked window
imagine Jethro fingering his trove:
great conches curling empty till his ear brings
titanic surfs to tunnels the silent snail
polished in solitude; bright rocks whose stain
of emerald or quartz shaft of shine the starfish
hugged beneath the tide.

Death seems nearer Jethro than it may be,
though in the village they say he's hale and sound.
Life seems precarious on his hillside,
battering windy breakers, by rot deepgnawed,
uncivil, ashake with joy and awe and wonder
at cragged Borealis
and the empty shell left on the shore.

In the Cove

There was no diminishing that day.

The sun in clarity of dew arose
Toward splendors unimagined before noon.

The day kept on becoming what it was,
The hour in being what it had become.

Then nothing dwindled. Where the tide fell back
The dazzled empire of the field enlarged

And we from the cliffside to the farthest brim
Heard gulls on offshore islands calling, calling

Against the lessening of the light
And the cessation of the fields of flowers

And the tide crawling toward the darker hours
And the black fir branchtips blotting out the sky.

A waning of one stillness and a coming
Of nothing near the soughing of the trees,

Changeless, rimmed by the sea's cold sway.

Moving among the Creatures

Moving among the creatures
As the new light

Surges down this cliff, these trees, this meadow,
Brightening the shade among the alders
And shrivelling the dew on leaves,
They are contented in their bodies—I can tell it—
The squalling gulls delighted to be turning
Widdershins, their shadows swooping
Over rocks where startled deer
Clatter, flashing spindly shanks
And delicate hooves while underfoot
Even the uglies in their sticky skins
Exult, the woodfrogs clunking all the bells
In sunken steeples, till at my
Thick tread
They leap and scissor-kick away
While the withering leech,
Shrinking, enlarging, waving
Knobbed horns
Makes the stem shine
With silver spittle where he's gone.
I trip on vines, stumble in potholes
And long for something of myself that's in them,
In the gulls' windy coursing, in the frogs'
Brief cadenza, even in the slug's
Gift to leave
A gleaming track, spun
From his own
Slippery gut.

The Summerhouse

Climbed uphill to the seashore summerhouse,
Domed and shingled cottage occupied
By certain predecessors in whose pots
Our porridge bubbles merrily. The waves
Crash beyond the windows. Without ceremony
They pack their things and are about to go.
Well, we will soon forget them walking
Dourly without shadows two by two.
It's our vacation, sheets dried in the sun—
Out from the floorboard, underneath the bed
With slightest scrape of scale on wooden grain
The flattened head of a silent copperhead
—A kitchen cleaver leaps into my hand,
Shining through the high song of your fear
The whacking silver arc of light descends
And head rolls, chomping, and the lithe

And lovely diamonds down the back writhe.
He, he, tall, returns, removes
A curved and grooved tooth and squeezes it
Into my palm.—'Here, it's yours now.'—'Thanks,
But might I not, as a memento, keep
The head?'—'Oh no, there's poison in the fangs.'
And now he's dropped the snake into his thermos
Of iced tea ('The place is yours') and driven
Down the sinuous twisting distant road.
And we've the sunny, salty, freshened air
And wind-dried linen sheets to spread.

JOHN TAGLIABUE
1923–

Born in Cantu, Italy, John Tagliabue received his B.A. and M.A. from Columbia University. His teaching career has included posts in Lebanon, Italy, Japan, Spain, Brazil, and in several institutions in this country; he has taught at Bates College in Lewiston since 1953. Among his volumes of poetry are *Poems* (1959 and 1969), *A Japanese Journal* (1966), *The Buddha Uproar* (1967), and *The Doorless Door* (1970), and he has contributed to numerous periodicals. In addition to his poetry, Tagliabue is the author of many puppet plays. He has given readings in Brazil, Japan, Spain, Greece, and Italy, and he has recorded his poems for the Library of Congress. Tagliabue keeps journals, often of poems, relating to his many travels. While his moods and styles have changed through the years, Tagliabue's poems remain a graceful and delicate celebration of life.

3 Poems on tomatoes & immortality

1.

ABUNDANCE,
and imagine when you press Them ! when you bite
Them !

They seem supernatural
but what could be more natural !
they are glowing, they are huge very huge luscious bright
shining red very red very red,
large to put it mildly, full juicy sumptuous the
summa theologica of vegetable summer,
brought over, about 7 of them, mellow, magnificent, as
if from another world, and
yet they came out of the earth just as they say Adam and
Eve did, but these are
so immediate so appetizing so holdable, when glories
become sensuous as these
then Nature in what seems her most operatic and supernatural
Mode can pronounce
TOMATOES.

2.

The fields of vegetables-and-literature Drenched

What happened when the rivers humidly and invisibly
entered the sky
and then came down like so many noisy
thick rivers?
were the Shinto priests preparing to shake their leaves
under a temple roof
or adolescent poets beginning to write were they having their
first emissions ?
surprised they took it upon themselves to utter words
like wet and I bet you
the gods are envious;
the summer world is receiving its fulfilment, the
tomatoes are doused, the vines like
the thoughts of Shakespeare
are responding to
THE TEMPEST.

3.

A future Italian envisions the miracles

The last tomatoes have been taken from the vines, the stick
upholding them have been pulled out
of the wet grund,
the cold air is bright and the frost is coming tonight
or soon;
from something before seed I'll call it song to bud to
green fruit, red fruit, lovely
to see, lovely to hold,
good to eat; and so now more than several dozen of those to
have become part of my green and red song.
But out there in the field they are gone and
winter is coming.
The birds are in migration. Dreams are taking directions.
Soil, soul, sun,
be patient, be active preparing your prayers
envision green then red
the future *pomodori.*

Vegetables Vegetables

For years, many, I've succumbed to them

Now a potato can be a Willendorf Venus,
all bumpy,

Bulky, earth mother as the professorial
mythology books say,
I prefer potatoes (to the professorial
abstractions I mean)
bumpy, huge, with delicate skins,
of the earth, and yet
related to sky, sun, rain, and to the genius
of all vegetables,
these enormous, at times hippopotamus like,
mind-boggling shapes
have much to do with nourishment, substantiality,
and organic poetry.
Wittgenstein and the Willendorf Venus are making out.

Lettuce does not let us alone

A green plot, or chlorophyll scheme, terrestrial
intrigue, vegetables
asserting themselves, my vegetables having their
say, characters
in a mystery play could not be more religious,
we are each others'
symbolists,
grass, fish, stars, actors in a Shakespeare Play,
exclamations in a
Hopkins' poem
rabbits, Easter ceremonies, the Seasonal Director
unseen is as wise
as can be, we
sometimes forget our parts, sometimes forget our lines,
then Thoreau is critical,
then all the best
poems from every where are helpful. Birds and the
theater of air and light.
Having a Sunday to think, co-operating we
made the world again.

Related to the Presents from the Mt. Vernon
poets and farmers

This time I carried it after the rain in the dark as if in
some Procession,
huge hieroglyph, as if it came from some other world and grew
into my hand,
we have thoughts of God like that, by the New England college
campus in Autumn,

by the ever strange and acceptable Nile. Or Any River. All the
while that this was happening,
consort and I walking in the dark with our raincoats on and
this enormous given
unto me Cabbage
in my hands
its leaves like ears of elephants or like the palms of
Egyptian trees,
leaves were
murmuring in different languages (we understood them)
and in different colors (we had seen their
beauty, orange, red, yellow, light green
for many dazzling days);
what were they murmuring ? Robert Frost or Tutankhamun
would ask;
the night and Nile not frightening and their future lives
all knew, and so did you.
Acclaiming as we were Recurrences, Cabbages, and gods, and
Chutes, and languages
all known our
walking
answered to all skies our presence. The gifts from friends
are recorded by
the Moon.

Another vegetable occasion to thank the Chutes

Ah, summer squash, light yellow, curved,
bumpy, luminous,
delectable, edible, an event to be
radiant about, increasing
desire, appetite, summer friendship.
Summer squash, summer squash.

PHILIP BOOTH
1925–

Philip Booth was born in Hanover, N.H., and educated at Dartmouth and Columbia. He has taught at numerous writers' workshops, colleges, and universities, including one year at Bowdoin, and has been on the faculty of Syracuse University in New York since 1965. Booth also considers Maine his home and has become a poet of the coast, capturing the speech and culture of a people living on the edge of land. Among his books are *Letter from a Distant Land* (1957), *The Islanders* (1961), *North by East* (1966), *Weathers and Edges* (1966), *Margins: A Sequence of New and Selected Poems* (1970), and *Available Light* (1976).

Barred Islands

Between their sandspit ends
we rowed, two spruce islands
moored in a blue Maine bay.
And under the Sou'west sky
we rowed ashore to swim
for love, a summer whim
when our limbs were all July.

Riding in on the tide
with shipped oars, jade
shallows under us, we
both looked down at the play
of sun on seaweed gardens,
swaying whorls in the currents
we neither could see.

And then the kelp-grown slope
slid up to meet us, steep
as a hill below our hull:
sand, stone, and clamshell
dredged by waves, time-
shaped by tide and fathom,
and then the tide was full.

We floated on hope at flood,
and over, over, the tide-
sunk bar; there where the run
of current, the waving sun,
showed clear on the waterglass
sand, on the seawind grass,
how the islands were one.

Raker

Now all the Fall is haze,
bittersweet with smoke
these elegiac days:
the raker leans on rake,
kneedeep in leaves gone bronze
and copper and dry browns;
he scuffs a golden wake
on lawn, his curbside blaze
both funeral pyre and fire
of his unspoken praise.

Shag

Under the slow heron,
flip tern, and swung gull,
six black shags run on
the water, each duck skull

filled with weathervane
thought. Toward east wind
they take off on the run,
splashing until the shag mind

tells spent feet to retract.
Then the seventh shag,
straggling, begins to react.
His head bobs. The fog

closing in, he raises
himself on gargoyle wings,
drops again, then rises
and runs as he bangs

the sea on all fours.
Slowly, then faster, he skims
the dark fir shores.
Momentarily, he seems

to join the first flight.
But he shoots away,
shaglike, his thought flat
black. All shags fly

low. Ornithologists know
more: the perhaps why
and improbable how
of shag flight. They

call them cormorants,
or latinize the North name.
I row slow in the dense
weather. This is Maine;

and I slap the split port oar
of my leaking skiff,
drifting among the fir
islands, the seabirds, as if

on vacation from knowledge:
six black shags, shagging;
August fog, me, a Maine ledge,
and the seventh shag, lagging.

Jake's Wharf

Days like this, off Jake's, the August fog
scales up on millpond mornings. Harbor gulls
float quiet as classboats in the leaning tide
(a gray gull rides the spar buoy on one leg
at noon); by four, blown home, they stand parade
on Jake's streaked roof, and summer moors as Sou'west
smoke furls in across the Camden Hills.

Come Labor Day, these weather-breeders end:
Jake's brightwork dinghies hauled, the mackerel sky
floods schools of rainsqualls on the wharf; September
tides wash through the boatshed where the wind
backs in Northeast; three driven days the timber
creaks, no boat puts off, and only the fish hawks,
cast from bent fir, fish down the spume-lined Bay.

There is another weather then, a day
swung hard Northwest, when every island spruce
stands sharpened in the wind's cold lens and rises,
like Blue Hill, in arctic clarity;

now lobstermen set traps where each wave blazes
in the splintered sun; upriver, seals
lie ledged across the tidal Bagaduce.

Days after these ebb gray without a thaw.
For some few men the winter sea is farmland
and front yard: off Jake's they drag for scallops,
hand-line cod, and tie up cold where tar
and marlin flavor talk that mends the traps.
Time closes in, like snow on cradled yachts,
now people from away have driven inland.

These are the weathers Jake knew to weather out
and wait for, slow in the woodstove warmth of his shop
where, days like this, he used to steam-bend oak,
or bend to plank a skiff, with his weather eye out
for a high March sky. But now, to a snow-swirl wake
of gulls, his lobsterboat swings cold at the mooring;
the wharf leans seaward in the ebb-tide chop.

Voyages

Crouched hard on granite,
facing a weathered sea,
I breathe as slow as rock.

Harbor is one way to look;
but voyages wash my eye,
and old tides rock my butt.

Gulls root on the ledge,
taught by every wind
how spruces tug; snails

hug the tideline, hulls
on their own horizon: bound
as I am to the very edge.

Stove

I wake up in the bed my grandmother died in.
November rain. The whole house is cold.
Long stairs, two rooms through to the kitchen:
walls that haven't been painted
in sixty years. They must have shone then:
pale sun, new pumpkin, old pine.

Nothing shines now but the nickel trim
on the grandmother stove, an iron invention
the whole room leans to surround; even
when it is dead the dogs sleep close behind it.
Now they bark out, but let rain return them;
they can smell how the stove is going to be lit.

Small chips of pine from the woodshed. Then
hardwood kindling. I build it all into the firebox,
on top of loose wads of last June's *Bangor News.*
Under the grate, my first match
catches. Flames congregate, the dogs watch,
the stove begins to attend old wisdom.

After the first noisy moments, I listen for Lora;
she cooked all the mornings my grandmother died,
she ruled the whole kitchen the year I was seven:
I can see Boyd Varnum, a post outside the side door;
he's waiting for Lora, up in the front of the house,
to get right change for his winter squash. Lora says

Boyd's got the best winter squash in the village.
When Boyd gets paid, she ties her apron back on
and lets in the eggman. He has a green wagon.
Lora tells him how last night her husband hit her;
she shows him the marks. All her bruised arms
adjust dampers and vents; under the plates where turnips

are coming to boil, she shifts both pies in the oven.
The dogs feel warmer now. I bank on thick coal.
The panes steam up as sure as November: rain,
school, a talkative stove to come home to at noon;
and Lora sets my red mittens to dry on the nickel shelves
next to the stovepipe. Lora knitted my mittens.

I can still smell the litter of spaniels
whelped between the stove and the wall; there's
venison cooking, there's milktoast being warmed on
the furthest back plate, milktoast to send upstairs
to my dead mother's mother. Because, Lora says,
she is sick. Lora says she is awful sick. When Lora goes up

to my grandmother's bed, I play with the puppies
under the stove; after they suckle and go back to sleep,
because I am in second grade and am seven, I practice
reading the black iron letters raised on the black oven door;

even though I don't know who Queen Clarion was,
I'm proud I can read what the oven door says: it says

Queen Clarion
Wood & Bishop
Bangor, Maine
1911

THEODORE ENSLIN
1925–

Theodore (Vernon) Enslin was born in Chester, Pa., and studied musical composition with Nadia Boulanger and Francis Judd Cooke. Enslin resides in Temple, Maine, where he devotes full time to his writing. He has produced dozens of volumes of verse, starting with *The Work Proposed* (1958) and including *To Come To Have Become* (1966), which won the Hart Crane Award in 1969. Condensing what he experiences in rural Maine into his poetry, Enslin bases his formal structure on sound and feels that each poem should be performed by being read aloud.

The End of the Lilacs

Copper,
          as if bronzed
for wreathes.
               Funereal tatters
at the corner
               of the house of November.

Ballad of the Goodly Company: Birds

They were singing a grey song
of flat words
               made dull
as the sun between clouds
                         wading
down the afternoon
                    now
this morning   the rain
                    makes
such a racket between
                    the eaves
and discarded metal
                    in the dooryard
I can't tell what song
                    from

the color of the day
                                        I would say
some shadings
                                up
from green.

Apple Tree Study

So bright—
there is fever in it.
That the weight of color
turns to light,
                              rises
in waves of incense
falls
        away.
And one sharp wind
climbs through
                                and over
shatters
                in
one
      sweet
    storm

The Fan Poem
1

How it opens to
    not quite a circle,
collapses to a ruled line—
    can never be
either of these things.
It will be made
    of paper,
mother of pearl, sea shells,
numbers of things
    which are destroyed
to make beauty.
It will still
                    wheel open
snap   shut.
                        It will move
backward as far as it goes
in another direction.
                                        It will balance
snap   shut.

2

Faint breeze that
stirs
    throughout
the warm night
catches
        leaf
after leaf
            the blow and
pour
    of the poplar
quaking and shaken
which passes
                in turn
to the window
                    or the sea tide
—scape—
corn in a rising field.

3

To speak out with power,
strength and no strength,
is the custom of wind
as it spreads
                outward.
Alone.
        The figures that resist it
                        the bent tops
of the trees turning
returning wrenched
                        at degrees
from the root.
                    It is passage.
It is the spread of a fan.

Cobwebs

Often—
in the morning
I have seen them
pulsing
thin blood
from the cold dew,
shredding
            and
tearing apart,

or throwing
filaments
-tentacles-
to catch on
to
something
for support—
burst finally—
the effort
            too
great,
or the cycle
complete—
              hiding
and curling away
from the sun,
holding in shadow
at midday
or longer—
              a slow life
that has little
                to do
with this,
but in some ways
                  it is
less fragile.
They will touch on it
only as a brush
against a face—
chance wetting,
breaking again,
but more strongly
entrenched.
They will outlast us.

CONSTANCE HUNTING
1925–

Born in Providence, R.I., Constance (Coulter) Hunting received a B.A. from Brown University and studied piano at New England Conservatory. She married Robert Hunting, a professor of English in 1948 and later moved to the midwest. The Huntings returned to New England to Orono in 1968. She has taught for the University and for its Continuing Education Division, and she is the founder, publisher, and editor of the Puckerbrush Press in Orono. Hunting's volumes of poetry include *After the Stravinsky Concert* (1969), for which she won the Indiana University Writers Prize; *Cimmerian* (1972); *Beyond the Summerhouse* (1976); *Nightwalk and Other Poems* (1980); and *Dream Cities, and other poems* (1982). In her poetry Hunting offers a close observation of the world transmuted through imagination and memory.

Fever

I take it my real child is ill.
The worm works in the rose, and fever
glisters in tower windows.
Can my thorn draw her poison?
Extreme caution must be exercised.
I must exercise extreme caution.
My medicine is very powerful.
It has already killed several.
I stand at the foot of her white bed
and tell her of her pet toad
whom she has named Mortimer, after
a friend of the family. I say that Mortimer,
patient, self-effacing, utterly reliable,
waits for her under the laurel hedge.
Her eyes are so bright!
Outside, the rain falls like fat gray slugs.

New England

Stones
are the sheep of these

hillsides
and fog
is the wool of these
stones

Poem Overheard in a Maine Doctor's Waiting Room

"I never go out in weather like this
I never go out in weather like this
I was married on the shortest day
of the year fifty years ago and that's why
I've never forgotten it
my great-great grandmother married when she
was sixteen two families pioneered
pioneers in Limestone
I get so cold at night
my bones ache and I can't move so I come here
and the doctor gives me something
they had no shelter for the only cow in Limestone
that first night so the young bride flew out
from the covered wagon and pegged a quilt
a brand-new wedding gift around the cow
during the night it snowed
and in the morning when they went out
they saw the steam
coming from under the edges of the blanket
the bride was milkmaid and that very day
the young lads and the bridegroom
built the shelter"

The Lost Boy

His photograph got in
with the family others. Nobody recognizes
him, not even the everybody's mother.
S. T. Wiggins, Ground Floor Gallery, No. 15
Commercial Street, Cedar Rapids, Iowa
is what's printed on
the back of the evidence.
Oh, the careful combing of his hair!
Two years old probably, he retains
his Buddha look, inscrutable, hinting at worlds.
Exquisite listening ear,
adze nose, his mouth judgemental, remarkable
in one so young; in a dress and sash.
A single booted foot protrudes beneath the hem.
Its angle I could kiss with reverence.
The fingers of the tiny hands dispose

themselves politically upon the fierce
upholstered arms of the chair that suffers
them, ending in tired lion's claws.
He has a power.
More than statesman, not much less
than transplanted god,
such a passenger
sits, a good baby, for the lens.
I should say before the First World War.
I told you, worlds ago. He does not whimper
or dwindle. He has disappeared from our mirrors
that he might have inherited: no,
he comes because he is gone,
having chosen perhaps to go with that clear
intimidating gaze
to lisp at Plato's knees, from Emerson
and Thoreau, Hawthorne among the sycamores.
Hedges of Osage oranges
stand between him and them. Nevertheless,
Negatives available for future orders.

INDEX